Virtually Christian

How Christ Changes Human Meaning
and Makes Creation New

Virtually Christian

How Christ Changes Human Meaning
and Makes Creation New

Anthony W. Bartlett

BOOKS

Winchester, UK
Washington, USA

First published by O-Books, 2011
O Books is an imprint of John Hunt Publishing Ltd., The Bothy, Deershot Lodge, Park Lane, Ropley,
Hants, SO24 0BE, UK
office1@o-books.net
www.o-books.com

For distributor details and how to order please visit the 'Ordering' section on our website.

Text copyright Anthony W. Bartlett 2009

ISBN: 978 1 84694 396 6

A CIP catalogue record for this book is available from the British Library.

Design: Stuart Davies

Printed in the UK by CPI Antony Rowe
Printed in the USA by Offset Paperback Mfrs, Inc

Bob Dylan's Ain't Talkin' copyright © 2006 Special Rider Music. All rights reserved.
International copyright secured. Reprinted by permission.

Cover design by Christopher Bartlett.

Unless otherwise noted the Scripture quotations in this publication are from the New
Standard Version Bible, copyright © 1989 by the Division of Christian Education of the National
Council of Churches of Christ in the U.S.A., and used by permission.

We operate a distinctive and ethical publishing philosophy in all
areas of its business, from its global network of authors to
production and worldwide distribution.

CONTENTS

For people who think our various Christian institutions and systems of belief need only a few minor tweaks or cosmetic enhancements, Virtually Christian will be like a jolt of hi-test espresso. They may not be ready for it, but it will wake them up. For people who already feel something in our faith community is deeply off track and in need of serious realignment, it will be like a well-crafted wine, deliciously combining insights from Jesus' life and teaching, medieval courtly love poetry, contemporary film, philosophy, biblical studies, anthropology, semiotics, and more. Tony Bartlett brings a needed voice to an important conversation emerging across denominations and around the world.
Brian McLaren, author/speaker/activist

In Virtually Christian Tony Bartlett makes a stunning presentation of Christianity as the transformation of desire—from violence to non-violence, from retribution to forgiveness, from competition to compassion, from acquisitiveness to giving. In a series of probing meditations—organized in terms of the contemporary world of signs and virtuality—he seeks to return Christianity to its founding experiences, recall it from eternity to time and the earth, redirect theology from metaphysics to the movements of experience, and reform the church from a hierarchical corporation to local communities inspired by the multiple movements of the spirit. The style manages to be fluent, personal, and testimonial, but also erudite, and it is uniquely cut to fit the persuasive call for transformation that it makes. This needs to be heard.
John D. Caputo, philosopher/theologian, author

What a tour de force! Like a highly skilled juggler, Bartlett puts many balls into the air, and then allows our eyes to rest on the extraordinary shape which comes into view as their movement together allows us to glimpse something entirely new. The result is an immensely exciting sense of what Jesus was and is really all about, has done and is doing, at last giving an anthropological account of how he has inescapably affected everything. Difficult in places, but yielding rich insights, this book is hugely suggestive as to who we are following and what will be the shape of our discipleship in the future.
James Alison, Catholic Priest, theologian and author

Bartlett gives a compelling interpretation of mimetic theory, arguing the cultural revelation of the victim is based in still more radical elements of compassion, forgiveness and nonviolence made culturally present by Christ. The transformative impact continues in contemporary areas of popular culture, as also philosophy and theology. In this last area Bartlett presents a formidable reflection, nothing less than the possibility of a "new reformation" through the sign-value of the gospel prompting a different nonviolent way of being human. Bartlett's argument draws out some of the most revolutionary possibilities of mimetic anthropology.

Rene' Girard, seminal thinker of mimetic anthropology.

*In memory of Carlo Carretto
who saw the world filled with
contemplation and shared its
light with those of us in the Spello
community 1983-84.*

Introduction

Every year there are multiple publications about Jesus, a constant comet trail of books spinning out from this extraordinary figure. Some are theological, some historical, some personal. Some come from an Evangelical side of Christianity, some from a Catholic, some from a place that is hardly on the religious grid at all. The present book arises from that different and suspect space. It's a book about signs and meaning, and it takes Jesus as a source of signs within our human web of communication. So much so that he changes human meaning itself. And in the same measure as that change happens there is an encounter with the God of Jesus, the God who is Endless Love.

Writing this book has been an amazing, even beautiful experience. Yes, it has taken time and travail. It touches on specialist topics, in particular theology, and there is always a trick throwing open the chapels of scholarship to the breezes of public conversation. I am not the first to say it, but writing in this instance often comes down to rewriting. Yet the final outcome, discovering and showing—and discovering *by* showing—how the figure of Jesus impacts our contemporary world, for the sake of peace and boundless love, seems little short of a miracle. I am convinced the book sets forth a true and thrilling dynamic of the prophet-comet from Galilee, in and for our time.

However, one man's miracle can appear to another as simply something weird. Standard theological publishing companies looked askance. The market niche they print for was not—they seemed to think—going to buy this. It was too off-center, too challenging, too non-traditional.

But surely we have to see there are many people out there for whom the old formulae are part of the problem? And at the same time these people sense there is still meaning to be found? The target group I am writing to is the steadily growing number searching for a spiritual way forward in a world overwhelmed by violence, and willing to find that forward way through the person of Jesus.

There are 7 billion hungry humans on the planet: mouths to be fed indeed, but even more than physical hunger, their hearts are hungry with desire. Our world cannot survive without a sense of meaning, in particular one that will lead us to the depths of love. Meanwhile we are sinking in an electronic whirlpool as it is driven ever faster by accelerated news, networking and entertainment media. We are fed an increasingly violent diet of desire by the universe of images and words wheeling constantly before us.

Yet this book is by no means anti-media. On the contrary it finds that the transforming sign-value of compassion, love and forgiveness brought by Christ is discovered progressively as our world of communication moves into overdrive. At the heart of the chaos of signs, especially in cinema and popular music, the sign of the nonviolent forgiving Christ can and will suddenly show up as the only way through, the only way to transform the violence into peace. A new human meaning appears at the core of our sign system, a meaning that is 'virtually Christian'. Although it may not be as plain as the explosion of images itself the evidence is there and when it is brought to focus through the groundbreaking anthropology of René Girard it becomes compelling. His basic ideas and their semiotics are laid out in chapter two, and their illustration in contemporary media in chapter three. Using Girard's thought in this holistic way provides the drive motor of *Virtually Christian*.

Traditional religious meaning has been controlled by metaphysical ideas of God, the soul, and heaven, with ultimate good, truth and beauty wrapped up in them. These are all presumably final categories which impart meaning to everything. The meaning I am talking about, however, is not located in this realm of ideas. It arises in the realm of signs, within the human reality of this world. A sign is always something concrete because it operates, as Girard tells us, within a cultural order birthed out of original crises of desire and violence. Our signs at some level always carry the birthmark of desire and violence... *Or*, alternatively, they can, because of Christ, signify the converse: compassion, forgiveness, love. And in the vortex of signs in which we currently exist these contrasting themes play themselves out with a rhythm both of gathering crisis and progressive transformation. In other words meaning is located in human actuality, and the question is always whether it turns to violence and death or to forgiveness and life.

The Christian theological discipline has a long and illustrious tradition in its own right and any new intervention will be carefully scrutinized. Therefore, a book that tries to be any kind of game-changer must at least implicitly speak to that tradition. This accounts for some of the more historical material included in the second chapter where the basic argument is set out. It also underlies the fourth chapter on philosophy and the fifth on the doctrine of Christ.

It's hardly possible to overstate the impact of Greek philosophical thought on Christianity—the thought that gave us our typical viewpoint of an ideal world beyond this one. The attempt to escape this perspective for the sake of a thoroughly this-worldly one must at some moment directly confront speculative thought and philosophy. That is why chapter four is there. I have been tempted to apologize somewhat for this chapter, viewing it as one of those required classes that students will endure rather than enjoy. But in point of fact it fits organically and dynamically with everything else and I think that makes it both accessible and vital. The chapter demonstrates just how powerfully the meaning of Christ has changed the intellectual and philosophical arena itself. This is a concrete effect, working against the abstract and boring associations of philosophy.

3

The fifth chapter changes the pace again. It delves into the heart of Christian theology, the doctrine of Christ and the doctrine of God. The approach I take is new and perhaps challenging but if I'm anywhere on the mark then this chapter may stand as the central architecture of the book. To see the divinity of Jesus in this-worldly terms is to reach and reveal the core of Christian meaning, overcoming the distortions of centuries. And the repercussions of this, and indeed the whole book, can then play out in a dramatically new understanding of what we call 'church' in the sixth chapter.

The final chapter, on the New Testament record of Jesus, serves both to underpin and illustrate this meaning. Once again there is an enormous field of scholarship standing around it, keeping a dyspeptic eye on its topic. A professional scripture scholar will throw up holy hands, saying 'Where are all the footnotes?' To which I will answer, 'Don't worry, they're in my head...' The point in a book like this is to present a coherent picture, not to engage in laser-sliced references. All scholars will admit they seek a coherent account and that there must be a governing hypothesis. The difference in this book is the hypothesis more or less covers the waterfront, and for the sake of architectural flow and simplicity I have worked to keep footnotes to the essential.

Finally my heartfelt thanks are due to my family, especially my angel wife Linda, my first and best colleague and friend, for unfailing support and encouragement; to my faith community, Wood Hath Hope, for providing the sounding-board for much of the content here and the pattern for a great deal of what is presented in chapter six; to Bexley Hall (Rochester) and Syracuse Episcopal Local Formation students for responding enthusiastically to this kind of theology; and last but not at all least to O-Books for opening the publishing world to a twist of the comet tail not framed by ancient constellations.

Chapter One

No Name for a Non-Violent God

I begin with a vision of extraordinary beauty: 'The earth robed in light like a jewel, like a bride dressed for her wedding…' Can we share the vision? Can we let ourselves be drawn to it?

Yes? Then let's look closer. Visible to the mind's eye we see all the continents and seas clearly marked. At the same time they are bathed in a patina of light. It feels as if the earth breathes, and we taste the air of its mountains, the salt of its seas, share the life of all earth's peoples. Yes, our hearts are caught in wonder at our planet!

But, as we gaze, there is also something strange; something is missing. There is no evident partner for a figure of such incredible beauty. There is no lover of the bride, no bridegroom. The earth appears alone, even solitary.

We ask, and the vision tells us. The partner for the earth's love cannot to be imaged, it is not an object of sight. What is happening is much more intimate, profound and dramatic.

The earth and her beloved are one, and their union is unseen. Their communion is hidden and it is the hiddenness which is the cause of the light. The light is the outward phenomenon of the mutual embrace of human life and eternal love. Their touch is complete, their joy boundless.

Here ends the vision. But as described it really cannot end, for it is already imprinted in our minds before we read it here. Pictures of a radiant earth against the sable of infinite space are known to us from the Apollo space program. When we see the photos from beyond the planet it is almost impossible not to catch our breath at the beauty of the earth, its quiet vigil in the trackless void. What space traveler coming in sight of the planet would not want to stop off for a visit? But there is more than just this to our pre-knowledge of the vision. Our collective imagination does not depend on space travel and the physical images it has given. The vision has a rich cultural source, one that is already ancient for us and with which, at a deeper level, we are even more familiar. It is engraved in our collective fantasy from the last pages of the bible, from the book of Revelation.

> Then I saw a new heaven and a new earth; for the first heaven and the first earth had passed away, and the sea was no more. And I saw the holy city, the new Jerusalem, coming down out of heaven from God, prepared as a bride adorned for her husband. (Rev. 21:1-2)

As the text continues it describes the holy city as like 'a very rare jewel, like jasper, clear as crystal' (21:11). It also has the city as a free-standing structure which is a perfect cube, fifteen hundred miles in length on each side. The color of jasper is earth tone, deep red, also green and brown, and in its natural state the stone is variegated. Running through the vast dimensions of the city these shades and hues are seen as pure as crystal. A shimmering earth as perfect design and dwelling, shot through with light, a truly stunning picture…

Yet the beauty of the biblical image does not depend essentially on the physical characteristics, rather on a deep intimacy that underlies them. 'See, the home of God is among mortals. He will dwell with them; they will be his peoples, and God himself will be with them; he will wipe every tear from their eyes. Death will be no more…' (21:3-4a). And later: 'I saw no temple in the city, for its temple is the Lord God, the Almighty and the Lamb. And the city has no need of sun or moon to shine on it, for the glory of God is its light, and its lamp is the Lamb' (21:22-3).

Here then is the partnership or union implied in our vision. The Christian bible tells us that it is God who is the intimate of the bride. But immediately we say this we hit a problem, and it is because of it that in the opening description above I adopted an approach to keep the partner oblique, unnamed. The partnership of God is a problem. It is in fact a general and fundamental problem.

The name of God is associated in all historical cultures with a continuous flood of violence unleashed on the earth. 'God' is a name which stands for the cumulative collective violence of the group given transcendent face and status. What group going to war does not have 'God on their side'? According to René Girard 'God' is in fact an unconscious name for the generative role of violence at the source of all culture, a signifier for the massive structuring effects of violence. Violence *is* the human sacred. Although all religion clearly also values peace and seeks it as its final goal the ambivalence or fuzzy edge between this and violence is profound and endemic.[1] As far as the bible is concerned, we can say that while it works radically to overturn human violence, very many of its cultural forms are still rooted in archaic violence, up to and including significant elements in the Book of Revelation. Perhaps all human beings dream of the perfection of the earth. But definitely not everyone wants the planet to become the home of God, and certainly not of the God of Revelation as most people understand that God to be.

So we are left in a stalemate: a vision of beauty founded in a divine intimacy, but a figure of God that shocks us with its violence and makes the intimacy repugnant. What possible way forward can there be? Is there any way of speaking that can bypass the crushing violence of the name of God, and still look to and talk of a communion of the human and divine? I would like to suggest one. I would like to offer a kind of language game that replaces 'God' with 'No-Name'. By using No-Name we can perhaps think of our vision of beauty without an immediate reaction against the divine 'other' that is joined with it.

Now, at once, I am aware of the objection: it is really impossible to replace the name of 'God'. Even as I use 'No-Name' the reader will back-project it with the word 'God' and allow all the old baggage to slip back in. Language is always porous and perhaps never more so than when dealing with ultimate questions and their meaning. But it is for that very reason I advance this 'No-Name': it is to make the porosity evident and open it to view on the surface of the text. If the old meaning flows in then also a new meaning may, and we can make that continuously the issue in the discussion.

So readily I admit, alongside No-Name will stand all the other names, God, Almighty, Father, Mother, Yahweh, Allah, Atman, Great Spirit, Holy Spirit, etc., etc. I do not pretend we can lose these, or that we should attempt to. They are rich generally in human resonance, and many of them in biblical resonance. Marcion, the first truly great heretic, was wrong to make an absolute or ontological divide between the name of God in the Old Testament and Christ, the God of the New, as he saw it. This is itself a violent displacement or division, re-establishing the very violence that he sought to reject in the 'angry and vengeful God of judgment' of the Old Testament. On the contrary, we can say that in the God of the Old Testament, and in all the ancient names of God, the deep truth of a nonviolent God is seeking to be born. Or, rather, in all relationships in and with and through those names, the nonviolent God is seeking to be known. And yet, having said this, it is good to have this other name, No-Name, because precisely it reminds us of what is yet completely new and not part of our old world. No-Name is a space where the new can flow, a vessel for the divine that is truly and deeply nonviolent, and may yet surprise the earth into its true beauty.

Light Below

At the same time as suggesting the language game we clearly do not have a change in the name of God as our only way to think in New Testament terms of an earth at peace. There is Jesus! It is very hard to attribute violence to the originator of the gospel, of the good news of God's forgiveness and love, of divine healing and welcome. Despite the fact that people refer to his action in the temple in the last days of his life as an exceptional yet conclusive 'proof' of Jesus' use of violence no serious bible scholar would look on these actions divorced from his whole ministry. And because of that we have to see them as a conscious and deliberate prophetic sign-action, taking control of the temple for a brief period to show how it stood in contrast to the direct relationship with God which he proclaimed, and to make the point with a definitive emphasis. The whip he plaits in John is used to drive the animals, probably with the sound of the crack alone. No one is attacked. No one gets hurt. And very soon the situation reverts to the status quo: the authorities take back control of the temple and decide on *Jesus'* suffering and death in order to control *him*.

Overall the event is to be seen as Jesus placing himself purposely and calculatedly in the cross-hairs for the sake of the truth, much rather than doing harm to anyone else. The consequences of his actions were indeed 'the cross', and supremely in the situation of crucifixion Jesus does not invoke retaliation on his enemies, or threaten those who reject redemption; rather he prays for their forgiveness. No, Jesus' whole life-story makes him unmistakably a figure of transcendent nonviolence. The problem lies elsewhere, with the way the cross is interpreted within the framework of a violent God. It is unfathomably ironic that the icon of human non-retaliation, Jesus' cross, gets turned in the tradition into a supreme piece of vengeance—God's 'just' punishment of Jesus in our place. My book, *Cross Purposes*, is about the way this tradition got formed and it represents just one of a constant stream of writing, gathering force at the end of the last century and continuing into this, questioning how this could be the meaning of the central symbol of Christianity.[2] I think the vigor of that question can only continue to grow, while the nonviolence of Jesus' response must at the same time stand out in greater and greater relief, in its own right and for its own sake. And for that same reason the argument at hand, of 'No-name' for a nonviolent God, can only be strengthened when we highlight the nonviolence of Jesus against the traditional violent concept of 'God'.

Now if we turn to the Book of Revelation—which we saw as a cause of offense in its apparent celebration of a God of violence—we have to say in all honesty that it is in fact a nonviolent New Testament writing, and profoundly so. 'The Lamb' is the general symbolic name given to Jesus in the book, mentioned 29 times, an image of nonviolence and the book's undisputed hero. The essence of the Lamb is not to use violence. When we first hear of it is 'standing as if it had been slaughtered' (5:6): it does not fight, it is slaughtered, and it continues exactly 'as if' it were something slaughtered (i.e. it does not lose this identity). Furthermore its followers do not fight, they also are killed. We learn that the Lamb holds the key to human history, opening its seals to reveal its purpose and meaning, including its intense inner violence. The Lamb is able to do this because it represents a completely different human / divine way of responding, other than that of violence. At the same time, precisely because of this revelation, all hell (literally) breaks out around the Lamb. The old world system—the Beast—does not remain indifferent to the intro-duction of a new way and the absolute challenge it makes, but reacts with continually redoubled violence. At the end of the book there is a final battle when the Beast and the kings of the earth with their armies are all slain by a figure called the Word of God, by the sword which comes from his mouth. But directly afterwards the new earth and the city of the Lamb welcome and heal these very kings and nations which have just been slain! The only figures not to be restored are the Beast and its prophet which represent the system of violence, the imperial order with its ideological apparatus of cult and worship.

No doubt there is a powerful tonality of anger running through the book, against the oppression and murder that the Christian communities were then experiencing at the hands of the Roman Empire. And there is pretty clearly a sense of emotional release offered by the images of destruction and vengeance unleashed against the forces of oppression. But the final structure of the book is redemptive and life-giving, and that has to be admitted in any honest assessment. The duality then is not between a vengeful God and a gentle Jesus, or an initially gentle Jesus and then a violent one, but between an actual world and culture of violence and a core message of forgiveness and nonviolence. The early Christians were sorely oppressed by the former and seeking desperately to hang on to the latter. If they use language and symbolism derived from the former to restore hope in the substance of the latter then the tension is literary and poetic, rather than two moods or identities of God. The book of Revelation was intended to have a cathartic effect on emotion, in order that the Christians who read or heard it could arrive, in their minds and hearts, at the transformed perspective where they welcomed and blessed their enemies. In other words it was and is intended to be therapeutic.[3] In contrast the split between Jesus and a God of punishment—which came to full growth in the Middle Ages—is ontological, and can only lead to a fundamental division in the Christian soul, with eternal love on the one hand, and eternal violence on the other. In other words, a spiritual schizophrenia.

This brief scriptural and theological stage-setting allows us to approach again the final vision of the book of Revelation but with even greater sensitivity and sense of wonder.

I saw no temple in the city, for its temple is No-Name and the Lamb. And the city has no need of sun or moon to shine on it, for the glory of No-Name is its light, and its lamp is the Lamb. (21:22-3)

In the new city built around the Lamb there is no temple, no separate 'restricted' area for the divine. And, really, there could not be a clearer statement than this one of the validity of the use of 'No-Name': God has always been too dangerous to let loose in the human city and has needed to be locked up in one place to be alternately placated and invoked for controlled releases of violence. This is the true meaning of the 'separation of church and state', keeping the deadly forces of religion locked up in a separate civil space and then allowing them to re-enter public discourse as and when needed. (For example, in George W. Bush's address at the National Episcopal Cathedral three days after 9/11 when he said: 'our responsibility to history is already clear: to answer these attacks and rid the world of evil,' at the same time as praying for God to guide and bless the nation.) Thus for there to be no temple in the new Jerusalem means that the time of God has ended and that of No-Name has truly arrived. The Lamb opens a human space emptied of all violence, and at one and the same time the meaning of God becomes the same—emptied of violence. The nonviolence of the Lamb has made possible a matching and mirroring nonviolence of the divine—and this is No-Name. It is because we have so very little idea of what would mean a human space emptied of violence, and the matching presence of a nonviolent God, a God of love, that it is appropriate to name God in this situation No-Name.

In this changed condition, the light of the city comes from an infinitely deep divine source, rather than external heavenly bodies with all their mythological associations of power and violence: *for the glory of No-Name is its light, and its lamp is the Lamb.*

Let us dwell for a moment in the understanding of light in a transformed earth. Light has a huge history as a metaphor for the divine. In visionary prophets we read of apparitions filled with light. In the gospels Jesus is transfigured and his face 'shone like the sun'. But it is when we turn to the Greek tradition that light comes into its full power as a trope. In Plato's dialogues we read how the intellectual soul in its ascent to the truth gains a vision of shining light, sharing with the gods the heavenly realm, and seeing there what is visible only to mind. There is also his famous image of the intellectual soul's ascent from the subterranean cave of sense impressions toward the light of the pure idea. It is our Platonic inheritance which must particularly ring warning bells because it sets up a separation or distance between the earthly and the heavenly, between the human and divine, between the falsehood of the senses and the truth of the intellect.

One of the reasons Plato's method is so effective is that it fits with a general human assumption that partners gods with the heavens, with astronomical entities, like sun and moon, and generally with everything 'above'. All Plato did was add the apparatus of intellectual thought and ideas to this 'above' and so fix in Western culture a powerful association of the two. (Think of our 'top universities', 'elite colleges', 'Ivy League', etc., and the vertical status attached to those who attend there.)

The bible clearly shares a general human preconception of the heavens as the realm of the divine, but, in contrast, it is radically concerned to break down this difference. This is the meaning of so much written in the prophets and it is definitively the case in the final vision of Revelation. So, then, here is another reason to keep the divine hidden in our vision: if we sought to portray it with some kind of image it would be inevitably thought of as a 'heavenly visitor', a god-figure from above and beyond rather than something truly intimate.

But as Augustine says, God is more intimate than we are to ourselves. What we are seeking to understand then is something that is deep in the ground of our being, deeper than being itself and than all simply intellectual understanding. The depth beyond being calls us to itself, as physical and conscious creatures living and breathing on earth, seeking to provoke in us the endless life that is meant for us. The figure of intimacy or depth creates an enormously different sense from the Platonic one of height. It is rooted in the actuality of human existence rather than in some other realm up in the sky beyond this one. It is hard perhaps for us to accept this because the theological tradition warns us to beware of 'pantheism', the identification of God and the cosmos. It tells us that God has to be 'other' than creation, and we automatically think that depth has to mean God is somehow down there, inside creation, while only height is truly beyond us. But being 'other' is just as little assured by height as by depth, if what we are thinking of is supreme power in terms of force. Power in this sense—and the intellect in alliance with it—exists on a continuum with the human world, and therefore height of itself proves nothing. What makes sure that God is 'other' is if God is infinitely nonviolent and we come to see that violence is a risk and product of creation itself. Nowhere is this more evident than among humans, but we may also speculate that the risk occurs at the animal level and all the way down to the atomic and subatomic. In a way it is 'built in'. However the present book is not concerned with a speculative question like this, only with the reality of the human. At the moment, therefore, here is the point to be clear on: God as understood by human beings can be deeply intimate to creation (more than we can imagine) but still 'other' from everything we know because God is infinitely nonviolent.

And so we move into the full depth of the meaning of the vision. If we think of God in this way—that God is in the depths of intimacy—then our feeling perhaps has more of dark than of light. And this would not be inappropriate in the tradition if we think of Luther's 'hidden God' or the 'shining darkness' of the mystics. Jesus said his Father 'is in the secret place'. There is a sense in which our contact with God is blind, and is known in and through our whole bodily existence, in and through the earth. This goes with the fact that in the vision the partner of the earth is not seen. We are talking about the intimacy of an embrace with eyes closed, like love-making, like the union of two bodies. The embrace with God does not need eyes, for it touches us at every level of our being, and deeper and deeper still...

At the same time light does have a meaning, an essential one for human existence. Light for us is seeing, and to say 'I see' is to say 'I understand' and sometimes in a powerful way, with a grasp of something that seems to go all the way through it. And thus the seer of Revelation described the holy city Jerusalem as having 'the glory of God and a radiance like a very rare jewel, like jasper, clear as crystal.' The new human city can be seen all the way through and without darkness or shadow in any part. It is the earth suffused through and through with the truth of nonviolence, without the shadow of rivalry and death, consistent with itself, with life, in every part. Light here is a light we have not yet reached, a light to come that will make present visibility dull indeed. To 'see' with this light then is both an intimacy and an understanding, one that tells the mind that the true, complete and final goal of the earth and its inhabitants has been reached. There are no further obstacles to overcome, no puzzles, contradictions or scandals to undo. 'The home of God is among mortals. He will dwell with them... Death will be no more...'

The vision is thus a reversal of our normal looking-upward understanding. Here we follow God's own gesture of coming down and understand with God's way of understanding, a glance of love that goes all the way in and through the earth and to its darkest corners. Down, therefore, is the new up. And the 'in', or innerness, of nonviolence is the new 'above'. The rest of this study will play out this perspective in terms of Christian anthropology, popular culture, formal theology, and finally ecclesial consequences. But now we can already see the basic reason why Christianity can and should always be considered 'virtual'. It is always a provisional version of itself, a sketch, a fantasy seeking to be fulfilled. Living just around the corner from its final goal its vision is filled with strange, wonderful images of the truth yet to come. In Christian thought the general term for this condition is 'eschatology'. Eschatology means orientation toward final things, the 'last things', and is a standard part of the Christian confession. In the Creed it is given in a nutshell and we repeat it automatically: Christ 'will come again to judge the living and the dead' and 'we look for the resurrection of the dead.' But immediately this seems woefully inadequate to what I'm attempting to describe.

The problem is both the automatic way these phrases are repeated and the image they communicate. The dominant picture is of final judgment and the sentence to be passed on each human being, deciding their eternal salvation or loss. This is a grim, legal picture, and produces a reaction that is basically like someone awaiting the results of an exam, to see if they have passed or failed. What is missing is an awareness of how the end is already playing out dynamically in the present. For the virtual character of Christianity is extraordinarily concrete.

If a baby is half-way out of the mother we don't say ritualistically 'Well, Lucy is going to have a baby.' We say 'Wow, look, there it is, I can see its head poking out! It's amazing!' This different attitude is in no way abstract or subjective, the effect of something we're just thinking about. The baby's head emerging from its mother already impacts the situation massively. The baby changes everything objectively in the present. In the same way the nonviolence of the cross pushes the envelope of the world in a completely new direction and we live in the space of its pushing. Nevertheless, by the same token, the baby is still not out yet; we cannot yet see its eyes and mouth, its arms and legs. And the envelope of pregnancy is still half intact and the pushing is still inside it. And so a half-way-out baby, though powerful, is still a virtual baby, and what is pressing at the cultural envelope of the world is concrete and virtual at the same time, a high-impact sketch of what it will be when it fully transforms our present frame.

The message of the gospel is thus a continuous trend in the world, a direction of pushing, and so every institutional claim and representation is necessarily provisional and even untrue when it claims 'this is Christianity'. It's untrue both because there is more pushing to do, and because that institution is only a restricted local (and perhaps very weak) instance of a much larger scene of pushing. In the next chapters I will go on to show how in the areas of history, popular culture and philosophical culture the pressure of the gospel is felt, so the churches are not alone, or even primary as agents of gospel change in the world. The gospel in fact is its own primary agent, and it works in many and various ways. The point then is for Christians to situate themselves in this overall geography and time of the gospel's pushing, rather than in any particular local scene. And in this way the local scenes—the churches—will perhaps themselves become different. Through a new or changed consciousness of what they are and how to situate themselves they will come to embody more clearly the transformation toward which the gospel is slowly pushing the whole world.

Meditation

No-Name: with this name we can begin to hear Jesus. We hear him when he says that no one knows the Father except the Son and those to whom the Son chooses to reveal him...We begin perhaps to understand what he means.

Jesus called God his Father. This surely is the same as Mother, but that on its own would make no difference to how we understand God. Jesus says we only know God in the practice of forgiveness, and by observing him, Jesus, in the practice of forgiveness: i.e. its ultimate and unconditional sense. 'He who has seen me has seen the Father.'

But Jesus also said God could be known from the character of the earth, its beauty and abundance.

Consider the lilies of the fields, how they grow; they neither toil nor spin, yet I tell you, even Solomon in all his glory was not clothed like one of these. But if God so clothes the grass of the fields, which is alive today and tomorrow is thrown into the oven, will he not much more clothe you—you of little faith? (Matt. 6:28-30)

We could trust the goodness of creation because it visibly demonstrates the goodness of its Maker.

So, what did Jesus think when he bit into a fruit, when he ate a crust of bread, when he drank a cup of water?

These things were not simply physical, quanta of calories, as we might judge them. Or pleasures for a moment's satisfaction. They spoke of God's work and love in creation, the same as the lilies of the field, the same as the birds of the air for whom the Father provided food.

Therefore, at some level, they were truly personal. They were a communication of God's creative Wisdom. They were God's concrete will for life.

Nevertheless they were products too of human culture, and so could be used unjustly, murderously. The poor were hungry. The plenty of the earth could stand as an offense and contradiction, as it did to Lazarus.

Also, Jesus knew the alienation of creation in its own right, the roaring lion, the marauding wolf, the bitter viper. Creation has been subjected to the risk of violence...

And it was because of all this, the communication of creation, both its beauty and its alienation, that he took it upon himself. He said concerning a piece of bread: 'This is my body.' He knew creation as deeply personal, and so he could overcome its alienation, carrying through a personal identification of nature with himself. And doing so he awakened the deep self of creation to a truly astonishing possibility, to becoming itself endless love, the love it was always intended to be.

Nor did he rest simply with what was presently living, with the current moment of what was breathing and growing on earth, but 'he descended into hell'. He went to the place of the dead, where all that has lived previously remains in its sad and dim memory of its brief instant of life. And he preached to the spirits of the dead in prison, in order that his communication of love might stretch back to the very dawn of time and engage its half-finished project in an astonishing second genesis...through love.

This is the final explanation of the beauty of the earth, of its radiant mysterious light. When Jesus said 'This is my body,' a light went on in the earth. God had spoken to its depths and so now speaks *from* its depths for all those who look upon it with understanding. If God had not spoken in this way the earth would remain bound to its endless risk of violence until its final doom. But now the home of God is among mortals and ultimately there can be no more death and no more sorrow. The pathway of history is now the understanding of the infinite depths of love at the heart of the earth, and the following of this utterly amazing truth to its conclusion.

God disappears from the skies. He now makes his abode in the abyss of the cosmos. Because of Jesus, God is now in the roots of our reality. It is because of the infinite nonviolence of creation created by Jesus that God is there, united boundlessly with earth.

Here is a parable for this truth. The story is about Buzz Aldrin, one of the first two men to walk the surface of the moon. It was Sunday, July 20, 1969.

Aldrin had carried aboard the Lunar Module a tiny communion kit, given to him by his church, including chalice, some wafers and a small flask of wine. That evening he radioed, 'This is the LM pilot speaking. I'd like to take this opportunity to ask every person listening in, whoever and wherever they may be, to pause for a moment and contemplate the events of the past few hours, and to give thanks in his or her own way.'

He tipped the wine into the chalice and watched it slowly lap against the side of the cup. Silently he read the words from John's gospel that he had printed on a card. 'I am the vine, you are the branches. Whoever remains in me and I in him will bear much fruit.'[4]

The astronaut did not celebrate his trip to the heavens by gazing further up, beyond to the stars, and thanking God up there for what had taken place. He brought with him products of the earth, filled themselves with the meaning of God. And he read about a vine that curls out of the earth to bring forth wondrous fruit. The story does not say so, but, surely, sometime when he was there, he looked down from the moon's barren surface upon the luminous beauty of the earth and gave thanks to God, all his thoughts flowing in that direction.

Chapter Two

The Sign that Means the World

The first chapter was in the nature both of a manifesto and a meditation, a visionary statement. Now we need to move to a more precise, analytic approach, although the vision's light remains always with us. An obvious place to begin is a question, and surely a loaded one. What is the character of historical Christianity in relation to the vision of the earth in communion with its lover No-Name and with Jesus the nonviolent one?

The question really does seem loaded, because Christianity has by far and away seen itself as a means of getting souls to heaven, not enhancing a relationship with the earth.[1] So, it may be assumed, many Christian thinkers will quickly pick off their mental bookshelves volumes filled with deviations and heresies, the type of what I am presenting here. These may be summed up under the name 'millennialism', meaning the false anticipation of God's kingdom here on earth. The history of Christianity is littered with deluded and dangerous attempts to force the coming of God's reign in history. But it's important here not to repeat a stereotyped reaction. We're living in a very different world from any other time in the past two thousand years, under great stresses of many kinds, both negative and positive. For Christianity not to try to realize its soul of peace on the earth is to contribute to great harm, but more important even than this, it is to ignore something that is coming to realization from within its own innermost character and story. For today, for the first time, Christianity is coming into its authentic character as *virtual*.

What does this mean? The statement is the heart of every-thing, and although I sketched the idea in the first chapter I need to explain it fully. By this word I intend to pull into a single theme a rich, layered event that is happening right under our noses. To begin to follow it through we need to do a kind of light-footed dance across the landscape of Christian history and the system of signs in which it lives and which are used to reveal its meaning (i.e. its semiotics). The image of dance is apt, because a dance is something seamless and whole, but to get to a facility with dance you first have to learn the steps patiently, one by one. What follows then is a series of steps for the dance, and I ask the reader to be patient and deliberate in following the steps in this way. What will result will be a pattern of meanings which add up to a different understanding of Christianity. Allowing ourselves to be pulled along by this dance, to enter its intricate choreography of significance and signs, will bring us into the compelling new thought of Christianity as virtual.

Dancing with the Stars

To begin then, Christianity is neither one thing or another! It is not the new earth, but neither is it the old earth. It takes a certain shape, yet progressively its shape is not certain. It is an impossible idea, but its impossibility becomes more and more its central possibility. Virtuality as used to describe Christianity says first that whatever the Christian movement is it is bound to have multiple forms. You could say that Christianity in essence is tied to simulation. It always amounts to a kind of cartoon sketch, a back-of-an-envelope design, seeking to give a concrete idea or shape to something in itself ungraspable and unfulfilled. And, by the very same token, it is productive of a never-ending impetus toward this impossible dream.

The actual history of Christianity of course shows this. There are countless such sketches in Christianity, any number of particular movements, churches, schisms, orders, covenants, reforms, revivals, spirituals, anchorites, communities, sects and splinters, from the great historical structures to the most esoteric little group. All of them claim something absolute and nonnegotiable in their chosen portrait and that is what gives them their special identity, their handle on the mysterious dynamic of the Christian faith.

We can certainly explain this from the future-directed perspective of the Christian message, from the general teaching of Christ's return and the full unity of God and humanity still to come. Anything with this powerful forward tug will have a built-in unrest to it. It will experience an undertow of challenge and crisis, resulting in a kind of nuclear half-life or splitting of forms in an open-ended search on what it means truly to be a Christian. Far from representing a wound in the Christian soul, a rent in the seamless garment of Christ, 'disunity' among churches is a natural condition of Christian existence. The phenomenon of Christianity possesses a plural and provisional character in response to what it's called to be and yet still is not. Moreover, the further it progresses in time the more this instability and changeling quality is likely to show. The existing multiple forms offer to Christians a template on which to consider still further ones. In this regard the attempt by a traditional institution like the Roman Catholic church to call all Christians back to physical unity within its fold is both a defensive expression of its own self-identity and a constant denial of the historical situation provoked by the very message it claims to represent.

However, what I mean by virtuality is not simply a riot of forms brought by the tug of the future. The term doesn't have simply a temporal sense, realized by historical shifts in Christianity. Virtuality refers normally to a very different theme than time. More than anything it is used in regard to the information world in which we live, especially the Internet. It describes the mushrooming of electronic communication through computers, broadband and satellites, with visual and audio terminals everywhere connecting the whole world to itself. The explosion of these media has given people the ability to connect with a twenty-four / seven stream of images and information, to the extent that it becomes an alternative way of being in the world. People not only spend hours online but they are able to enter constructed virtual worlds with persona or 'avatars' which interact, play, fight, buy, sell etc. Virtual property, including game roles, status, and narrative, are sold across the web. I have a friend whose son is paid to travel the world and play in game tournaments on behalf of others who will then experience the pleasure vicariously online. In other words the world of electronic communication has become another 'real' layer of reality shaping people's lives and destiny.

Yet this intense world of signs is just the latest, complex mode of the universal human capacity for symbol making. Virtuality can also stand, therefore, for the way human beings have always existed within some kind of sign system, within a visual and verbal order. This could easily be humanity's distinctive defining feature. Today that symbolic order has reached a level of extraordinary development and depth, but it has always in one way or another been proper to human beings. Think of almost any form of ritual, its garments and colors, its movement and center, all a symbolic system giving shape and meaning to the world. Architecture of whatever level, from a circle of stones made by children, to the Forbidden City of Beijing, a replica of the abode of the celestial emperor surrounding the North Star, is a shape of meaning which we literally live within. The sign indeed means the world to us.

Philosophers recognize this, that it is impossible in fact to separate the thing from the sign. They have become more and more resigned to not being able to do so. And many of them are not just resigned. They see this as the distinctive quality of human existence. To be inside a sign is to be human.

Today we are in a frenzy of the sign. To the Internet we have to add movies, a slightly older but still enormously vibrant form of symbolic communication. Movies bring us into a narrative world, but they are more than just their story. The movie screen possesses a spectacular immediacy of color and form, of texture and movement, of bodies, faces, eyes and souls. To watch a movie in a darkened theater, or even at home, is to drown in a hyper-world which is a sign in its own right, a sign gathered together from signs. It is a sensuous experience which makes everything somehow more essential, powerful, alive. Movies as an experience displace the world, make the symbolic order greater than the real. And so we live inside movies both at the immediate level of watching them and afterwards because of their enduring impact on us. How often have you heard someone giving the meaning of an extraordinary time-stopping experience say, 'It was like a movie?' Or heard a reference to a specific movie scene or dialogue to tell the story of something that happened in 'real life'? 'It was like that movie, you know, it has that guy in it who was in *Stage Beauty*, what's his name? In this movie he's a sort of mystic druggie who begins to turn his life around and he likes to pass this woman's house to overhear her singing gospel songs through her open window, you know, attracted by something completely other from what's he known...'[2] Etcetera.

And of course we should add T.V. and radio in all their formats of news, sports, talk shows, game shows, reality shows and advertising. So much of the same kind of thing can be said about them, of their power to construct our lived world, and I don't mean so much what is actually said in these programs. What is actually spoken is more and more swallowed up in the stream of speech and image itself, leaving only a sense of staging, of the spotlight itself, and of who can command the spotlight. As a character in the movie *To Die For* (1995) says, 'You're nobody in America unless you're on T.V. On T.V. is where we learn about who we really are.' The majority of people really don't end up on T.V. for fifteen minutes of fame, but like in the movie *Requiem For A Dream* (2000) many people construct their self-image by a fantasy of doing so, or at the least in reference to what they see there.

Generally speaking T.V. and radio constitute the most existentially empty or indifferent regions of the contemporary world of signs. News, fashion, chat, sport, and advertisements follow each other so relentlessly it seems that everything is disposable and everything is for sale. But by the very fact of its unending presence and immediacy it says that this is where reality lies and where we personally can find it. In some households the T.V. is never switched off, becoming a kind of extra member of the household, perhaps the most important one.

Behind this modern screen-centered world, however, there is a further level of the technical multiplication of signs, one with a less obtrusive character yet still immensely important. Behind all electronic media there stands first the printed word, the Gutenberg revolution. This is generally considered a more 'serious' level of meaning, certainly less visual and much more designed to enlist our internal imagination in producing its effect. Written words depend on language and its ability to speak 'inside our heads' without recourse to externally visible signs, only the words themselves. Language and writing are really the most mysterious phenomena in the sign world and there is an immense amount of literature devoted to understanding them. One thing that is striking is the way language seems to arrive whole and complete, a kind of ready-made software for the brain before software was ever thought of. It constitutes more than anything the sea of signs or signification in which we swim. Outside of it human life is inconceivable. But if we then add to this basic fact of spoken and written meaning the ability to reproduce it by movable type on the written page, and for great numbers of people to be able to read exactly the same thing as others, then you have another and primary level to the explosion of the sign world around us. Gutenberg is the beginning of the automated multiplication of the sign that has flooded our world in a fathomless deep. It shows the depth of the seas in which we swim, seas which have been added to by successive tributaries covering it with ever more impetuous waters, until the image or visual sign becomes an overwhelming flood.

Circling back in our dance to Gutenberg brings us smartly face to face again with Christianity. Gutenberg is the classic linkage between the Christian movement and the concrete universe of the sign. As we know the translation and printing of the bible helped the Reformation put the scriptures into the hands of ordinary people. Along with a reading of the literal sense it enabled each individual to gain an authoritative meaning, right there on the printed page. This is itself a 'sign', again a sign made up of signs. The book achieves transcendent importance, mediating personal freedom or 'justification' before God. More than any other single feature it was the physical fact of the scriptures that mobilized the immense changes of the Protestant Reformation. If the printed sign helped provoke this upheaval in Christianity could not the visual explosion of the Internet etc. mean a similar shift? Will not the new technologies of the visual work in some similar way to advance the significance or sign-functions of Christianity? Here we have arrived at the critical point. Here is where we begin to plumb more deeply the meaning of virtuality in connection to Christianity.

From the reasons I have given it easy to understand that Christianity has a natural sympathy for the world of the automated sign, for the projection of its meaning through the printing press. There is, I believe, a parallel upheaval in respect of the visual media, but not a parallel way in which it is playing out.[3] Christian institutions or churches employed the sign of the printed page to project their meaning, a meaning which was already particularly a matter of language, of verbal signs communicating a 'good news'. But the new virtuality of the visual media is doing something that seems to have a life of its own. No one social institution is able to control it or exploit it for its own ends. Evangelists may use it, but with nothing like the privileged feeling with which the bible claimed the printed word. It really appears to be a 'free' medium, with basically anyone, anywhere, being able to plug in and use it. However, exactly in this freedom, within this life of its own, visual virtuality is carrying through a Christian revolution.

In order to show how and why this might be, we will turn directly to the reflections of a unique anthropological thinker, René Girard.[4] Girard represents another step in our dance, involving something of an enormous leap or flip backward, into a distant space at the very dawn of human signs and significance. Once we have accomplished this primal jump then our dance of Christian meaning and signs can become little short of extraordinary, taking on a movement that we could hardly have imagined. To learn this step demands a little more concentration at this point perhaps, but its effect is truly breathtaking.

Girard provides a seminal account both of the origins of culture and of the role of biblical revelation in disclosing them. His thought demonstrates the subversive effect of the Christian gospel, and above all of Christianity's central sign of the cross and resurrection. According to Girard the story of the passion and crucifixion of Christ has broken open the traditional cultural order based on violent sacrifice and the rules and structures that flow from it. This loosening of culture is momentous, involving a radical interference in our system of signs and the possibility, I believe, of a system that is entirely new. At the core of Girard's anthropology is what he calls mimesis, i.e. competitive imitation. I will explain this thought in a moment, but at once I want to foreshadow a twist I will make on his key idea that will constitute the Nijinsky leap in the dance! Alongside competitive imitation I want to highlight giving and compassion as the other possibility of human imitation, one that through Christ has become rooted in the semiotic universe. Compassion is frequently drowned out by competitive imitation and the violence it induces, but nevertheless the Christian gospel has made compassion central or thematic to human history, even if against the historical grain. After I have presented Girard's thesis I will go on to draw from Christian cultural history a vibrant understanding of how the compassion and giving of Christ have changed our relationship to creation through a transformational sign system. The giving of Christ has entered deeply into the world, producing at the world's heart the powerful engine of Christian virtuality—what might be called the world's once and future meaning. We are now very near to the really thrilling part of our dance!

Origins of the Sign

Girard tells us that in common with all nature, but to a truly critical degree, human beings are imitative. They are able to imitate everything and anything. This leads to humanity's potent capacity for learning, but at the same time it invites the possibility of an imitation of one human by another. Girard first recognized the phenomenon in certain key works of Western literature. These masterpieces reflected an author's shift from naive description of romantic desire to an account where desire is mediated, where one person's desire infects another with the very same desire. From this Girard deduced a three-cornered structure, consisting of the model and the object which the model seeks, and the subject who is brought to imitate that same vector of relationship—and so undergo 'mimetic desire'. Let me give my own very basic example of the pattern: the time when my four year old daughter was playing with her four year old friend. There were three toys to play with, a scooter, a tricycle, a little car. When my daughter got on the scooter her friend insisted that was in fact what she wanted. When my daughter then moved to the tricycle her friend discovered an overriding preference for the three-wheeler. When my daughter then chose the car her friend realized after all it was the car she needed. And so my daughter returned to the scooter... but there's no call to continue, you see what I mean! Here is mimetic or imitative desire immediately recognizable in children, but what Girard under-stood from these novelists was that it was a structuring principle of human relationship as such.

Although in the instance I describe my daughter was a model of discretion, and no battle erupted, it is easy to see how very easily there could be a mutual feedback between model and subject, each reinforcing each other's desire. In which case a fight seems inevitable. Everything happens so fast and so deep that the ache of desire within is felt as most properly the subject's own and is not at all something coming from the other. In consequence when the other moves to grab the object, s/he is taking away what is most properly and necessarily the subject's 'own'. The potential for rivalry and violence is plain.

The next stage in Girard's thinking was an inference backward to the first emergence of our ancestors, evolving from the line of primates or higher apes. The early hominids were equipped with a greatly increased neural capacity for imitation which both overrode instinctual restraint and lacked—as yet—cultural controls. There were no adjudicating parents or babysitters on hand! There is now a big hole, an open possibility, where before there were instinctual dominance and submission patterns. In this situation imitating the gesture of the other toward an object is the birth of desire itself—an awareness of the hole inside one and the need to fill it precisely with that object. The 'discovery' of this bottomless pit was of course acutely dangerous and led 'naturally', and yet unnaturally, to violence. Without either biological or cultural controls the result of these mirroring and converging movements of acquisition could only be lethal violence.

But then, in the midst of this primitive scenario, Girard hypothesizes a dramatic and terrible solution. And again it is something both natural and unnatural. In primary groups of hominids, on a timescale up to a million years ago or more, a conflict between two can rapidly involve others, in swift imitation of the intense desire on display, until all are drawn into a fearful brawl of all against all. Think of the school-hall swarm around a fight, but without teachers or monitors to restrain it! It is an event of catastrophic proportions, comparable in evolutionary terms to the Big Bang or the first self-organization of the cell out of an indifferent soup of molecules. For precisely in this moment of threatened annihilation there arrives a saving mechanism, truly as if a god had appeared. One of the group for whatever reason appears weaker or more provocative than the others, or perhaps she simply trips, and then all of the terrible violence quickly falls on her. As Girard says, in an all-against-all one can quickly stand for all, assuming monstrous proportions. It is a single experience of hatred and fear and once the individual is singled out s/he becomes responsible for the whole evil event. The result is automatic and horrifying: the single surrogate or scapegoat is beaten and killed in a group murder without precedent, and the moment s/he is dead a new, totally astonishing peace prevails. (I hardly need emphasize the hypothetical character of the scene, but it has been played out with numbing familiarity in historical humanity, from stonings, through lynchings and pogroms, down to the unremarked assassinations of day-to-day conversation. All Girard has done is to extrapolate it to the beginning of human experience, in every sense.)

The qualitative break in the continuum of animal awareness creates the basis of the human. It is the gaping void of annihilation and its miraculous healing over through the single victim which provides the origin of the sacred — the victim becomes the god, a being of awesome power. And at the same time it is the primordial event of the sign. By its scorching effect it produces the first actual 'thought' separated from immediate sensation, an 'abstraction' that means something enormous, impalpable, transcendent, divine. It hardly yet has a name, but it certainly has a reality, one which opens up the world as a field of consciousness, separating out a 'something' from everything else. And the moment it is repeated by a group in some kind of semi-intentionality for the sake of its benefits, then it gains the power of ritual, of reiteration, of recognizability. The experience of the primal murder provides the mental electric storm which burns the transcendent circuits into the brain; but only when the event is re-enacted will it find its necessary flag or signal by which the thought, the abstraction, the story of the god can be summoned to mind. For, as Girard argues, the re-enactment will carry certain characteristic gestures or sounds which will then stand for the event and evoke all its mysterious power. And around those gestures and sounds, like the pole star at sea, the chaos of sense impressions will piece by piece find their own distinguishing marks or signs. Like decoding, but in reverse (i.e. the creation of a code), once you establish a sign for one element of meaning you can begin to multiply meaningful signs across all of a given surface—by virtue of the original act of signification. It's conceivable that basically organized primitive syntax and working vocabularies were established within a matter of months after the first ritual repetitions.

Here then is a step in our dance which has an apocalyptic shape to it. It amounts to the stars falling from the sky, because, looked at this way, the human sign loses all its Platonic purity and height, its 'immaculate conception' as Girard terms it. Instead it becomes a deep well in which first we spy the power of desire and then the event of the surrogate victim / scapegoat as the primary signified around which coalesces all meaning.

Human cultures have continually talked about their gods: can we now understand that as a way of (mis)remembering the incredible phenomenon of the birth of meaning itself? And if this is the case what then would be the latter-day consequences if a sign should arise from the midst of history reproducing the contours of that original violent phenomenon but actually as a gesture of infinite forgiving love? Would it not easily embed itself in many hearers, awakening an atavistic memory of the most 'natural' thing in the world, but this time not as horror, but astonishingly, stunningly, free of violence? And would not this transforming sign then progressively, century by century, have a multiplying, productive effect on the world of signs, communicating its positive relational value to all other signs? Would it not initiate a secret slow epistemic shift, changing the very character of human meaning? Would it not be, in other words, the heart of the virtual, setting in motion the changeling world of signs as such?

But with these last few sentences I have leaped well ahead, unable to hold back from the last brilliant passes of the dance. These thoughts are quite a bit further than Girard himself goes and I need to come back into step with him so I can properly introduce this transformative anthropology. Girard has created a truly epoch-making intellectual advance, a synthesis of biological evolutionary processes and the singular phenomenon of the human spirit. He has still one further element to teach us, and it is in this respect that his thought—inescapably I believe— opens the way for the more radical argument I am suggesting in these pages.

The Bible Effect

If culture depends on a founding murder it is highly improbable that culture will be able to identify its own ultimate source. How does the eye see the blind-spot by which it works? How can you find the Archimedean point to upend the universe itself? All the same, there are some moments in culture which get very close. Girard identifies Greek drama, the great tragedies of Sophocles and Euripides, as effectively aware of the role of the scapegoat, based as they are in ancient Greek ritual. In other words there is necessarily some awareness of violent origins in collective human consciousness, if only because we keep doing the same thing over and over. And yet we have a vested interest in keeping it from the forefront of our minds—and so the Greek dramatists only go so far and at the last moment sheer away from what they have revealed. However, in these circumstances of prevailing cultural mist there rises to view one cultural tradition which does consistently and radically unearth violent human foundations. It is only because of that tradition—as Girard asserts—that we have a progressive awareness of these foundations today. The Jewish and Christian biblical traditions are unique in speaking for the victim; and above all the figure of Jesus the Crucified has served to disclose and vindicate the multiple victims of history, those at its foundation and those throughout its course. Because of the spread of these traditions throughout the world it is now impossible to ignore the victims we make, from the victims of genocide, through those massacred in war, to those subjected to discrimination, to individual abused children. This is a massive shift in human consciousness and it has only one reasonable historical source, the Jewish and Christian scriptures and their *de facto* dispersion through global culture.

They are the subversive force progressively breaking down traditional mechanisms based on sacrificial repetitions of the founding murder and the cover-up that goes with them. Girard is very clear that the bible has had this unique effect which thoroughly pervades our contemporary world. But in these conditions there emerges a stark choice. After the Christian revelation there are no longer truly effective scapegoats and so, in Girard's own words, 'the virus of mimetic violence can spread freely'. Thus, 'Either we choose Christ or we run the risk of self-destruction.'[5] I do not disagree, but the way his analysis narrows simply to this statement cuts out a great deal of the field of contemporary reality. It becomes a kind of negative scholastic or churchy judgment on the world. All the deep genealogy he has labored over at this point becomes two dimensional and misses the profound transformative changes Christianity has brought about. In short Girard has produced a structural genealogy of violence; he lacks an equivalent genealogy of compassion.

In contrast I have already pointed toward a positive implication of the revelation of Christ in the world that counters that
of violence. The desire for the object demonstrated in Christian
culture is not simply possessive; it is also contemplative and self-
dispossessing, and this contemplative desire may well
accompany and parallel the spreading virus of mimetic desire.
My argument then is both more radical and more hopeful than
Girard's. I believe, in agreement with Girard, that in the world of
signs under the pressure of the gospel the inherent violence of
human culture is more and more exposed to view. But alongside
this there is the cultural 'other' of the revelation of violence
which is the possibility of compassion and giving arising in and
from the very same chaos of signs. We are assisting at the most
profound semiotic revolution worked by the Christian message,
more profound than the use of the printing press, more profound
even than the revelation of violence. Why? Because Christ is
changing the nature of the sign itself. Christ is working at the
level of the virtual to bring about his kingdom of love. I want
now to demonstrate this, to show within the chaotic world of
signs the process of an amazing change.

The Truth about Romance

How did the West produce the intense world of visual signs?
What were the underlying forces that favored the multiplication
of signs? It is generally understood that there is close
relationship between capitalism and Christianity. Especially
through the Protestant Reformation the Christian faith produced
a huge shift to the individual, a man or woman separated out
before God. Sociologists and historians recognize that by means
of this ideological transition the individual no longer existed
within a containing order of duties and rights controlling the
distribution of wealth. Wealth instead became a marker of
individual divine blessing. Thus the Reformation led to the

typical figure of the righteous business man, the mill-owner who made big profits during the week and with them endowed a church for giving thanks on Sunday. More recently we have the emergence of the 'prosperity gospel' which applies the same basic formula to everyone. As they say in these churches, 'prayed for and paid for', neatly chiming relationship to God and personal financial success. Thus Christianity has underpinned the multiplication of material wealth for individuals. But a consequence of this is the thickening of the world of signs. Prosperity is a sign of God's favor, and this is shown, signified, by the actual goods, the houses, clothes, cars, etc. Against this metaphysical background, however, the goods very quickly attain their own social value and produce the well-known contours of the consumer world. Once they were declared divinely willed and good they could act as self-referential signs in and for themselves. People don't have to give any thought to theological justification to derive meaning from the latest car model, from the good-life associations of household items, refrigerators, fitted kitchens, plasma T.V.s, and now from the plugged-in cool of the digital world, computers, cell phones, iPods, G.P.S. and so on. So it is that our Western culture has developed a class of signs with a powerful inner content of validated desire.

You could say then that desire creates a 'lining' around the surface, or just under the surface, of an object so that it works dynamically as a sign. The lining is put there by people and says in effect, 'Here is the object to possess and the fact that both you and I desire it makes it powerfully significant.' We are very close here of course to Girard's mimetic desire; the only difference is that it is played out in a systemic collective form, in the world of economics, the marketplace of buying and selling. Here is another aspect then of our world of signs. They are not just about information. Many of them—perhaps today almost all of them— enlist our mimetic and possessive desire to achieve and communicate their meaning. However, the moment I say this a reaction surely sets in. People have a sense that the contemporary phenomenon covered by the word 'desire' is richer and more many-sided than sheer possessiveness, and immediately I will also agree. I said 'almost all' signs, not all. I believe in fact that before the motif of possessive desire at work in Western society there is an earlier, underlying and more wonderful level which it presupposes. In this case Girardian desire, although enormously cogent, is only a partial description of the historical and anthropological facts. Before people in the West learned to desire things as consumers they learned to do so as contemplatives!

I refer to the eleventh and twelfth centuries as a uniquely fruitful moment in the production and meaning of desire. These centuries saw the first development of romantic feeling. They witnessed the new poetry of 'courtly love', fostered as the name suggests in the aristocratic courts of Europe. Among the ideals of this poetry was a passionate relationship to the beloved held in a state of imaginative suspension rather than fulfilled in action. While, naturally with human beings, the facts can easily turn out very different from intentions, the way the literature worked and attained an endless fascination was because there really was an element of distance and dispossession in the affirmed desire.[6] To think of courtly love as always a covert route to seduction, is to import a far too modern, suspicious approach. It fails to recognize the powerful cultural restraints of the time—the way desire between men and women in the petty nobility would be morally and practically controlled—and thus the real, spiritual breakthrough which felt legitimacy precisely in this situation. No doubt there was a frisson of the forbidden in much of what went on, but my argument is not that courtly love was ever 'pure' but that it was it was based on a real modification of desire introduced into the human universe.

What was discovered was a way to maintain the object deliberately on the virtual level— desire both released and held in abeyance. This adds another and strictly transformative layer to the meaning of virtual and specifically in relation to desire. It makes possible the possession of something in imagination only and the deliberate forfeiture of its object in order paradoxically to stay in relation to it. In the process the object and the other become valuable in their own right. All this happened in the elite circles of the courts of France, England, Germany, but it was celebrated in story and song, and became one of the under-girdings of Western culture allowing the release into the public domain of the object of desire. Prior, then, to capitalism and the economic liberation of desire there was the mobilization of inter-personal desire. It happened in a way that held in check its destructive potential, enabling instead a non-possessive moment, a contemplative refusal to move to the violent act of possession.

There is much discussion about the cultural sources of this phenomenon, Arabic, Greek, Celtic. There can be little doubt of these influences: it is no accident that the growth of passionate feeling arose very soon after the First Crusade when Europe had opened itself to an exotic southern world. But the taproot has to be the Christian gospel; its cultural theme of selfless love predated these new elements in European experience. External influences rather became the rains which nourished a seed already present. How other would the new teaching have been able to gain such ready acceptance in a culture ruled by church and state in alliance, and then even to challenge that culture? There was a natural resource in the affective devotion to the saints and to Jesus, and a similar intensity of devotion inevitably became directed to the ordinary human.[7] Eleanor of Aquitaine, the paragon of courtly love at the courts of Angers and Poitiers, was a grandchild of Guillaume, duke of Aquitaine, the first known troubadour. In many of Guillaume's love songs 'the vocabulary and emotional fervor hitherto ordinarily used to express man's love for God are transferred to the liturgical worship of woman, and vice versa.'[8] The layering of Christian feeling and the new romantic spirit is also witnessed in the *roman courtois,* the epic stories filled with legendary material and hinged on figures of woman, mystery and quest. The best known are the Arthurian cycles in which the image of the Holy Grail is probably the most enduring single figure of the overlapping of Christian and worldly themes. The Grail is at once a dish for the host of the mass, the chalice used by Jesus at his Last Supper, and the ultimate symbol of questing desire in almost any context.[9]

According to a number of scholars the theme of the Grail was promoted by contemporary growth in devotion to the host of communion, alongside Cistercian mysticism and its passionate desire for Christ. We can see in fact St. Bernard of Clairvaux, the founder of the Cistercians, working from the other direction. He took the frankly erotic love poetry of the biblical *Song of Songs* and in his commentary made it a parable for the love of Christ and the soul. He thus affirmed a deep harmony between Christian desire and human desire, and from the side of human love. Anselm of Canterbury, a slightly earlier figure working in the last quarter of the eleventh century, stands at the headwaters of the scholastic movement with writings of enormous intellectual weight. But he also anticipated the romantic development. He wrote prayers of deep affectivity, including addressing Jesus as 'mother'. Those addressed to the Virgin Mary are seen as among the earliest examples of a devotional attitude that would grow to a mighty flood in European Catholicism. They were in fact written at the request of his monks something like twenty years before the first stirrings of courtly poetry, turning on its head the common notion that the church used the theme of courtly love by shifting it to the Virgin Mary. Anselm's monks already held an affective relationship to the mother of Jesus and they got their literary master to put it in writing.[10]

Arguably these monks prepared the way for the troubadours. Once these church figures gave human expression to love of the divine it was entirely plausible for 'secular' poets and writers to work in the other direction, looking toward the spiritual to model love of the human. As already suggested in fact the imitation is then able to run in both directions, from the divine to the human and the human to the divine, and we can see an example of both in the work of a German writer of this period, Hartmann von Aue. In one of his stories, *Der Arme Heinrich*, there is a village girl who gives her blood for the love of her lord after the pattern of Christ, and subsequently she is rewarded with a vision of Christ in the form of a peasant.[11] Finally, toward the end of the period, there is the classic example of Francis of Assisi, perhaps the figure who more than any other brought together creation and love in an indelible joyous bond. His *Canticle of Creation* is a testament of an overflowing love for the object without a trace of acquisitiveness or violence. Francis translates into a cultural heritage with repercussions way beyond his time. The frescoes of Giotto, Cimabue and others, celebrating Francis' life, demonstrate a simple vividness and delight in the world which went on to influence generations of artists, leading into the upwelling humanism of the sixteenth century. And it was Francis who also gave us the *preseppio*, the first recorded crib with the infant Jesus in a manger which he erected at Greccio, perhaps his greatest artistic achievement in his own right. In one marvelous *coup de theatre* he placed the Christ in the middle of an earthly scene, without any sense of division or levels of reality between divine and human. He thus communicated the desire for Christ also to the ox, the ass, the shepherds, and the precious gifts of the kings.

If we look at later medieval depictions of the scene, for example Van der Weyden or Filippino Lippi's *Adoration of the Magi*, it's as if an explosion of wealth has hit the canvas but it is held suspended in something utterly new through the embrace of the dispossessed child. A riot of signs becomes an electrifying silence of love. Colors, cloth brocade, gold, jewels, horses, cattle, privileged and poor men, all are shown innocent and life-giving by their relationship with the infant Crucified One. The feast of

Christmas has maintained the sense of transformative giving, of the earth and its objects freed from violence, to this day.

The common thread always is the interchangeability of Christian and human devotion, and the effective anthropology which binds them together must be the non-possession of the object at the same time as a most intense relation to it. It strikes me as a highly fragile phenomenon in its secular realization; it was so easy for courtly devotion to topple over into rivalry, jealousy, possession, all the usual suspects. But the fragility does not count against the actuality: for a brief window of time in Western culture the object was beheld in a contemplative freedom, eagerly affirming the absolute value of the object without moving to lay hold of it. At an actual individual level the layering of contemplative freedom and affirmed desire becomes impossible to track: how pure was it, how genuine in any given case? But it is not necessary to answer these questions, because so long as the accent is on the theological roots of the experience we are on safe grounds. If we recognize the effective translation of Christian contemplation into relationships of human desire then in principle the phenomenon is possible. And we only deny this if we divide the world up in a dualist way between super-natural things and natural things.

At the formative level it is the gospel actuality of Jesus and the system of signs produced by him that stands behind the whole experience. It is the story and message of Jesus which creates a cultural novelty, a fresh sense in the eleventh and twelfth centuries of a love both boundless and non-possessive. This is the essence of contemplation. But if we were to single out one Jesus sign that mobilized this amazing emotion it would be the bread of the Eucharist. As already mentioned devotion to the Sacrament was experiencing at this time a growth in popularity, involving reservation for prayer, processions, windows built in the cells of anchorites with a sightline to the church tabernacle, openings or *oculi* made in the walls of the church apse so the faithful could venerate the host from outside, visits, genuflection, etc., etc. If we understand this from the perspective of sign rather than 'real presence' we won't immediately get bogged down in a controversy that only came later and after the church had applied substantialist language to semiotics.[12] When the Jesus of the gospels identified with the bread, saying 'This is my body', he in effect produced a sign 'lined' with desire that really was desire but which had no term in capture, conquest, violence. Because the limitless nonviolence of the cross was anticipated and signaled in this 'thing' then all reference to it, in devotion, would necessarily experience itself without violence, as non-possessive love. How indeed is it possible to desire something without limit and at the same time without violence? Only if the object itself somehow invites you to surrender in 'communion' with itself, with its own limitless self-giving. Only if the object has within it an infinite depth of love into which it invites you.

This is the semiotic character of the bread of the Eucharist and Anne Astell has shown in important detail how it worked. She points out how the aesthetics of the period did not draw a rigid distinction between seeing and other modes such as touching, tasting and eating. Eating the Eucharist was thus to gain a 'vision' of Christ, but reciprocally, 'Gazing upon the host in adoration meant a real physical contact with it, a touch, as light rays emanating from the Host beamed into the eye of the adorer; and vice versa, as rays from the beholder's eye extended themselves in a line of vision to the Host.'[13] But this vibrancy of the sign was not simply the result of a more holistic aesthetic. Because the limitless nonviolence of the cross instituted this sign the devotion to it must at some level experience itself without violence. Shared light is in fact a metonym for the nonviolence of the Eucharist, the mutual in-pouring of nonviolent selfhood, without barrier or pain. It was intimacy without violence, therefore, that provoked the intense popular desire to see, to behold, to consume, to be united to the host.[14] This experience was the engine of the contemplative meaning of the Eucharist in this period and it served to broadcast and reinforce a wider cultural wavelength of non-violent desire. The Eucharistic bread's immediacy and generosity of impact within the actual cultural world, combined with a parallel sense of devotion to the human beloved, produced in Europe a first breakthrough phenomenon of nonviolent desire.

It doesn't count against this moment of transformation that it was swallowed up in a tide of political and military violence which, if anything, was worse in Europe because at some level it was repressing precisely this new-found nonviolence. Christendom has always had a bad conscience about itself that it can only deal with by greater and greater paroxysms of 'justified' violence. But no matter the violent reaction, at that moment of time, perhaps for a day, or three score of years, a cultural transformation was experienced in all its mysterious freshness. It then bent its head and plunged down into the depth of Western culture, but not before it had left its mark on literature and art and very probably commerce as an enduring possibility of nonviolent desire. And so, standing behind the Reformation and its theological freedom for acquiring the things of this world, there is a deeper and more basic anthropology of desire in relation to the object. The twelfth and thirteenth centuries saw a striking eruption of this desire and it gave birth to a class of signs which in their anthropological structure provide objects emptied of violence. Because Christian contemplation necessarily implicates the real world—not some purely spiritual world beyond—it cannot help communicate a positive desire to the world in general. Before there is capitalism there is in fact love. This conclusion allows us to see the question of virtuality at a depth which is immensely positive and offers tremendous hope for the contemporary human world.

Yes, for sure, on the surface it is hard to see this hope. There is a huge gap separating the medieval religious experience from contemporary virtuality. The latter comes at what looks like a terminal distance from gospel roots, appearing rather as a feature of sophisticated capitalism. It has become the virtualization of goods and wealth where exchange of things is stripped down to the ghost of its ghostly self, inspired more than ever by desire. The digital world presents a global market where the exchange is of signs, with no physical content at all, and yet still and always for the sake of wealth, success, status. And, as a by-product, this virtual world can create a detached mode of existence in its own right. Virtualization now projects a super-agitated sphere of images in continued exchange and motion, referring apparently only to itself. We ask, therefore, to what end? Whatever the values of medieval contemplation back then, what could possibly be the Christian purpose now of a world hyper-filled with possibilities of greed, or the hypnotic effects of on-line existence? What is the point of all these images or signs bursting up like clouds of steam on a pot of boiling water, creating shapes and forms to be replaced almost at once by others? With this latter-day question we have reached the heart of the meaning of the virtual character of Christianity. Girard shows us the built instability of our world of signs filled with desire. But what is known as romanticism may in these circumstances come back in a new and much more radical form. It may come as the event of nonviolence and forgiveness. In its first form it was the effect of Christ communicated obliquely in a hierarchical world and its contemplative power was quickly sidelined by the onrush of violent desire. In its second coming, the image of Christ has become culturally self-selecting, at the heart of a chaotic cultural whirlpool, as an increasingly urgent choice for compassion and forgiveness. And so the true power of contemplative desire is revealed. Let me explain.

The Photon of Compassion
The cross is the most potent subversive image of the biblical

tradition. Christianity as a religion takes off from the fact of the crucifixion and its paradoxically twinned reversal and validation by the resurrection. The resurrection didn't just undo the death of Jesus, it affirmed the value of everything he had done including voluntarily and nonviolently surrendering himself to death. It is because of this affirmation that all the surrogate victims of human culture are declared innocent, while an individual's participation in that violence is challenged to be forgiven and changed into love. I made an attempt to map these existential changes arising directly from the cross in *Cross Purposes,* and the key feature I found there was what I called the abyssal compassion of Christ. Essentially this meant that no matter the level of violence and abandonment which Jesus suffered he responded always with forgiveness. In other words there was an answering passion of love within the human abyss of violence. This concept now presents enormous relevance for the discussion at hand.

The compassion of Christ is the necessary triggering agent of the revelation of the victim. The cross is absolutely not an intellectual or scholastic event. Against the impacted forces of violence and denial it cannot possibly 'work' by presenting a pure Platonic form or 'intelligence' of the truth. It has to meet the actual neural forces of violence with an answering neural pathway of nonretaliation and fore-giveness. (Breaking the word open in this way allows us to see the crucial giving of the self— forth-giveness—at the heart of forgiveness). Only in this way will the aggressor / sinner discover his violence, not affirmed and strengthened in mirrored violence, but literally undone and dissipated by the infinite self-giving of the other. This is entirely intelligible at the anthropological level; it is the simple wisdom of 'turn the other cheek'. What I *feel* when someone does not retaliate to my aggression is a softening of my own response, mirroring the letting-go of the other: it does not mean necessarily that I will forsake my violence but, helplessly, its edge is taken from me. What makes Christ's turning the other cheek infinite is the formal abyss of violence into which he was thrust and the way his nonviolence within this pit is raised up to new life. He is the single victim of the religious, political and mob forces around him in a moment of acute historical crisis, and as such his story carries an enormously impacted symbolic value. He is the chosen victim of both imperial and religious ideologies filled at that point with a critical accumulation of historical violence. But at every level he does not retaliate, and it is precisely this response which is raised up in resurrection. The historical abyss of violence is turned upside down, its violence shaken out, and it becomes instead an endlessness of life, the infinity of love.

If this is the psychology and ontology of the cross then it stands behind and accompanies every disclosure of the victim. It would be impossible for the cross to reveal the victims of history if this neural compassion did not act as a perfect mirror or non-reciprocating 'photo' of the violence inflicted on them. The silvered backing of a mirror never shows itself and so it reveals all the world, while mimetic mirroring is always 'me' showing myself exactly the same as the rival, the aggressor, and thus the victim never appears. If there was any retaliation in the cross then its perfect reflectivity or light-sensitivity to the true colors of this world, above all the face of the victim, would have disappeared and it would have simply have fed back the turbid muck of human violence. It is this cosmic 'photo-sensitivity' of Jesus' compassion and forgiveness that makes every sign of the victim work. And yet despite this it still remains largely invisible because the world as it stands cannot recognize it. Despite the revelatory labor of Jesus the world simply sees the face of the victim, or, more accurately, the face of anger of the victim, for it operates on the basis of an intellectual and emotional light still dense with culture's violence. As the gospel of John says, 'He was in the world, and the world came into being through him; yet the world did not know him' (1:10).

The statement is precisely accurate in respect of our actual contemporary world; this world is deeply structured by the intervention of Jesus but that structure is seen somehow as our own invention, a product of Enlightenment reason and our entrepreneurial drive. But the fact the world does not understand this does not change the essential dynamic of the world as Jesus has caused it, i.e. the progressive transformation of the sign which means the world. We can conclude, therefore, that the world cannot claim immunity from Christ. Nor can its ignorance last forever, for its ignorance is literally a self-contradiction. Elsewhere the gospel of John says, 'And I, when I am lifted up from the earth, will draw all people to myself' (12:33). The text goes on to say that this refers to the manner of Jesus' death. Thus the cross exercises a progressive attractive power over humankind, so setting a limit on this world's ignorance. Really, it is the attractive power—not intellect as such—that will overcome the ignorance. And nowhere is this more manifest than in the realm of multiplied images.

We have come to the core point of the meaning of Christianity as virtual, its critical role at the heart of the contemporary universe of visual signs. We are at the pulsing center of the dance! Girard's general description of mimetic origins shows how essential desire is to the deep structure of meaning. It lurks within the sign system like a coiled dragon at the bottom of a glittering pool. But I have described how in a consumer universe desire has become a standard surface feature of goods, a 'lining' giving them their social significance. The dragon has risen to the top of the pool and is lashing it with its tail! So it is that in a world propelled by mimetic desire one image succeeds the other in an increasing warp tempo. Here is the world of fashion, of advertisements, of the latest toys and devices, of movies and shows, of stars and paparazzi, of the fifteen minutes of fame which is more and more like fifteen seconds. Frequently these images are violent, signifying an intense crisis of desire, either for entertainment's sake, or in deadly earnest. And somewhere in the middle, between the two, there is the talking-point violence of politicians, commentators and pundits, half-way between virtual and actual. In such a pinwheel galaxy there cannot be any lasting difference to mark signs: so long as they are fed solely by this swirling angry axis.

Thus it is that in this toxic plasma, our symbolic world, there can be only one truly differentiating sign, one absolute exception. Among a semiotic chaos of desire and violence it is the photo-sensitivity of Christ's compassion that separates itself out and rises to the surface, providing both meaning and truth. Why? Because the whole spinning universe of signs is a twisting away from the self-giving of Christ and the more it spins and dissolves away from that center the more it must reveal it. As any process which decays or explodes it must resolve into its original element. This is the character of the historical-cultural revolution carried out by the gospel. But Christ is not simply an objective process, he is a personal historical agent. It is appropriate, therefore, to name him the 'photon' of compassion, the elementary particle or principle of absolute giving by which light shines at all, by which this universe of vision was set in motion in the first place. At one level this is a faith-statement, a product of personal belief in Jesus. But it has also emerged in the argument as a transcendental statement, i.e. a rational account of how our contemporary virtual world is possible at all. Without the photon or light source of Jesus our contemporary world of signs would not be conceivable, would not exist. Finally it is also, and more and more, a statement of cultural fact. As the world craters deeper and deeper into its abyss of desire and violence perceptive artists, writers, commentators begin to discern the revolutionary figure at its heart. In the following chapter I will lay out some of this cultural evidence. At the moment, however, I want to bring to as sharp a point as possible the findings of this one, to summarize the thought on which the book turns.

Einstein Eyes

Compassion is the single crucial difference in an infinite world of signs because it is the contrasting motion that set this contemporary world spinning in the first place. The nature of desire has been volatilized into a billion billion fragments in contemporary culture, but this has happened because of the original impact of the cross. The release of desire is more basic, more original, than the revelation of the victim, and the latter in fact could not take place without the underlying conditions of the former. Other cultures have produced forms and images of desire, of course, but these were contained within structures of duty and deference, and restricted generally to aristocratic or urban elites. The culture the West has produced is the first that seems to survive more and more on desire alone and on every plane. And the only convincing original source of this extraordinary development is the core vision of the gospel, proclaiming the existential goodness and nonviolence of creation, down through every level of violence. This is highly paradoxical but it is the only coherent explanation given Girardian premises.

Progressively, therefore, the only true difference in this chaos of signs will not be a return to rules or hierarchy, but the sign of compassion by which the whole flux was first prompted, the abyssal compassion of the Crucified. The sign that destabilized sacrifice has prompted the mobilization of desire, and this was not just a byproduct. Rather it is the core purpose of the cross, the mobilization of desire in order that there might be a transformation of desire. There cannot be a universe of love without first a universe of desire. Returning to rules and law is an outdated attempt to contain our violence against the massive contemporary thrust of unleashed desire. It is a solution for an older world, not for this one. It is only the present infinitization of desire and then its progressive transformation that can promise a genuine hope for all human culture and existence.

How then would this work in practice? The very chaos of the

signs, their frenzied tempo, produces eyes which look away, but it is almost impossible to do so in our world. Wherever we look the same chaos is before us. So ultimately perhaps we stand before it and instead of looking away we look deeper, perhaps drawn in by a sense, after all, there is some other motion behind it all. We continue to seek out a true difference, but we do so not by distinguishing, separating, but following the signs into their primal blur which then astonishingly may reveal a heart at their heart. They melt away, dissipate, to disclose love, to show the photon or light source of compassion. Love moves in a different direction—it is centripetal rather than centrifugal—yet it was its absolute giving that first released the possibility and then the chaos of desire. To see this requires what might be called 'Einstein eyes.' Einstein had the ability to sit in his room and see things in the universe which then took decades to show experimentally. And now, little by little, we all see what he saw. What I am saying is that just as Einstein shared a startlingly new vision of the physical universe by penetrating the data and math available to him, now on a much broader semiotic level people are capable of seeing a startling new version of the meaning and role of compassion in the world. The multi-colored light of the fantastically-spinning semiotic disk cannot help but resolve into the gentle nonviolent light of compassion, which first set it turning. The light-source of absolute self-giving becomes the contemplative principle of a transformed human universe. You have to look to see it, and you have to look with contemplative eyes, but it really is there! (Think perhaps as a quick pungent example the *South Park* cartoon of Jesus and Santa Claus engaged in shocking violence over the meaning of Christmas. There is not just irony here but pathos, the actual nonviolence of Christ subtly undermining the scandalous images.)

The contemplation of the nonviolent Jesus first gave courage to human culture to release a universe of signs filled with positive desire, but at the same time the possibilities of rivalry, greed and violence were made endless. If we build onto the release of desire the revelation of the victim we see how the latter both prevents the 're-hierarchizing' of culture and provides multiple opportunities for anger in the one who has been hurt and his/her desire for vindication. Virtuality in turn speeds up the process, both multiplying and diffusing the violence. In this fantastical world the patient face of Christ is disclosed as the true point of light. As I suggest, violent desire in a world impacted by Christ has always been a swerve away from Christ, so when the swerve exhausts itself, swerving from itself, then the true motion of Christ must emerge. When this happens, when compassionate forgiveness is revealed as the final and first sign value of the world, then the effect is away from pure signification toward a dramatically new way of being human. It becomes the arrival of compassion in the immediacy of the lived world. Human beings are invited to pour themselves out in imitation of the Beloved. Self-giving compassion begins to govern concrete existence, and so bring about the new creation our Eternal Beloved has always intended.

This book is not about political or economic matters, like ecology, poverty, human rights, land use, health, etc. It does not set out an agenda or programs for reform. What it supplies is a new basis for understanding Christian faith in the world, and if this were to become in any way persuasive or standard it would most surely have enormous impact on these matters. Chapters five and six on the doctrinal figure of Christ and on the church will develop the thought more fully in core areas of Christian belief and practice. They will continue to seek this epochal shift in Christian awareness. Before we get there, however, we must turn to the concrete evidence for virtual Christianity as it arises in the contemporary world. In the fourth chapter I will show its impact in the field of thought and philosophy, a place where you would necessarily assume some effect of the movement I am suggesting. In the chapter immediately following here I will present some of the more ephemeral evidence taken from popular culture. Fleeting, it is true, movies and songs are here today gone tomorrow, but they will be replaced by others. We may examine the ones we have, knowing they are the cutting edge of the virtual where more than anywhere we can detect the changes I am talking about. In order to close the present discussion, therefore, I will give one salient and quite stunning example because it may demonstrate the argument in one.

Wall E

It's a cartoon film called *Wall E* released in 2008. The story tells of an earth abandoned by humans, leaving behind a polluted planet choked with mountains of trash. The sole remaining figures of 'life' are a small beat-up robot, the Wall E of the title, and his companion, a lone cockroach. The grubby little machine continues faithfully to tidy up, compacting blocks of trash with which to build further giant mounds of rubbish. Meanwhile human beings have literally taken to the heavens, flying around space in an enormous luxury spaceship, and so glutted with food and computerized entertainment that they are unable physically to get off their hovercraft loungers or emotionally to conduct real relationships. Back on earth a hi-tech probe arrives in Wall E's neighborhood to research whether plant life has regenerated, the original intention having been for the space-cruising humans to return to earth once life reappeared. Wall E names the probe robot Eva and falls in love with her. He shows her a single green seedling he has discovered and she promptly locks it up inside her glittering body and shuts down awaiting her return transport to the space liner. The story unfolds from there, taking both robots up to the mighty spaceship with the all-important sign of life inside of Eva. This literally vital piece of evidence prompts a fierce struggle between the ship's computer, which has been secretly programmed to continue indefinitely in space, and the captain who at last comes to grasp the wonder of life on earth and to want urgently to get back there. His key allies in carrying through his dream are the two robots who by now have formed a relationship.

The ironies pile up and it is impossible to miss the bitter hints of inverted biblical models. Instead of Adam and Eve we have two robots; instead of a garden we have a waste land; instead of an earthly paradise we have an endless cruise in empty heavens; instead of organic life we have meaningless gratification; instead of human beings enjoying relationship a robot teaches another robot to love and through him she learns to reciprocate.

Humanity has been both dehumanized and de-terrestrialized. In this situation there is absolute need for a new beginning and it has to come from somewhere other than inhuman humanity. The robot Wall E thus symbolizes paradoxically but accurately the astonishing novelty of transforming compassion in the midst of historical human defeat.

Wall-E is a hero of abyssal compassion. He continues to work in the pit of the world for a biblical 700 years when all else have fled to the Platonizing heavens. He continues unfailingly to love his 'other', Eva, until she learns the ability to love too. His disruptive presence among the humans begins to awaken even them to the possibility of relationship. His own life is ultimately destroyed in the crucial struggle to deliver the seedling to the ship's scanning mechanism and so activate humanity's homecoming to earth. In turn Eva brings him back to life—raises him from the dead—through her own offered touch of love. There is no mention of Christ throughout the movie, and there is no need. It only takes a little inter-textual reflection to see the figure of the Crucified, but the point precisely is not an apologetic or doctrinal one. The sense of redeeming compassion falls like light from the screen because the movie itself is an authentic anthropological event. It is the education in new humanity which shines forth from the figure of Christ in the virtual world. It is the photon of compassion.

In light of this amazing example we may now perhaps summarize. In movies, on the web, on TV and radio, there is always the possibility of an image of compassion arising from the seminal presence of the Crucified, one that will produce a response of compassion in an individual. It is another way of stating the possibility of conversion, a surrender of a way of life and collapse into a new one, like Saul on the road to Damascus. But rather than happening religiously and formally it is happening progressively and organically. We must still opt for it—there is no determinism here. But the point is people do opt for it. They can do so reactively within the context of violence, projecting further crisis and violence, and many do this. But many others at multiple unpredictable points of our human geography opt for it positively. And this is the emerging cultural sign of Christ that brings hope to our earth.

But what in this case does it mean to be a Christian? In a frame like this where does 'church' begin and where does it end? I will show in the fifth chapter how the encounter with the Crucified and Risen One is an event of infinite nonviolent compassion and necessarily a meeting with God. It is of course a deeply religious event and it will shape itself in some form as church, but perhaps not in the way that has been understood in the past. What I have done so far is shift the locus and key of the crucial encounter, from the traditional religious sphere—the separated 'spiritual' areas of the soul, heaven, etc.—to the lived human world under the long-term impact of the gospel.

In the meantime it is enough, and more than enough, to recognize the epochal shift that is taking place right under our eyes. The old order of meaning is accelerating before us to the point of complete meaninglessness. But its very acceleration is the product of a subversive compassion which it cannot help but reveal, and with an increasing tempo of recognition. It is this tempo that produces a steadily gathering human change—the one Jesus always intended. It is the dawning of new creation.

Chapter Three

Motion Pictures

The Italian film *8 ½*, directed by Federico Fellini (1963), a movie about the making of a movie, tells the story of a director called Guido who because of creative block cannot finish his project and is constantly harassed by people wanting decisions. The screenplay is bracketed by two big crowd scenes, one near the beginning and one at the end. The first is of a health spa with long lines of people climbing up steps to a formal semi-circular stone bar where glasses of healing water are dispensed, very much like a communion service. The final scene shows the whole cast of characters, those who are part of the film-within-the-film, plus the many others who make up Guido's chaotic world. They are brought together by a circus ring-master with a circus band, and then the director at last takes over. He makes everyone form a circle, holding hands, and they follow each other round in a simple but beautiful dance. In both scenes, beginning and end, religious figures are prominent, nuns, priests, and a cardinal. The cardinal is featured at the mid-point of the story when the spiritually confused Guido is granted an interview with him in a private section of a vast sauna. Among clouds of steam and billowing cotton sheets Guido tells the cleric bent with time that he is not happy. The aged prince of the church replies it's not the director's job to be happy in this world and then repeats four times, in varying Latin formulae, 'There is no salvation outside the church.'

The irony is that Fellini put the church figures—including this central scene—within his movie, so it could be said that there is nothing outside the movie, including the theme of salvation. The whole movie is a nonstop dreamlike swirl of images and relationships, weaving vivid memories of Fellini's Catholic childhood with adult sexual escapades, and of course the problems of the stalled film. At the end everything culminates in the slow compassionate dance. I watched this movie in 1967, as a member of a film club in the Jesuit-run seminary I attended. It has recently been re-released in DVD, confirming its status as one of the most influential movies of the 20th century. Watching it again I understood perhaps the most important thing I had gotten from it. It was the way the visual world of cinema was able to show something as rock-like and ancient as the Roman Catholic church, and make it part of something else, something fluid, evocative, open.

Even if it was only for a couple of hours that really was enough. At some level there was a field of imagination and images able in one scene to change the dimensions by which I saw the world. Growing up in something of a one-family Catholic ghetto in post-war England, and heading from there to seminary, this power of film to place me so rapidly in an utterly different space became enormously significant. I loved the works of Fellini, Godard, Ritt, Buñuel. It was not escapism but liberation, a way of totally reimagining a world otherwise seemingly set in stone. Now, many years later I still see the same value in film but I also understand it in a broader context of history and theology. Over the centuries, from magic lanterns through zoetropes to film projectors, the tricks of light and persistence of vision have enabled us progressively to produce alternative worlds in which the spectator can drown for an hour or so. But those worlds also stay with us. Paradoxically what I was immersed in I also carry around inside me, so it can truthfully be said that our whole perceptual world is altered by film. My mind is a fish swimming in a deep sea of images inside my head!

It might be claimed from a materialist point of view that a movie is still only a mechanical device which continues to enhance the power relations of those who own it and run it. But

I have shown that deeper than the mere mechanics of film-making there is an undertow of signs which is in the process of changing our human meaning. Film is surely the most vibrant of the visual media and the one that attracts a great deal of creative talent because of the promise it contains of creating a total world. As such it is the medium most likely to represent the most frenzied stage of the dance of signs I described in the last chapter, all the way through to the light source of compassion at its heart. Movies, because of their intensified vortex of signs are likely again and again to put this differentiating particle up on screen in what might be called moments of cinematic revelation. Incidentally, the banner example I gave in the last chapter, *Wall-E*, contains a wonderful deep-space waltz between the compassionate robot 'Adam' and his beloved Eva. As they dance through the stars Wall-E is carrying a fire-extinguisher which he uses as a propulsion jet, leaving behind a stream of bright particles.

What I want to do now is present a log of these moments of cinematic revelation. I will give a report of what I see as data, of when and where the particle we are claiming shows up. The same account can be given of other popular media, like music, music videos, TV (particularly satirical cartoons), even fashion and fashion accessories, and of course literature. I will include a few examples from closely related areas as we go ahead, but to cover the whole field adequately would require a book in itself, and probably more than one, especially if literature were surveyed. Movies instead serve as the signature example in a study developing an overall account of the emerging radical difference that is the sign of Christ. They represent the evolutionary leading edge which illustrates what is happening in a much broader range of life-forms on the planet. By the same token, my movie log is not intended as exhaustive; there are certainly many instances it leaves out. And for sure it does not pretend to cancel the vast range of movies where there is no such revelation. Thus it cannot claim its results as mathematical proof, as a hard sociological fact outweighing all counter evidence. Rather its argument is structural, connecting with all the other bits of evidence the present study provides. For that very same reason it also should not need stressing that I am not referring here to doctrinally motivated works, pious Christian movies, stories, songs, etc. The difference in feel between one of these and what I am documenting is immediately recognizable. What I am showing is a human phenomenon, an anthropological shift that appears spontaneously in artistic formats, without doctrinal agenda. In consequence, it is possible to take the examples I give as something like Fellini's circle dance in *8 1/2*. Fellini put together a movie from disparate bits about making a movie, but they had a coherence, displayed in the final glorious scene. I have taken scenes and themes from different movies and as I set these scenes moving before your eyes they can have the persuasive force of artistic data combining to an intuitive truth. It is a picture of cinematic revelation which combines to produce itself the light source of compassion.

As we go forward I will also mention movies which employ motifs on the way to this cinematic revelation. In other words their screenplay recognizes and incorporates the dramatic energy on this road. I will refer to some of these to illustrate the point and build the overall picture, but essentially I will illustrate the fully captured particle as sign of human transformation. Finally, after I have assembled this evidence from the semiotic world of cinema, I will in fact make a short foray into music videos and the lyrics of popular songs. Once again these areas represent a leading edge of popular culture and again the examples will project the structural argument. The revelation of Christ arises within these artistic forms showing the same culturally transformative energy as in cinema. At the point of human impossibility brought by violence the compassion of Christ shows itself as the emerging human sign of a way forward.

Aliens and Robots

Outer space provides a picture-perfect setting for cinematic revelation. Its vast emptiness allows the imagination to expand, inviting images of what has never been seen or even thought. There is a breath of the infinite among the stars. Arthur C. Clarke and Stanley Kubrick's landmark *2001* (1968) sought in those immense distances the answer to human intelligence and the purpose of human life. Its extraterrestrial black monolith jump-started into thought a wretched tribe of primates and then finally embraced their spaceman descendant, Bowman, turning him into the cosmic 'star child' in a great circuit of intelligent life. As one critic said it this is a 'shaggy God' story: the questions usually answered by 'God'—including conscious intelligence—are worked through with material (if mythic) explanations. The movie also suggested anthropological motifs, particularly of the constant presence of the enemy. Not only is the first intelligent act by the tribe of proto-humans the use of a weapon but, much later, out in space the super-computer Hal turns into a deadly rival of the humans. Later science fiction movies found the enemy computer a rich vein to mine. Films like the *Terminator* series and the *Matrix* trilogy are premised on the destruction or enslavement of humanity by a race of highly developed cyber-netic machines. But before the computer became the sci.fi. villain of choice there was another deadly enemy—the one called *Alien*.

The original *Alien* movie (1979) spawned three further movies in the franchise, but it is the third in the series that we are concerned with here. *Alien 3* (1992) follows the first two movies in depicting a creature from deep space of horrific appearance and lethal force. Part giant scorpion, part shark, part leech, part doubled phallus and vagina, nothing like this had been seen before. This was a haunting violence nesting in the recesses of distant planets but at the same time deeply familiar to humanity. The Alien continuously seeks to deposit its eggs inside flesh-and-blood so the host humans can nourish its young from larva stage to murderous independence. The movies establish a dramatic symbiosis or interchangeability between transcendent violence and human beings, and the virtual identity of the two serves to provide the recognition and fascination of the series. The working model of the Alien's head was a highly complex machine, with hundreds of moving parts and joints, including the form of a human skull as the face, and then a second 'shark' mouth with its own teeth striking out of the main mouth. In most of the scenes the physical figure of the Alien was portrayed by a very tall actor wearing a latex costume. The director of the original *Alien*, Ridley Scott, comments 'It's a man in a suit, but then it would be, wouldn't it? It takes on elements of the host – in this case, a man.'[1] In other words the character of the Alien is in some way understood as derived from human beings.

In the first two movies the unrelenting battle with the monster is only resolved when the leading protagonist, a woman officer called Ellen Ripley, manages to expel it through explosive decompression of a space shuttle or air lock, out into space. The motif of expulsion into the void provides the feeling of annihilation of the evil creature now separated from humans in the abyss of space. However, the third movie makes Ripley's situation more complex. Following the final events of the second movie the survivors enter cryonic sleep aboard their spaceship but are suddenly ejected in an escape pod and crash land on a small planet, the home of a penal colony. Ripley is the only one left alive. It then turns out that one of the creatures had managed to get onboard their craft and Ripley herself was implanted with an Alien. It is in fact the embryo of a queen and so capable of laying more eggs.

The commercial company responsible for Ripley's space travel wishes to preserve the specimen, for use as a biological weapon. Its representative attempts to persuade Ripley to undergo surgery to have it removed intact. Ripley refuses and commits suicide, throwing herself backward into the colony's giant furnace just as the Alien queen bursts forth from her breast. As she plummets into the fiery abyss she assumes the shape of a cross, her arms spread wide. It was a Jewish friend who pointed out that Ripley is visibly the Christ figure and the scene has iconic Christian significance. (By one of those uncanny fun facts or coincidences the scene was also shot on Good Friday.[2]) At this point, therefore, the engine of absolute violence which has proven impossible to detach from the human group is literally crossed by the core of the gospel. It is a fleeting moment but one that has been built up to consistently by the overlaid elements of the plot. The constant overlapping of the monstrous alien form and its human enemy / host has informed us that the Alien is essentially a human thing. It lives among us, in us. We are its father and its mother. Meanwhile, on the surface of the plot, the Alien's biological character, growing its young by parasitism, brings us to the point where the lead protagonist has become the Alien's surrogate. The commercial company can resolve this situation by a kind of Caesarian birth, but Ripley refuses because of the company's military purposes and her knowledge of the Alien's unstoppable violence. She can therefore be seen to make an ethical decision, but the cinematography has no wish to leave it simply at the ethical level, the heroic gesture of someone who will not bring plague into the camp. The character of the plague has been constantly imaged as always already part of the human make-up—i.e. everyone still has the plague whether Ripley expels herself or not. So the response has to be something more, something systemic.

It is a moment of cinematic revelation which all the creative forces at work have led up to, the narrative genres of horror and science fiction, the power of a star actress, the skill of directors, the sophistication of special effects, and above all the logic of violence itself. When Ripley plunges to her willed death there is only one figure capable of giving dramatic vindication to her action at the depth of crisis to which the movie had come.

Christ's absolute self-giving into the abyss of human violence is the single cultural image that could mark that acute cinematic violence and change it into something meaningful, something that exceeded its brute destructiveness. Once the *Alien* movies had troubled the waters of human violence to this point there was no other way to bring a positive emotional depth, and so it was the cross which was invoked, whether or not the screenwriter or director consciously embraced the process or not. This is what I mean by the light source of compassion bursting on the screen by an inevitability which it alone provokes. And it is true: no sooner is it up there than it seems to disappear. The fourth in the *Alien* series, *Alien Resurrection*, seems deliberately to invert the figure. It makes 'resurrection' refer to the company's cloning of Ripley's DNA and the regeneration of the Alien specimens from her restored body. Thus the logic of violence reasserts itself, against compassion. But that does not matter. The after-image of Ripley's plunge is sealed on the retina of the world when it has eyes to see.

Terminator 2: Judgment Day (1991) arrived in the cinemas a year before *Alien 3* and that image was already inscribed or burning in its screenplay. In the *Terminator* stories the narrative thread is an apocalyptic war initiated by computer software called Skynet which gets control of cyberspace and unleashes the world's nuclear weaponry against humanity. A small group led by an individual called John Connor constitutes the resistance of humans against the computers and their machines. The device that binds the stories is the sending back in time of different 'Terminators' or robotic killers to destroy Connor, or his mother before him, in a pre-emptive strike at the resistance by the cyber regime.

It's clear that the figure of transcendent violence has found a more credible persona than an outer-space polymorphous insect. But the unfolding of a radical logic remains the same. The second movie, *Terminator 2: Judgment Day*, is where it occurs. The original Terminator has returned from the future again, but now programmed to protect John and his mother, Sarah, against a newer shape-shifting and near-indestructible model. The guardian Terminator, however, manages to make the newer model fall into a pit of molten steel, destroying it. Then he tells John and his mother that he too must be destroyed to prevent his technology being used to create the computer system which will unleash the apocalypse. He cannot self-terminate so Sarah must lower him on a winch into the incandescent melt. And this she does. But again it is not simply a matter of quarantining the plague. During the course of the story to this point the previously unfeeling robot had begun to learn about human emotion, its strangeness and its value. He responded to the boy John who told him to stop killing people, restricting himself to destroying the police vehicles chasing them. Now as he sinks into the furnace he gives a 'thumbs up' signal, a positive relational gesture within his willing surrender of his own systemic violence. Again this gesture is not intelligible without the cross. It is not the fierce death of a hero, but a relationship that reaches out from the abyss of violence, thereby freeing the spectator from being sucked into it in turn.

More than simply *Alien 3's* cross it is in fact the resurrection. Nonviolent forgiveness in the midst of violent death has no cultural precedent except the cross and resurrection, and that is why this is another moment of the photon of compassion. There is in fact a still earlier version of the Christ-like death of a robot / alien, predating *Terminator 2* and demonstrating the deep genealogy of the image. In Ridley Scott's *Blade Runner* (1982) Roy is a rogue robot or 'replicant,' visually indistinguishable from human beings. He is one of a number whom an operative named Deckard has the job of 'retiring', i.e. killing, after a robot revolt. Only Roy is left and he is rapidly dying from his own built-in term of life. To restore briefly his fading connection with sensation he drives a nail through his hand, an unmistakable image of the Crucified. Then in a final scene when Deckard is at

his mercy and about to fall to his death Roy reaches out—
inexplicably—to save him. It is a moment of intense compassion,
visually proving Roy's denied 'humanity'. The figure of Christ
provides the symbolic warrant for the claim, standing behind the
cinematic image as the rejected yet compassionate one.

Similar to the *Alien* franchise, the violence of subsequent
Terminator movies continues while 2's single 'after-image' and its
revelation remain. But now we have just intersected with another
twist or inversion around the figure of the enemy or the alien: the
robot who appears more human than the humans and the
compassion of Christ as its symbolic warrant. If a robot can be
seen in the guise of Christ, then robots can surely achieve an
authentic humanity. It's worth pursuing this side path a short
while in a movie where the story is about a robot figure seeking
exactly this goal. For along its route the movie approaches very
closely a moment of cinematic revelation. *A.I, Artificial
Intelligence* (2001) tells of a robot boy called David designed by a
cybertronics company to mimic human emotion, including 'love'.
He is tested with a couple whose real son is kept in suspended
animation awaiting a treatment for a deadly disease. The mother,
Monica, warms to David when his 'imprinting protocol' is
activated so he develops feelings for her. But then very shortly a
cure is found for her original child. The 'real' boy returns home,
at once becoming David's rival. The mother abandons David in a
wood, along with his friend Teddy, an automated toy. They
become part of a large number of unregistered robots, living free
but prey to mobs of human beings who in a world of ecological
disaster blame their troubles on them. Captured, they are taken
to a 'flesh fair' where robots are set on fire, but they escape. The
story now turns to a retelling of the nineteenth century tale of
Pinocchio, the puppet who wanted to be a boy, but told reflexively
through David himself. The robot boy has heard the story and,
after escaping the mob, sets out on a quest for the 'Blue Fairy'
who has the power to turn a pretend-boy into a real one. He

makes his way to Manhattan, now totally under water. Just as Pinocchio was swallowed by a fish in the depths of his long alienation, so David dives in a submersible craft to speak his wish in front of a submerged Coney-island attraction which he takes to be the fairy herself.

Yet it is not a magical figure which becomes the agent of the boy's wish. While keeping a two thousand year vigil in front of the statue, repeating and repeating his desire, the seas freeze over and humans become extinct. At the last evolved robots from the future discover him, dig him out and offer an answer to his prayer. Using a single hair preserved by Teddy, they recreate his longed-for mother figure, Monica. Her resuscitation can only happen for a single twenty-four hour period, but it's enough for David to be with her for one glorious moment. As the evening draws in she tells him she loves him and has always loved him. She gently falls to sleep for one last time while in her arms David falls asleep for the first time, going 'to that place where dreams are born'.

Steven Spielberg who took over the script for this movie from Stanley Kubrick impressed it with a gentler sensibility while retaining Kubrick's fascination with both artificial intelligence and dystopian humanity. The resulting focus on the robot, David, and his endless search for love becomes paradoxically a parable for the age-long human struggle with alienation and abandonment. David's sojourn in the depths of the ocean praying to a 'god that cannot save' could be Kubrickian cynicism, but the figure also has the biblical precedent of Jonah (as the Pinocchio story also implies); and what comes after is bathed in the light of an at least partial resurrection. The wondrous androids who in fact make this possible are gentle and non-threatening in manner and, while sleep is the final image of the movie, they first supply a somehow everlasting experience of love for David. In other words the end of the movie is deeply ambiguous and unresolved. While the movie lacks the transforming gesture of the cross the photon of compassion seems to tremble above and around the resurrection scene where violence is no more. When I first saw the poster for the movie in New York city the name *Artificial Intelligence* struck me as ironic. Obviously it refers to computer processing but did it not also hint at the artificiality of our present vaunted human intelligence? That what we claim now as intelligent is not 'real', and we are all longing for true intelligence, for the intelligence of love?

Matrix of Rivalry

If we have looked so far at sci. fi. movies which seem almost helplessly to throw out moments of revelation the *Matrix* series is designed purposely to arrive at them. The trilogy (*The Matrix, The Matrix Reloaded, Matrix Revolutions*) was released from 1999 to 2003 and even though following closely in its footsteps it represents a clear step-up on the content and style of the *Terminator* franchise. There is the same plot basis of a computer that has taken over the earth, the eponymous Matrix in place of Skynet, and there is a human resistance, this time located in subterranean spaces and a city buried deep in the earth. But now humanity is also integral to the existence of the computer, their bodies kept in a vast architecture of pods, sedated and fed with streaming images of 'real life' from the Matrix, while their body electricity is harvested to power the machine world.

The symbiosis of cybernetic machines and human existence is one of the features that make the movies so different and disturbing. It prompts the question of how much are we controlled by the multiple sources of 'information' in our lives. And a more general question also develops, of the ultimate status of what we consider to be human meaning and freedom. The very strong implication is that at a certain core level we construct the meaning of our world; thus the human resistance to the machines is never simply military but is also mental, and progressively more so. This is a decisive plot advance and, alongside the comic-book angles and special effects, it produces a fascinating strangeness and intensity. The CGI (computer generated imagery) includes what is called 'bullet time' which is the ability to interlace images of bullets in flight with real-time frames, appearing both to slow down and speed up normal human action. Members of the resistance have the ability to get back into the Matrix (via an electrical port surgically placed in the back of their necks) and, by means of the special effects, we see them carrying out gravity-defying actions, walking on walls and ceilings and leaping across rooftops. This serves to underline the sense of 'mental truth' determining our existence in the 'real world'. Progressively human reality is shown to be virtual, i.e. open to radical change of perceptual and actual meaning.

Adding to this very contemporary sense of human existence the storyline produces a relationship between two enemy protagonists which goes well beyond the hints of interchangeability in the *Alien* series. Their reciprocal identity becomes a plot device on which the whole story finally turns. I need to outline the somewhat complex character of this reciprocity in order to set the scene fully for its astonishing resolution.

A member of the resistance named Neo develops his abilities in the Matrix to an extraordinary degree, to the extent that he is able to battle hand-to-hand with the Agents who are human simulation programs within the Matrix able to alter at will its laws of space and time. Neo, however, shows a progressive ability not just to exceed, as they do, the laws of physics but to control the Matrix itself, to decode and interrupt its information sequence. As such he becomes the single greatest enemy of the Agents, especially their leader, Mr. Smith. After the big battle at the end of the first movie when Smith is defeated by Neo, Smith becomes a rogue program refusing to return to the Matrix mainframe to be deleted. Later on he says that his new found freedom is some kind of infection he got from Neo. At the same time he has lost his previous sense of strict purpose, so his freedom means nothing. Instead, he seeks to gain meaning by cloning everyone he encounters in the Matrix as himself, and he seeks ultimately to do the same to Neo. In effect Smith wishes to overwhelm and to win. He has become a virus pure and simple, threatening even the Matrix and its primary hardware or 'Source'.

All of this only becomes clear step by step during the second and third movies. In the meantime the human resistance is facing a last-stand battle to defend its stronghold, Zion, now located by the enemy battle craft, the Sentinels. Also Neo has been told that he personally represents the surplus of a programmed anomaly in the system intended to keep humans happy—i.e. an element of freedom. Although a mysterious prophecy said he would be the one to bring full freedom to humans his real purpose—according to an original designer of the Matrix called the Architect—is to return to the Source and re-set the Matrix to its original equilibrium. If he doesn't do this all humanity will die. Neo does not believe the threat and when he is given the choice he opts to save from death another member of the resistance called Trinity, rather than obey his supposed destiny. Finally, in the company of Trinity, he heads toward Machine City to negotiate with its godlike figurehead, Deus Ex Machina. If Neo can defeat Smith who threatens the Source itself then the machines must call off their attack. Trinity is killed on the journey, surrendering her life for the sake of Neo's mission. Neo continues on his own to make his bargain. The 'Ancient-of-Days' Machine agrees. Neo is plugged back into the Matrix on a bed of cables and the stage is set for an apocalyptic showdown between him and Smith.

Neo contends with Smith in a battle of the giants watched by a vast glowering crowd of Smithian clones. At first the two seem evenly matched, exchanging blow for blow, charging at each other like bullets, through rain-drenched streets, up into space, across the face of the city, intersecting with lightning, propelling each other to great distances only to see the other return with ever greater ferocity. Finally there is a shocking impact and Neo falls. At the bottom of a crater he lies inert but slowly gets to his feet. Smith asks him why he continues to fight. He suggests rhetorically the standard motivations of freedom, truth or love, only to dismiss them in Nietzschean fashion as perceptual figments, constructs as empty as the Matrix itself. But then, immediately, as if in a parenthesis, he adds that only a pathetic human mind could invent something as wishy-washy as love.

Neo answers simply that he chooses to continue. Once again, therefore, they fight and once again Neo falls. Smith then hesitates, puzzled. He wonders if somehow he has seen this before and whether this is in fact the end. He asks himself if he is meant to say something, something about things that have beginnings also having ends. One more time Neo stands, but something has also changed for him. For the first time Smith is confused, fearful. He charges at Neo and he finds him non-resisting. He drives his hand into Neo's body and brings about the cloning he always sought. Neo becomes just one more Smith. Smith asks Neo / Smith, 'Is it over?' His vanquished opponent nods. The scene cuts back to Neo's real body in Machine City and he seems to convulse in death on his bed of connector cables. An image of Neo's body is embraced by a form of light, perhaps the Source. From the center of Neo's physical frame the dark shape of a cross then forms the core of a brilliant emanation of light, and, directly after, Neo's actual body assumes the T-shape of the Crucified. Cutting back to Neo / Smith we see all the cloned Smiths filled with light and explode. The same thing happens finally to Smith himself. A bright cross of light spreads from the battle zone throughout the Matrix cityscape. Back with the machines the godlike figurehead says 'It is done.'

Agent Smith was always himself a construct, something devised by the Matrix. Attaining freedom he can find no reason for his existence except endless rivalry. Neo, a 'real' human is pitted endlessly against him, his own freedom defined by this battle. What is different about Neo is that he is obeying a deeper motivation related to a freedom of belief and love. At a certain point in the fight, as we have seen, it is Smith himself who alerts Neo to the 'end', meaning perhaps both the term of this conflict and its goal. At once Neo surrenders resistance and is absorbed as one of Smith's 'dead ringers', one of his dead world of sameness. Directly after the image of the cross multiplies three times across the screen. It is unmistakable, and its significance cued by the quotation of John's gospel, 'It is finished'(19:30). Jesus' surrender on the cross defeated the devil, the rival, the prince of this world. The name of Satan, and its Greek translation *diabolos* (anglicized as devil), mean rival, adversary, enemy. The effect of the cross is to subvert rivalry itself, thus defeating Satan.

What the *Matrix* trilogy gives us is a single parable of human virtuality, the way in which we construct our world out of signs, out of images, and at the same time out of rivalry. It does not say this world is unreal, simply that it is continually constructed by these forces. It then suggests that there is a deeper construction going on, made up of belief and love, one which the 'Matrix' world finds insipid, and yet secretly guides everything. For ultimately the Matrix has to surrender to this construction in order to survive the threat of its alternative—terminal rivalry. The greatest and essential shift in reality is achieved by the self-surrender of love, and this is the meaning of the cross. Or, rather, it is the cross that has first produced and revealed this meaning, this shift. The *Matrix* series, especially the third movie, is a triumphant cinema of the photon of compassion, displaying the guiding meaning of the Crucified at the heart of our world, bringing resolution and peace to a universe of hyper-violence. Many influences from different cultures can be seen to be present in the series, and there is definitely an astonishing breadth to its religious world. But the final showdown of Neo and Smith is mainline New Testament and the reiterated marker of the cross makes it unavoidable. Everything is conducted in comic-book scene-setting and a video-game atmosphere. The relentless fighting, cut-away editing and rock-rhythm pacing are not the New Testament, but that is itself the point. Within the vortex of our contemporary sign world the cross distinguishes itself as the final meaningful figure revealed in the final frame.

Smith, the quintessential rival, seems himself to be the leading agent of his own ultimate defeat, sensing all the time that something is happening to him he can't quite control. What is happening in fact is the 'inevitability' of love, bringing about the annihilation of the rival through the annihilation of rivalry itself. It is the inexhaustible return of the rival which cannot end, which throws up of itself the sudden devastating truth of another end, the one that comes by means of voluntary defeat. The light of compassion shines here very much in its inner structural sense, bringing about the change of basic principle by which human enmity and violence perpetuate themselves. But the way the redemptive logic bursts out of the futile endlessness of the old principle is pure photon! When the rivals are crashing into each other in the sky and all the world is turned into the uniformity of hostility then the cross shines through as the virtual yet inescapable truth. Only the cross can bring an end to the endless semiotics of violence.

The movie should be read as a seminal contribution to a theology of Christian virtuality—meaning that the Christian tradition is a radical shift in the human sign system, simultaneously showing the violence that lurks deeply within it and the possibility of something wonderfully new and true beneath that again. Jesus never fought anyone with martial arts or any other kind of violence. But he is having a transforming influence in our world of images driven ever faster in their whirl of desire and violence. The *Matrix* trilogy is probably the hottest virtually Christian ride you could take, but these three movies are not by any means the final word. They are not the last or the deepest cinematic encounter with the transforming semiotics of Jesus.

Meanwhile Back on Earth

The crime-thriller movie *Face Off* (1997), directed by John Woo, has a thematic device comparable to the rivalry between Smith and Neo. The plot details are not important except to know that two deadly enemies—one a crook, the other a cop—come to swap actual physical identities by an extreme type of cosmetic surgery: each gets the other's face. The medical procedure by which this occurs is completely far-fetched, but the point of enemy doubles is not. Once the interchange of faces has occurred the actors assume the persona of the respective enemy and the audience must continually interpret the figure of one with the personality of the other. The effort is emotionally satisfying because everyone knows intuitively the way intense rivalry makes you the living double of the other. The crisis of doubles is finally resolved, of course, by the killing of the bad guy and the cop regaining his original face. That does not happen, however, without the photon of compassion making its appearance within the heart of the crisis. A prolonged shoot-out takes place in a chapel, and this is the moment in which the film suddenly says more than its surface plot. As all the while a hail of bullets splinters the chapel altar, the camera returns obsessively to the figure of the Crucified above it. It seems little more than a stylistic device but why does it happen? It seems the confusion and hatred between the two is so pronounced that the Jesus figure emerges out of the loss of differentiation as the only real *other* in the conflict, the true 'enemy'—of the violence itself. There is a confirming doublet of this cinematic Jesus moment when the cop eventually prevails over his double, killing him with a spear gun: the criminal is seen in the same physical position as the figure on the cross shown in the chapel. At the bottom of the vortex of violence where it is impossible to tell me and my enemy apart the figure of the Crucified appears as saving differentiation. My hated other, who is myself, is seen suddenly as the forgiving Christ and thus I am returned to myself in peace. Again, whether the director consciously knew what he was doing—or even perhaps gave it an entirely different interpretation—does not matter. Cinematically the burden of peace at the heart of intense hostility is placed on the figure of Jesus, and that is the light source of compassion at the core of our virtual world.

The following examples will continue to develop the cinematic role of Jesus in 'more real' settings than the fantastic worlds of science fiction. *Face Off* provides an apt bridge with its regular cops-and-criminals format but also the futuristic exchange of faces. What is striking is the continuity of cinematic revelation expanding more and more from the semi-mythic world of sci. fi. into ordinary human worlds, pulled there by the revelatory energy of the Crucified.

Changing Lanes (2002) is a great example of a recognizably ordinary world: it tells the story of two men involved in a fender-bender on FDR drive in New York City. Gavin is a successful young lawyer, the other, Doyle Gipson, a recovering alcoholic and absentee father trying to put his life back together. The lawyer's hurried writing of a check to cover the accident, rather than giving insurance details, doesn't sit well with Doyle who is trying to go by the book and 'do things right'. From there on the inevitable rivalry sets in and everything escalates uncontrollably, involving computer-fraud, false imprisonment, attempted murder. As the movie advertising has it, 'One bad turn deserves another.'

In these circumstances just as in *Face Off* the Crucified takes on the role of the revelatory other, but this time it is more developed and emphatic. Everything takes place on a single day which is in fact Good Friday, the day Christ's death is commemorated. The figure of the cross assumes a constant presence, seen a number of times, and especially in a service of veneration inside of the church where Gavin goes for advice. There is also a picture of Jesus in Doyle's new house. What saves the movie from being a piece of religious propaganda is that these elements are always allusive rather than thematic. For example, the church scene where Gavin is looking for advice on life's meaning produces an antithetical frustration. He doesn't get further than his own bitter diagnosis, 'Maybe God wanted to put two guys in a paper bag and let 'em rip.'

Ultimately there is a moral revolution on the part of the men against their own behavior and a shift towards reconciliation and a new start for both. But it is not religiously mediated. Rather it is an anthropological movement from violent reciprocity to letting-go of violence as the best mode of human living. The Good Friday story and the symbol of the cross have been revelatory of anthropological transformation within the contemporary human crisis. The symbols are evident enough to be deliberate, but they are still occurring as cinematic revelation, as an artistic upwelling allowing a different human truth in a situation of lethal crisis.

In the first scene of the movie *Crash* (2004), Jack, a black police detective, has just been rear-ended. He speaks in monologue about people in L.A. being deprived of human touch, how they are cut off from each other by metal and glass. He thinks they therefore crash into each other just to make contact, to be able to feel a little. Toward the end of the movie, Jean the bored ignored wife of the District Attorney, speaks on the phone to a presumed friend. She says she is feeling angry and goes through a list of things that could have caused her anger, including having her car stolen. Yet she concludes it's really none of them. Instead she is simply angry, all the time, and has no idea why. Her friend replies she has to go and the conversation ends abruptly.

This rolling isolation and anger that Jack and Jean express are what drives the movie and literally crashes cars into each other and shoots guns at people. It is clear then, right from the beginning, that this is a movie about human relationships in a violent slice of our contemporary world. It does not come as a surprise then that the photon of compassion shows up in the screenplay. The movie garnered the 2005 Academy Award 'Best Picture', as well as 'Best Film Editing' and 'Best Original Screenplay'. It was seen as a major upset, coming from behind to gain the coveted first prize.

It's as if the Academy voters suddenly felt here was the statement of an absolutely contemporary theme (more contemporary even than the gay cowboy romance, *Brokeback Mountain*) and within a country at war not just in Afghanistan and Iraq it had to claim first place. On one level the movie is about race, covering the simmering interactions of a wide range of peoples, black, white, Chinese, Latino, Iranians, Koreans. But more than this the real thematic is the uncontrollable rage that bursts from the broken seams of these relationships. The movie cuts from one individual's frustration to the next, with moments of both redemption and violence interspersed almost randomly, so that there is no one element of plot to pin our hopes or desire for revenge on. We remain in the midst of maelstrom but with flashes of possible alternatives that could make things very different.

The referencing that opens the revelatory alternative is derived from two sources, Christmas and two statuettes of St. Christopher. The story takes place over two nights some time just before the Christian midwinter festival with all its embedded imagery. At one point there has been a car chase with police following a luxury S.U.V. with two black men in it, cornering them in a residential cul-de-sac. The black men are very different, one is a television director, the other is a car thief who has just tried to steal the director's car, the one they're riding in. The director is angry and ready to go down fighting because of a previous incident in which he was deeply humiliated by a racist white policeman. As they screech into the dead-end we are confronted with a Santa Claus with his hand held up. Right behind Santa on a wall is the mural of the Christmas nativity which glimmers for an instant before we return to the action. A young policeman on the scene happened to have been the partner of the racist cop and witnessed the incident with the director. He intervenes desperately and manages to stop an escalation to what threatens as inevitable bloodshed.

Later in the movie, however, the same young policeman, this time off-duty, gives a ride to a black youth (he is incidentally Jack's brother). On the dashboard of the car is a magnetized statuette of St. Christopher. As the conversation progresses the cop mistakes the young black's attitude for one of disrespect; he pulls over telling him to get out of the car. The youth attempts to defuse the situation. In fact he also carries a statuette of St. Christopher. As he reaches into his pocket to bring out the icon the policeman thinks he's going for a gun and pulls out his own, shooting and killing the youth. The physical reminder of Christ—Christopher, 'Christ-bearer'—becomes by a horrible irony the situational trigger of a killing. The situational figure of Christ in the cul-de-sac seemed positively to signal peace-making and reconciliation. Now, however, it causes death. The clear choice of the figure—it could just as easily have been an emblem for a sports team—produces the photon of revelation by ironic inversion: what could / should have been the peace of Christ becomes instead the horror of gunfire. There is indeed a kind of subversive irony in all these cinematic revelations. They appear against the grain, halting and reversing the vortex of violence. But here it is classic irony, the collapse of a conventional value into its contrary. The effect here is to point up the deep truth of what is merely conventional, creating an authentic moment of cinematic revelation.

The movie has numerous other subplots. A particularly poignant one tells of an Iranian immigrant attempting to shoot a Mexican-American locksmith he blames for a break-in of his store. Instead he appears to kill the man's little daughter but in fact his own daughter has substituted blanks in his handgun and the little girl is 'miraculously' saved. Again the supposed super-natural enters into the world in anthropological terms. The movie ends with a kind of peace, inhabited by the irony that pervades it. But, as I say, this irony is rich in revelation.

It is possible to continue this parade through examples like *Goodbye Solo* (2009), *Gran Torino* (2008), *Eastern Promises* (2007), *Children of Men* (2006), *Pan's Labyrinth* (2006), *21 Grams* (2003), *End of Days* (1999), *Stigmata* (1999), *Dead Man Walking* (1995), and all the way back to *Bad Lieutenant* (1992). Some are clearer than others but all in one way or another display the semiotic in-breaking of the Crucified. *Dead Man Walking* tells a real-life story and reflects the responses of actual human beings, but its final scenes quite naturally play out on the semiotic level. Sister Helen Prejean befriends a death-row inmate, Matthew Poncelet, and accompanies his terrible journey toward execution. The nun acts as a catalyst for a final non-retaliatory attitude on the part of the condemned man. But cinematically it is the images of execution by lethal injection, of Poncelet spread-eagled and dead on the table in a shape approximating a cross, which carry the movie's revelatory power. The camera pulls up from the scene of execution merging the image of Poncelet's body back to the scene in the woods where the murders of which he was guilty took place. The figure of his body fades and is replaced by the image of one of his victims spread out in the same fashion. The impli-cation is unavoidable: victims of human violence are indivisible, whether they are innocent or guilty. And it is the photon of the cross that produces the implication, allowing the screen to merge the guilty and innocent under the single theme of compassion and forgiveness.

Cinematic Blood of Jesus

Bad Lieutenant has the riveting scene where a drug-crazed corrupt cop sees Jesus come down off the cross and stand there silent before him. The cop shouts obscenities at the Crucified but Jesus' complete nonretaliation (along with the parallel behavior of a nun in the story) has the dramatic effect of changing the policeman's attitude. He sets free two youths who have stolen drugs, sending them on their way out of the city and inviting the drug boss' revenge in their place. A more recent movie using some of the same motifs is *In Bruges* (2008). It tells the story of two hit-men, Ken and Ray, sent to the Belgian city of Bruges after a job; there they await further instructions from their boss, Harry. They visit a church in which is kept a phial of Jesus' blood, brought back from the Holy Land during the Crusades. This blood is said to liquefy in times of great stress and it fascinates the older of the pair, Ken. He invites his partner to join the queue to touch it, explaining to an unwilling Ray, with the use of an expletive, that 'It's only the blood of Jesus of…Nazareth…' Ken then discovers that their purpose for being in Bruges is for him to kill Ray as the necessary consequence of a hit-gone-wrong when Ray mistakenly killed a young boy. Ken is in two minds but cannot go ahead with the murder. He then puts the young man on a train out of the city, to get him away from Harry and the old criminal life. Harry comes to Bruges to finish the job himself, but first he must settle with Ken. They meet in the great bell tower of the main plaza of the old city. Ken refuses to fight, saying he's prepared to take the consequences but he had to give the young man another chance. Harry then is unable to kill Ken because he's 'gone all Gandhi on him'. However, he shoots him in the leg saying, 'Do you think I'm going to do nothing to you just because you're standing around like Robert (expletive) Powell?' 'Who?' groans Ken. 'Robert Powell out of Jesus of (expletive) Nazareth,' replies Harry.

The dialogue makes the scene a doublet of the visit to the church of Jesus' blood, and fills in its meaning by merging the figures of Jesus and Ken via explicit movie references to nonviolence. A struggle then ensues when Ken finds out that Ray is in the plaza below, and he is shot again by Harry who hurries off to kill Ray. Ken hauls himself back to the top of the tower leaving a trail of very graphic blood. He then pitches himself from the tower to warn and save Ray. The story ends in a film-set of medieval mummers into which Ray and Harry, in pursuit, stumble and where Harry continues his killings. The strong implication is that contemporary violence is on a simple continuum with medieval violence, a matter of being stuck eternally 'in Bruges'. Meanwhile the 'blood of Jesus' cries out for a different resolution. It has a glistening cinematic liquidity filled with compassion, calling out for radical transformation from a pit of violence stretching back in the history of the Christian West.

The movie's mention of Robert Powell, the actor who took the part of Jesus in Zeffirelli's *Jesus of Nazareth* (1977), brings us in a conscious cinematic reference to films that tell the story of the gospels. Not surprisingly for a sign that continues to intrude into movies there have been numerous movies devoted to the original written account of that sign. The story of Jesus affecting so many movies must be itself cinematic. Some of the earlier Jesus movies approached their subject with exaggerated awe, but the anthropological revelation within the story opened up progressive artistic choices about how to portray the gospel drama. In Cecil B. DeMille's silent film, *The King of Kings* (1927), one of the first appearances of Jesus sees him surrounded by a halo, as through the eyes of the little girl whom he has just healed. In *Ben Hur* (1959), a story taking place in the time of Jesus and interlaced with episodes from the gospels, the visuals of Jesus are from behind him, or showing only his hands or feet. *King of Kings* (1961) presents Jesus in a more human light, accenting his ethical teaching and clearly showing his face. At the same time it features a very blue-eyed 'white-bread' Jesus who fits the imaginations of a dominant white audience. *The Greatest Story Ever Told* (1965) again shows Jesus clearly but the figure appears impassive and all-knowing, reflecting the transcendent Jesus of John's Gospel. Zeffirelli's made-for-television *Jesus of Nazareth* has a lush Italian feel, easy on the eye. His Jesus (Robert Powell) is humanly very gentle and attractive, but it has been noted during the whole movie Powell never blinks, a strong visual hint at transcendence. We have to wait until Pasolini's Marxist-tinged *The Gospel According To St. Matthew* (1964) for a screenplay that shakes the pious or dogmatic representation of Jesus. The young Basque student Pasolini used for the central role presents Jesus as a driven character, talking relentlessly to camera, almost in anguish, as he attempts to communicate all he has to say ahead of what is to befall the world and him. There is also a vivid realism to the acting (using mainly locals from towns in southern Italy where the film was shot) which in turn increases the urgency of the dialogue, almost all of it taken from the gospel of Matthew.

Pasolini's realism, however, did not carry over to the crucifixion which in the movie still has something of a devotional look, with a lot of focus on the ravaged face of Jesus' mother. Martin Scorsese was the one who finally and decisively ruptured the pious membrane surrounding the cross. His movie *The Last Temptation of Christ* (1988), based on Nikos Kazantzakis' novel, depicted Jesus in a dream-state abandoning the cross, coming down from it in order to enjoy the pleasures of marriage and an ordinary human life. In the novel the 'temptation' was almost instantaneous, lasting only for the moment it takes for Jesus to utter the sentence, 'My God, my God, why have you forsaken me?' But in the movie it occupies a considerable amount of the running time and for that reason physically breaks the sacrificial necessity of the passion and cross. Because of this the crucifixion gains much greater realism, just before the dream and when Jesus finally and willingly returns to the instrument of torture. Although there is no accent on graphic suffering the existential decision Jesus makes allows the viewer to feel the terror and loneliness of his action. We are faced with the brutal reality of the crucifixion and the scene is set for *The Passion of the Christ*.

This movie was a blockbuster success, winning audiences across the world, ranking number 41 for all worldwide grosses, and number 2 for an R-rated movie (behind only *The Matrix Reloaded* (which it outdid in the domestic USA market). At the same time it was deeply controversial, banned in a few countries, and tagged by the accusation of anti-Semitism to the extent that none of the major studios would back it or distribute it. Mel Gibson, its director and co-producer, used his own company to finance it and it was distributed by an independent agency. A major reason for its controversial nature, which also ran up the meter of the anti-Semitism charge, was its intense graphic violence. Roger Ebert who gave it four out of four stars said it was the most violent film he had ever seen. Gibson defended his movie saying it was based on the gospels and that it was everyone who had put Jesus to death. Far from being anti-Semitic, it was a movie about love, hope, faith, and forgiveness.[3] Gibson now finds it difficult to make people believe the sincerity of such statements after his drunken anti-Jewish rant on the occasion of his arrest. Nevertheless, I am personally convinced the integrity of the movie remains. It is worth pursuing a small sidebar of analysis here in order to understand why this is so, and how the movie radically supports the overall argument I have developed.

Everything about the movie has become highly personalized around Gibson, and helplessly so. This was such an exceptional and disturbing vision that the anxiety and distress it produced had to find a focus, and Gibson of course was massively the architect. Even the name of Mel Gibson associated with a depiction of the passion was enough to set warning bells ringing for some people. He is accused not just of anti-Semitism but sadism, a perverse delight in cruelty, already manifest in his other films but brought here to a point of refinement. Yet none of these categories fit what is really going on. The movie risks them all, leaping across the abyss of Western history and culture, but that is not what it is about. Girardian categories were not well-enough known to provide a ready tool box for commentators, but there can be no doubt that what *The Passion of the Christ* represents is pure sacrificial crisis. Essentially the meaning of such a crisis is the violence which erupts when the polarizing and stabilizing power of temple or societal sacrifice is disrupted from within or without. What results is a boiling pot of violence with nowhere to overflow and disperse. Classic examples given by Girard include a community overwhelmed by plague or bitter rivalries, but the model he gives which is really applicable here is of a warrior returning from war.[4] Heracles returning from his battles, still steeped in the haze of bloodshed, is an extremely dangerous individual, capable of bringing his craft of killing right into the heart of the community. The warrior covered in blood cannot stop shedding blood. The war, however, we are talking of here is not actual but cinematic, and so the crisis is a *cinematic* sacrificial crisis.

Mel Gibson is without doubt one of the biggest cinematic warriors of the twentieth century. As both actor and director he has focused on brutal conflict; in the post-apocalyptic *Mad Max* trilogy; in the thundering shock-of-battle *Braveheart* he both directed and acted in, and which ended with the bloody torture of the charismatic rebel leader he portrayed; in *The Patriot* where he is first peaceful and then fiercely violent, leading a militia against the British in the American Revolutionary wars. Gibson came to the story of Christ's passion covered in the virtual blood of cinematic battles. And that it is to say nothing of the huge arena of bloody cinema that surrounds him, one which he did not make but which acts as a constant context for his own violent movies. It seems both incredible and yet entirely credible that Roger Ebert should have said this was the most violent movie he'd ever seen. What about *Saving Private Ryan, Killing Fields, Kill*

Bill I & II, Sin City, Gladiator, History of Violence, etc., etc? In *The Passion* only one man is tortured and killed; in these others hundreds and hundreds are. And yet of course for Ebert, like the rest of us, all the violence of these movies passes under our radar like blood on the Tiber after a night a good night in the Coliseum. So long as someone else—either villain or hero—is doing this violence to another violent person then we slip into blameless participation in dynamics that have been with us since year one. Here is the guilty party, ultimately he will get his just deserts, or if he doesn't he should have, and history will ensure so. The gospel does not permit that option and it is exactly its bottomless pit of nonretaliation transferred to the big screen that makes the violence so unbearable.

It is certainly possible to see many things wrong with Gibson's depiction: he short-circuits Jesus' ministry and teaching, concentrating myopically on the last twenty-four hours of his life; he merges Mary Magdalene with the woman taken in adultery; from a historical point of view he allows the Roman governor and his officers to take absurdly minimal responsibility; and this imbalance feeds the impression the Jewish authorities were the main agents. But what is never acknowledged in the rush to judge the movie is Jesus' unimpeachable attitude of forgiveness and nonviolence evident throughout. One of the few flash-backs to Jesus' actual teaching ministry gives the crucial Sermon on the Mount commandment of love for enemies. In the course of the actual crucifixion Jesus twice prays to his Father to forgive his persecutors, and one of the times emphatically in the face of priests and leaders of the people. It is this reaction by Jesus which simultaneously thrusts the violence back on the viewer—we are in fact not permitted to fantasize revenge on the perpetrators—and invites us into that unimaginable pit of forgiveness. Standing on the edge we cast around frantically for someone to blame, and yes, of course, it has to be the person who put all this up there, Gibson. And thinking exactly within the mindset of violent Christendom—not the onscreen Jesus—we conclude further that Gibson's necessary subtext is: 1) it is the race of the Jews who are responsible, and 2) he subscribes to a grossly exaggerated atonement theology which emphasizes our sin and makes Jesus both a sacrificial lamb and divine superman able to bear unsustainable violence.

But if we see this all for what it is, an event of Christian virtuality, then our assessment must be very different. What we are seeing is the runaway train of onscreen violence exploding at full force against the photon of compassion, and Gibson as artist and director creatively intended this out of his personal pit of cinematic war. He is the cinematic Heracles bringing it all back home to the cinematic Jesus. And this, I submit, is the real reason why Pilate and his centurion are given such benign treatment. Rather than reading it as a deliberate historical distortion we should see it as a cinematic gesture of healing, peace and nonviolence for the blood-drenched warrior (however 'undeserved'). And the side-plot of the death of Judas—criticized again because much of its material is not in the gospels—serves to illustrate the essential mob-nature of violence, including the mob-character of Satan himself. Far from blaming the Jewish people this insight is strictly anthropological and sets the scene of human violence in its fullest context and deepest nature. In other words, once we abandon dogmatic perspectives, of either a doctrinal or liberal stripe, we can suddenly see revealed the whole cinematic logic that brought us to this point. The steady progression of Jesus movies, each time less pious and more virtual, has come face to face with the catastrophic human violence which cinema progressively invokes under the provocation of the gospel revealing and reversing violence itself.

This was a movie waiting to happen. If Mel Gibson had not made it, someone else would have, or one pretty much like it. Gibson with his violent movie past, his directing skill, his heavyweight production and financing power, and his particular brand of Roman Catholic piety—well, you could say the lot fell on him. From the perspective of the argument of this chapter and of Christian virtuality in general, what we can conclude is that *The Passion of the Christ* does not simply follow the artistic development we have traced to this point. It is not simply a more-or-less-conscious distillation of compassion from the vortex of violence. It is rather a cinematic moment of truth when the world of virtuality becomes artistically aware of its own dynamics. At this moment the vortex of violence is hurled deliberately and visually against the actual story of the gospel—including a non-survivable and intolerable twenty-minute scourging. It erupts like a tiger from its cage and tears the photon apart and yet the photon survives. Jesus forgives his enemies and, as he says in the screenplay, 'Behold I make all things new.' It leaves the viewer very little place to go, not because it is dogmatic but because it is virtual, full both of the violence of the virtual and its paradoxical heart of nonviolence. It is the sign of the Son of Man showing forth in the contemporary universe of images, and in my opinion an irreducible moment of cinema.

Switching on the Music Video

If we now make a sideways shift from cinema to music video we can see the basic logic of the argument repeated, adding another key area of popular culture visibly under the impact of the Crucified. Madonna is reputed to be the highest earning female performer of the 20th century. In her 1989 music video, *Like a Prayer,* she used the image of crucifixion. It shows an African-America nailed to a cross; Madonna comes to his aid, rescuing him from the instrument of torture. The image-spinning pop diva was clearly sensitive to the role of the cross in confronting human violence, but she is not simply making a grim political point, just as little as she is promoting the Christian icon in any church sense. She is enrolling herself in the motif of compassion derived from the cross and she can do so because it is now a freely available, dynamic image within our cultural repertoire. Her 'Confessions' tour of 2006 was the top-grossing tour ever by a female artist, with 1.2 million people attending 60 shows. In a number of the shows she appeared wearing a crown of thorns and lying outstretched upon a great white cross which was then gradually raised to a vertical position to the ecstatic applause of her fans. One of the songs performed during the mock-crucifixion was 'Live To Tell.' During the song a huge written number, 12 million, appeared above the stage: the legend then explained this is how many AIDS orphans there are in Africa. For a savvy entertainer like Madonna the mise-en-scène could never simply be do-gooding. Rather it's an ambivalent mix of politics, sexuality, gender issues and, once again, an emerging transformative anthropology which she is smart enough literally to ride upon. The light source of Christ's compassion becomes another spotlight which she uses to illuminate her body, positively, generously, bathing her in the reflected, referred attractiveness it gives. It is this light which gathered all the other meanings of her daring 'crucifixion' and triggered the enthusiastic approval of her audience. Unlike in the movies where the light source almost always resolves narrative issues of violence Madonna's appropriation seems to major on the kind of positive desire emerging in the Christ figure which we saw first in the Middle Ages. In this respect she utilizes the consumer-value possibilities of the Christ figure. But at the same time, as she also demonstrates, these are always organically connected to the overcoming of violence.

She is not the only pop musician to mix the two references. Hip-hop and rap artists made the wearing of large crosses and crucifixes a fashion statement, and there is in the African-American context a powerful element of identification. The MTV video for the single *Hate Me Now* (1999) by Nas, featuring Sean Puffy Combs, shows Nas dragging a huge cross through a stone-throwing crowd, images of which shift from first-century Palestine to contemporary NewYork. Nas ends on the cross crying out to the Lord, in unmistakable imitation of the gospel. Kanye West is a politically outspoken hip-hop artist whose *Jesus Walks* (2003) became a radio and concert favorite. It features a rap sequence by the artist invoking the protection of Jesus and a chorus chanting in the background. Then in February 2006 Kanye repeated Nas' visual identification, together with Madonna's sense of style, appearing on the cover of *Rolling Stone* in a reddish cloak and wearing a crown of thorns. It's hard to say who influenced whom, Madonna hip-hop, or the other way, but in Kanye the use of the Crucified as identification of suffering has merged seamlessly with its employment as pure visual image with all the benefits described for Madonna.

And it seems like everyone is doing it. The last single and video made by the country singer Johnny Cash, *Hurt* (2002), inter-cuts sequences of the singer with images of Jesus, again crowned with thorns. Perhaps we should say that it all goes back to John Lennon with his remark measuring the popularity of the Beatles against that of Jesus, and then his *Ballad of John and Yoko* telling Christ (and us) that he is going to get crucified. There does seem to be always these two elements in play, popularity and identification, the revelation of suffering and a deep human magnetism. The pop star is cast in the category of innocent victim radically affirmed in the image of the Crucified, but at the same time there is with Jesus an irresistible quality of attraction. Just as in the Middle Ages he is the intimation of a world transformed in love, but now this is not simply associated with goods-for-sale in indirect generative fashion. The figure of Christ a.k.a. Kanye West adorns the cover of *Rolling Stone* and it would not do so if it did not have its own direct power to sell a product. Pop stars like Kanye and Madonna know that and unhesitatingly wrap themselves in it.

Listening to the Words
Music videos carry a huge stress on image but they also contain

words and this prompts us to make another quick shift, this time to pop lyrics and lyric writers. Here is an important field of express meaning in relation to Christ, but it is difficult to comment on in detail since the words of successful song-writers are jealously guarded by copyright. This was true of the lyrics penned by the artists reviewed in the section above. However, if we can perhaps take just two examples of outstanding writers in this connection, and basically tell the story of their catalogue it may serve to make the point.

Members of the band U2 are both successful musicians and, in one way or another, personally confessing Christians. They are not a 'Christian band' in the sense of a group who set out to write songs about faith with guitar accompaniment, but neither are they invoking the iconic attraction and sales-value of the figure of Christ in the manner of Madonna. The actual message of the gospel plays a central role in their body of work. They started as a straight-up rock group, fronted by the impassioned tenor of singer Bono and the whipping guitar of The Edge. Hits like *I Will Follow* (1980) and *Where The Streets Have No Name* (1987) are stadium pieces with driving beat and haunted vocals. At the same time a song like *Sunday, Bloody Sunday* (1983) deliberately contrasts the violence-laden emotions of the Northern Ireland troubles with the message of Easter Sunday. The true challenge is to realize the victory that Jesus won on that first crucial Sunday. U2 have always regarded their music, and that of other popular music authors too, as framed in a spiritual universe. Evidently the Easter message provides for them the shape of that frame.

But Bono has also always maintained an ambivalence toward organized religion. U2's own songs can be specifically and clearly about Jesus, even to the extent of addressing him directly in their lyrics. But they work in a world which exceeds the scope of the churches and their professional religiosity in the same manner and by the same degree as the shape and significance of a movie theater would exceed a church.

To address Jesus directly in the pop-music context is to relate at once to his virtual role, to respond to his presence and action as a sign in the amped-up world of signs. But song lyrics that speak to Jesus in this world can have a much more nuanced expression than the cinematic revelation of nonviolence at the heart of violence. They inhabit something of a halfway position between prayer and the visual sign, and as such they can give a much more sensitive response to the problem of a world still awaiting transformation. They can express the interior tension of human existence caught between violence and forgiveness.

Songs like *I Still Haven't Found What I'm Looking For* (1987), *Peace On Earth* and *When I Look At the World* (2000) may therefore be read as a kind of prayerful manifesto of the photon of compassion. They are a person-to-person version of the sign-system or semiotics of forgiveness and compassion as they play out in the frenzied world of signs. As prayer they make the revelation of compassion directly religious, even devotional, but their religion and devotion do not relate to the metaphysical dimension normally reserved for these activities. They belong fully instead to the human world as it groans in its travail of violence, sign and change. Their religion is a matter of human, cultural transformation, speaking of war, injustice, pain and hope. By the same token their compositions are not political rants or bitter laments, mere songs of protest or pathos. What they are is a direct artistic amplification of the self-revelation of Christ in the world, an audio version of the photon of compassion as it struggles slowly and steadily to disclose itself in our world of signs. The band U2 is culturally significant because it serves as a meter of the virtual Christ in the lives of actual artists who continually and deliberately chose to base themselves in this event of disclosure. That's why I said they are confessing Christians in one sense or another. That also means they perhaps don't go to church. And neither would they neces-sarily explain themselves in the terms I am using. What they surely would say, however, is they draw no private / public or spiritual / secular distinction between their relation to Christ and their lives as rock stars. Their church is the world they know, in its state of virtual Christianity, and their confession is to articulate over and over the artistic and human sign-value of Jesus in the world.

U2 songs don't escape a sense of personal pain on the part of the artists themselves. This would seem to be inevitable in an artistic life straddling a personal vision of the world transformed and the actual world as it continues to see itself. Their art sensitively records the real impact of Christ, the light source of compassion, but immediately recognizes the distance that separates the world from genuine surrender to it. The dissonances of such an existence lead us directly to the consideration of one further musical artist, the most exceptional of his era. But in his case the accent falls not so much on the sign-value of Jesus in the world but on the full spectrum of human experience as the world comes under the pressure of that sign.

Silver River

The first full Bob Dylan album I listened to was *Bringing It All Back Home* (1965), his own first to use electric guitar. My brother brought the record in its *zeitgeist* sleeve to show to me in seminary and then he took it back home with him. I had to wait till I went home myself on vacation to listen to it. If Fellini gave me a swirl of images inside my head Dylan gave me a swirl of images inside my ears, with the resonance of a uniquely expressive voice. His looping lashing delivery, at the same time caustic and prayerful, became a constant companion as I walked my own road. Standouts for me on that album were *Gates of Eden* and *It's Alright Ma (I'm Only Bleeding)*. They offered a coruscating parade of images with uncertain reference but a crystal clear sense of social disillusion, spiritual malaise and deep human longing. *Gates of Eden* speaks of exclusion from paradise, regardless of any precise application Dylan may or may not have had for the idea. And who is the 'Ma' in the song title and refrain but an unspecified 'other' to whom a secret prayer for compassion is addressed but without much confidence in a response?

From this point onward Dylan's writing never lost an edge of personal alienation and separation. *Desolation Row* (1965), *Shelter from the Storm* (1975), *Not Dark Yet* (1997) are some of the deep cuts in a landscape rutted with pain. And throughout it all the theme of violence as a constant threat to the human condition is never abandoned. After the early classics like *Masters of War* (1963) and *A Hard Rain's a-Gonna Fall* (1963) it continues to surface, in *Knockin' On Heaven's Door* (1972), *Señor (Tales of Yankee Power)* (1978), *Blind Willie McTell* (1983), *License To Kill* (1983), *John Brown* (released 1995), *Things Have Changed* (2000), *Tweedle Dee and Tweedle Dum* (2001), etc.

It is not surprising given this attention to the human crisis that Dylan should at some point have found Christ. In the late seventies Dylan became a born-again Christian and recorded three albums with explicitly Christian lyrics. Some of the most memorable songs are *I Believe In You* (1979), *When He Returns* (1979), and *In The Garden* (1980). They are generally called gospel, but they go beyond the historical roots of the genre, reflecting an intensely personal and direct response by Dylan. However, his confessional approach did not last long, and by 1983 he had returned to a much more ambiguous and even hostile relationship to Christianity. Dylan is famous for his unquantifiable persona, both as individual and artist, and this was just one more instance of not being able to put him in a box. For the same reason it would also be wrong to say that either the meaning of Christ or the ongoing possibility of relationship has disappeared from his songs. Once again it is a matter of the artist straddling the borderline between the world of signs, deeply attuned to Christ, and the present regimes of the world, including Christianity. But with Dylan it comes in a more acute form than with Bono. We might say for Dylan there is fundamentally a *Blowin'-in-the-Wind* style of transformation by which Christ touches the world, but it is by a *Gates-of-Eden* alienation that he came to see Christ inhabiting the churches and then even also his own life.[5] Dylan's artistic experience can be said perhaps to reside entirely in the virtual part of virtual Christianity, i.e. as pure sign or significance, in whatever way it presents itself, but without any surety of faith to stabilize it. In which case Dylan may be read as a kind of weather vane of Christian virtuality, shifting to all the quarters of the compass as the winds blow from it, against it, or tack somewhere in between.

This is undeniably true of his general use of the bible as cultural resource. Regardless of any event of conversion, Dylan has continued to mine the biblical text for metaphors, motifs and motive force. It amounts to a kind of primal phenomenon for him, woven in his songs from start to finish. Starting from the universally known *Blowin' in the Wind* (1963) we can see it reappearing in *Highway 61 Revisited* (1965), *All Along The Watchtower* (1967), *Quinn The Eskimo* (1967), *Father of Night* (1970), *Changing Of The Guards* (1978), *The Groom's Still Waiting At The Altar* (1981), *Every Grain of Sand* (1981), *Ring Them Bells* (1989), again *Tweedle Dee and Tweedle Dum* (2001), all the way to some of his most recent work, *Spirit On The Water* (2006), *Thunder on the Mountain* (2006), and the astonishing album, *Christmas In The Heart* (2009). But it is the climactic heart-sick journey of *Ain't Talkin'* (2006) that grabs the attention. The quality of reflection in this song, coming late in the five-decade-long journey of his career, warrants remarking finally on these lyrics out of all he has written. They stand as a kind of comment on just about everything that has gone before. The refrain takes us deep into New Testament territory despite the apparent despair of the lyric. The first and third lines of the quatrain remain the same throughout the song, while the second and fourth change. Here, for example, is the third chorus: 'Ain't talkin', just walkin' / Through the world mysterious and vague / Heart burnin', still yearnin' / Walking through the cities of the plague.'

The walking while not talking , and with a burning heart, may be recognized as references to the disciples on the road to Emmaus, listening to Jesus explain the scriptures to them. 'Were not our hearts burning within us while he was talking to us on the road...?' (Luke 24:32). All the same the song begins with the cruel scene of Cain, happening now in the garden of Eden and — with fierce writing economy—twinned with the figure of Christ.

> As I walked out tonight in the mystic garden
> The wounded flowers were dangling from the vines
> I was passing by yon cool and crystal fountain
> Someone hit me from behind

We remember that 'a river flows out of Eden to water the garden' (Gen. 2:10), and simultaneously the image of wounds and vine cannot help remind us of Jesus and place the redemptive figure in that primary context. Yet it makes no difference: Cain is still murdering from behind. This Christian failure is reinforced by the final verse which evokes (and negates) Mary Magdalene's encounter on Easter morning when she takes Jesus to be the gardener.

> As I walked out in the mystic garden
> On a hot summer day, hot summer lawn
> Excuse me, ma'am, I beg your pardon
> There's no one here, the gardener is gone

Nevertheless Dylan continues his endless Emmaus journey to the last: 'Ain't talkin', just walkin' / Up the road around the bend / Heart burnin', still yearnin' / In the last outback, at the world's end.' Despite every failure he has no choice but to keep going with the burning and yearning within him. In the final absence of the one figure of who could give meaning to the journey the longing for that figure somehow continues to provide significance. It offers a meaningful sign. And so in the song's very desperation the figure seems to return. In respect of Dylan himself it is difficult to draw conclusions, but in the context of his oeuvre and the overall study here things are much simpler. The work of indisputably the most significant singer-songwriter of the 2nd half of the 20th century and beginning of the 21st is laced throughout with the mysterious sign of Christ. Dylan's body of writing would be unthinkable without the bible generally and the gospels in particular. And the depth of ambiguity of his relationship with Christ fits the context and character of the photon entirely.

The revelation of the sign of Christ arises in denial of the world and is denied by it, and yet it also mobilizes the world in its deepest spring. The world moves toward it in the same measure as it moves away. An artist like Dylan knows all this and cannot help but give expression to the full range of possible reactions. A medium like the movies can use the photon for dramatic purposes without having to take a stand, but a spinner of words like Dylan may always be held to account by the things he said. He thus changes his words continually to avoid them trapping him. But this is not for reasons of vanity. Rather so many of the changes of his writing encompass the deep ambiguity of the world as it is faced with the transforming humanity of Jesus. Time and again the world fails before this ineluctable human sign and Dylan is a remorseless chronicler of its collapse. But in that moment of failure and like a silver river seen from the air the figure of Christ suddenly reappears and glimmers unfailingly. This Jewish-Christian-Secular artist who is called the Shakespeare of popular song stands as persuasive witness of the dynamic meaning of Christ at the heart of our contemporary culture, at the heart of our world of signs.

Chapter Four

Alpha to Omega

The lines of Christ's presence at the heart of our media world have been depicted in bright strokes, with coloring from both medieval and contemporary forms. It is necessary now to step back a little from these eye-popping visuals and fit the same phenomena within a more traditional intellectual perspective. This has of course the benefit of strengthening the argument, but also of letting it join more closely the two millennial tradition of thought about the Christ. Established Christian theology has been carried on within the context of Western philosophy and speculative thought and this chapter will be meeting and merging with that context. We're making a substantial shift in the tenor of the argument, so we should gather our natural wits to focus as we do. Let me restate then specifically what it is I am doing.

In the previous chapters I have given an historical and popular-culture account of the virtual, arguing that Christ is revealed or, more precisely, draws close to us through it. The argument set up a strong sense of movement, of the vortex of images and the agency at its heart which is the self-giving of Christ. The sense of this movement was something that could be gained immediately, at first hand, by going to the movies, or by watching a music video. And it was my deliberate intention to begin at that level, because the way you think about something always depends crucially on the point at which you start your thinking. What comes first comes after. Thus the beginning point at which the book now stands is the lived world of our 21st century humanity, especially its visual media, not some purely intellectual truth. Christian theology has always had the reference of the lived world—because it was there that Christ was always experienced—but it made final sense of that reference by fitting it within a world of eternal truth largely inherited from the Greeks. I believe that the inherited intellectual world has itself been profoundly influenced by the revelation of forgiveness and love in the Crucified. It has in fact slowly been shifted into a dynamic sense of movement, away from static concepts and eternal truth. I want to demonstrate this by bringing into the conversation pivotal thinkers for whom movement is central. I will discuss the path which movement takes in their thought and draw out some detail of its content and implications. Essentially I will argue that it is Christ who is the generative source of the movement in their thought. And then, reciprocally, we will begin to see the irreducible role of movement for our contemporary theological and faith universe. Rather than finding our world made out of fixed 'things' in a traditional way we will come to sense it as much more essentially fluid, dynamic, open to trans-formation. Building up this framework will then allow us to situate the idea of virtual Christianity more securely and demon-strate it more compellingly. If Christ is the source of actual human movement presumably it is to draw human beings to himself, and in terms of historical fact.

A World in Motion
Movement was a puzzle to ancient philosophers. Some of them discounted it, thinking it little more than illusory, others saw it as real and primary. The world we are in today is bedazzled by movement. For contemporary culture it is not a question of deciding movement's philosophical status. Rather it has become a way of life in its own right, a super-medium, one that contains an almost unlimited number of variations on its essential theme. It would not be exaggerated to say that movement has become today the primary mode of human existence, one unimaginable to our forefathers and foremothers. From car travel to jet travel,

from radio waves to broadband, from barter to digital trading, the world finds itself aboard a speeding train that no one has any idea of how to stop or really any desire to do so.

Of course damage to the environment itself could slow the train catastrophically and war could wreck it completely, but these doomsday possibilities only serve to demonstrate how crucial movement is to our life and how nearly impossible it is to imagine a modern world without movement at the center.

Related to movement is time. Aristotle saw time as motion which is measured or numbered, like the apparent circuit of the sun in the heavens producing a day, or an hourglass an hour. Augustine proposed a more subtle psychological sense. Human beings are the measure of time, not motion its own measure. Thus the human mind expects the future and remembers the past and so produces the sense of the present between the two, even though the present constantly vanishes away. What holds steady is not 'the present' but our attention in the midst of past and future. In this frame the basic experience of movement, of moving through time, is always a deeply human thing.

But if Augustine is right—if the soul spins the facts of time almost like the spider its thread—then what is happening today when the collective human soul has created infinitely multiplied webs in which to experience movement and time? Has time been expanded to include much more of itself? Is our sense of time much richer than before? Or is time spread so thin that it has lost a great deal of its human value and become instead a meaningless, even soul-destroying, succession of atomized sensations. Or, are perhaps both things true? Is it possible that even as we multiply the situations and occasions where movement occurs—and so run the risk of emptying every movement of purpose and meaning—at the same time the heightened pace of everything suggests that we are being carried necessarily toward something different, something new? And that we sense—or at least hope for—this possibility in our madcap dash from one thing to another?

Thus movement becomes the key question of our age. Where is it leading us? What is its purpose?

Evolution and Christ

One of the first places to start looking at the thought of movement is the contemporary scientific worldview of evolution. Evolution has movement at its core, and whether that movement is random at source or in some way goal-directed, the important thing at this point is the vibrant sense of movement it provides. To say a life form 'evolved' tells us that an adaptive change took place which—regardless of whether by organic feedback or accident—always looks like a positive change, something affirmative. We never think that the evolution of a species is a bad thing; we call it the 'success' of that species. In which case biological change, or movement, is experienced as a basic existential value.

The theory of evolution is the default scientific view of our culture and has irreversibly influenced the way humans look at their cosmos. When I was growing up, going to a Roman Catholic school, I was taught there was no problem in putting the theory of evolution and the doctrine of creation together. My religious education teacher would say that the process of evolution would 'redound' even more to God's glory than if creation happened by divine *fiat*. As well as being impressed by the word 'redound' something in me entirely agreed. It seemed to token a much smarter and at the same time much more loving and freedom-giving God if creation took place over vast eons of time and by processes intimate to the material world rather than forced upon it as if by a divine laser.

To add to this boyhood experience one of my first real educational discoveries in seminary was a lecture on Teilhard de Chardin, the French Jesuit priest who earned the wrath of church authorities for merging together evolution and the life of the spirit. (De Chardin was silenced during his lifetime but his major work was published after his death.) What really struck me about the presentation was the overlapping of physical life with the traditionally more disembodied, other-worldly thought of spirit. Somehow this seemed to fit entirely with the physicality of Jesus and of the message of the bodily Resurrection arising from the gospels. And the way it felt to a nineteen-year-old it brought vitality to the dull concepts of theology and a sense of hope to the harsh world of history. De Chardin argued that within the development of external physical life there was always a parallel growth of a 'within,' an interiority. 'Since…the natural history of living creatures amounts on the *exterior* to the gradual establishment of a vast nervous system, it therefore corresponds on the *interior* to the installation of a psychic state coextensive with the earth. On the surface, we find the nerve fibers and the ganglions; deep down, consciousness.'[1]

According to de Chardin there is *de facto* a curve toward consciousness in evolutionary genesis and this suggests to him a built-in impetus or inner principle, a reaching up toward thought, to personal communion and to love, to what he calls an Omega point. This point he sees coinciding perfectly with the Christian teaching of the unity of the earth with God through Christ. It is not important to develop de Chardin's detailed argument, either as regards evolution itself, or the way they might fit with traditional Christian doctrine. What counts is the excited sense of recognition de Chardin obviously felt as a Christian looking at the grand story of evolution he had come to know as a biologist. There was a sense of already having seen what he was looking at. He says explicitly he saw the New Testament teaching of all creation in communion with God 'so perfectly…[to] coincide with the Omega Point that doubtless I should never have ventured to envisage the latter or formulate the hypothesis rationally if, *in my consciousness as a believer, I had not found* not only its speculative model but also *its living reality.'*[2]

In other words it was his direct experience as a Christian that provided the original template for a thought of evolution. So, very quickly we have come full circle: rather than having to adjust Christianity to a world full of movement we have discovered the sense of cosmic movement emerging from an original Christian sensibility. Darwin's thought obviously followed a different route, progressively abandoning Christian belief because of the contradiction, as he saw it, between the words of scripture and the teachings of science (especially the antiquity of geological formation compared to six days creation). But once again the immediate question is not the rightness or wrongness of the thought of evolution as such but the way it has injected movement into the contemporary worldview. And in this respect we can see how Darwin's atheism and secularism has served to accentuate enormously the freedom or immanent sense of movement in the world—not dependent at all on a divine shaping or control. So, what we end up with is this intensely interesting flux back and forth between a Christianity naturally productive of a sense of movement and an equally powerful assertion of an entirely independent materialist or worldly sense of movement. In either case movement is the common denominator and is the hugely determinative context in which theology finds itself. A theology that says Darwin was essentially wrong and the scripture literally true may be understood from this perspective as a reaction against movement in favor of vertical divine power and control. In this viewpoint time means almost nothing; it is merely the minimum necessary space of freedom wherein human persons may, under God's prompting, decide their place within a rigid eternal framework.

I will delay until the next chapter the examination of what a theology of movement might mean for the traditional ideas of God and the world. For my instincts these categories taken in abstract are not the primary theological question, in the sense of providing the shape of theology in themselves; they do however demand and get attention at a secondary moment. What is primary is the actual condition of movement in which the world finds itself, and where this has come from. As already illustrated in the case of de Chardin it is very possible to find biblical revelation as the immediate source of the sense of movement. At the same time, on a cultural level, the sense of movement gives evidence of itself in its own right. It is the sea in which we swim, the contemporary condition of human existence, and to want to negate it in favor of vertical divine control seems, in this light, simply reactive and defensive (and in practice increasingly violent). It is within this overall cultural context—which again is open intuitively to identification as Christian—that I see the general idea of evolution as convincing, rather than seeking mathematical conviction in the science as such (particularly, in the two solitary Darwinian principles of random mutation and struggle of species.) However, once the general proposition is accepted, it then allows us to consider various elements of the science with objectivity. It allows scientific data to stand forth more coherently and lucidly. In this light, then, we may now ask what we may learn more specifically about movement from evolutionary biology?

Evolution and Soul

When de Chardin describes the birth of thought in the world he does so in decisively collective or bio-structural terms. His concept of thought has none of the stale individual intellectual-soul character derived from Greek philosophy. The name he gives to it mimics the names given to the various layers structuring life on earth, for example the hydrosphere and the biosphere. It is the *noosphere* or 'mind-sphere' and here is his evocative description.

A glow ripples outward from the first spark of conscious

reflection. The point of ignition grows larger. The fire spreads in ever widening circles till finally the whole planet is covered with incandescence. Only one interpretation, only one name can be found worthy of this grand phenomenon. Much more coherent and just as extensive as any preceding layer, it is really a new layer, the 'thinking layer', which, since its germination at the end of the Tertiary period, has spread over and above the world of plants and animals. In other words, outside and above the biosphere there is the noosphere.[3]

I am not the first to see here a prophetic description of the Internet phenomenon, the layer of satellites and computers girdling the earth allowing simultaneous aural and visual 'thought' by humans. In this context the concept of a noosphere reaching toward its Omega point looks very similar to the argument advanced in the second and third chapters that the figure of Christ is slowly distinguishing itself as the critical point of meaning in our digital world. I will return to this again but for the moment what is important is the general understanding afforded by evolutionary science. For de Chardin the technical advance of the Internet would simply be the latest and logical outgrowth of a possibility that was there from the beginning. For him thought and intelligence were always a collective or phylogenetic emergence, always something that happened to the whole class of hominids together, never simply to individuals.

There is now a recent and very exciting scientific development which falls within the range of evolutionary biology and shows the potential of science to enrich a theology of movement and virtuality. It demonstrates the intensely shared nature of human consciousness and this is a phenomenon already sketched in our primate cousins. In the early nineteen nineties a research team led by Giacomo Rizzolatti and Vittorio Gallese, in Parma, Italy, was studying motor neurons in an area of the premotor cortex of macaque monkeys, using brain electrodes.[4] By chance and to their complete amazement they discovered that the same neural pathways that were used to carry out complex goal-directed actions, like holding, grasping, tearing, were activated when the subject monkey observed another individual (human or monkey) performing the same actions. The *observation* of an action in another led to the activation of the identical neurons used in *performing* that selfsame action. The name the researchers gave to these dual function neurons was 'mirror neurons', and thus was born an area of scientific inquiry which commentators say will have the same impact on psychology as the discovery of DNA had on biology.

The really remarkable thing is that the object of the activity (e.g. a piece of fruit or a bright object) could never produce the neural response on its own; it had to be held and used by another. In other words what was being mirrored was always goal-directed activity, the object and its manipulation by another, never the object on its own. Moreover, the activation of these neurons was automatic, independent of either the intention of the observer or the will of the observed. At the level of the neurons, therefore, there is a shared world, independent of the decision or wish of either protagonist. Further research, using less invasive methods, demonstrated (of course) the same phenomenon in humans, and to a much greater degree both quantitatively and qualitatively.[5] The discovery then has an astonishing range of implications in the sciences of human life which the researchers were not slow to realize: from learning to language, from maternal function to morality, from empathy to philosophy, the consequences of a borderless self-other universe are themselves almost without borders.

But for our immediate discussion what is noteworthy is the confirmation of de Chardin's thesis—that the nervous system as exterior system carries with it an 'interior' psychic state which is as much a part of biological evolution as the exterior. The existence of mirror neurons in the primates demonstrates that the 'spiritual' self or soul—the self that merges, beyond boundaries, with the other—is part of their experience too. What we can also extrapolate from these neurons is that the universe is already a 'shared' phenomenon. In order for one organism to be able to 'repeat' the other implies at a primordial level that each separate part is somehow a part of the other. The mirror effect of the neurons cannot be fully 'in' the self (a kind of third-party spectator in the brain looking at its own screen with the mirroring going on intellectually inside its tiny head, and so on infinitely) but *between* selves. The first primate mirrors the second because they've already learned they are part of each other, and this 'learning' cannot happen unless it was somehow always already there! There can be little doubt, therefore, that the whole of creation in some way is already a unitary system, connected to or 'mirroring' itself in every part, and that it has indeed reached upward, in a redoubling or refining manner, to the point where that connectedness becomes 'seen' in and by the primate and hominid brain.

Here then is another strand in the theme of the virtual: I am virtually you, and you are virtually me. And, moreover (evident at a second reflective moment), I am virtually the universe, and the universe is virtually me. For if a hominid has come to itself only with and through 'the other' (hominid) then it is impossible for it in some way not to experience the whole world as 'personal'. The meaningful world has always been mediated by another, and so it must always retain a sense of mediation. It is either 'for me or against me'! It is easy then to understand the extremely volatile conditions created by a plurality of individual anthropoids each with such 'universal' pretensions, and so Girard's hypothesis of original violence becomes very credible. For of course we do not lose sight of the fact that while the mirroring is taking place between organisms those organisms still remain distinct and self-affirming. There is in fact a fearful paradox involved in super-connectedness (mimetic consciousness) involving individual agencies. How do you reconcile the continuing drive for self-assertion by the organism (Darwin's competition to survive) with the emergence of an over-the-top ability to imitate the other? I am indeed neither one thing or another: I am neither a drive-controlled organism competing safely within biological dominance-and-submission patterns, nor am I so connected to you that I can willingly subordinate myself to your good. This is the point, therefore, where anthropology must take over from neuroscience, and Girard's hypothesis of original violence resolved in the surrogate victim brings full coherence to the evolutionary pathway. It's only when the super-mimesis of the emerging hominid is traumatized and cauterized by a meta-physical event of violence and its resulting peace that culture arrives. Something greater than all of us appears, able both to contain and control the explosive mix of competition and imitation.

The Yes and No, and the Yes Alone

We are arriving at a sketch of evolutionary movement which offers, I think, profound theological possibility. To appreciate it we have to underline and draw out the pivotal development presented in the Girardian hypothesis in the second chapter. The total experience of the surrogate victim is both remembered and misrecognized in a mythological frame. As the guilty source of all evil and then the benign origin of all good the surrogate victim appears as a god. And truly s/he is divine, for in her 'switch' from evil to good she makes available an on / off switch with astonishing world-creating and world-ordering power. First the on / off switch produces a rule-bound universe: there is an area of behavior which must at all costs be avoided if similar crises in the future are to be averted and peace maintained: therefore don't do that / do this! The world of prohibitions grows naturally from the terror of the primary event producing a proto-cultural line in the sand, a 'no' on one side and a 'yes' on the other. Take, for example, the universal prohibition on incest. Imagine the situation before the prohibition was in place in a particular group, the rivalry and violence that were provoked on one catastrophic occasion and the significance that the surrogate victim would then have attained (perhaps the unfortunate sister disputed by two brothers, or one of the brothers himself). S/he would have spoken deafeningly of the 'evil' of such relations and automatically generated attention to the outward boundary where—and only there—sexual relations were permitted. But simultaneously this cultural development could not have emerged without the language to say it. There had to be two primary words, a primitive set of vocalization, which came with the event and which created the signals both for the crisis, with the meaning of 'bad,' and for its resolution, with the meaning 'good'. These signals should not be conceived in any ideal way but simply the sounds wrung from the group by the exhaled trauma of the two primary moments. But that was enough. The event necessarily contains, therefore, the generative binary of differentiation: bad and good, and then by an essential multiplication, 'no and yes', 'that and this', 'there and here', and so on, infinitely, into the universe of language. Girard has taught both these results—rules and language— but to my knowledge he has not noted how critical the on / off is, the essential role of the binary switch contained in the primary scene. I am now seeking to draw attention to this implication and its remarkable consequences. In both cases—rules and language—the switch of yes / no overcomes 'undifferentiation', the loss of difference between individuals because of imitation and the dissolution of a world constructed only by instinct. Now rules and language provide an essential structure and a world of difference.

Setting the evolutionary scene in this way we are in a position to offer a theological pathway of great simplicity and at the same time enormous vitality. One of the criticisms of de Chardin and other thinkers who emphasize movement is that they underestimate the power of sin and hence the need for redemption: you would not think that anything could seriously go wrong on the grand evolutionary journey to the Omega point. By inserting Girard here, and by means of the 'hard' biological science of mirror neurons, we open the evolutionary picture fully and formidably to sin. The world comes about through murder and the lie that covers it up. This in itself is entirely consistent with the account in Genesis.

Unlike the dominant theological tradition which has given exclusive weight to the 'sin of the first parents' and so relegated the other stories in Genesis 1-11 to a sideshow, contemporary biblical scholarship is able to see these stories as so many parallel accounts of a single human condition of alienation from God and from each other. They should be read as so many facets of a single prism. The Eden story can claim to come first ontologically, in terms of our ultimate condition of separation from God, but not chronologically as 'the very first historical event'. A much more plausible candidate for that—for the emergence of actual history—is in fact the story that comes next. In this light the story of Cain and Abel can be seen as a 'real-time' doublet of the more mystical Garden of Eden story containing its inner meaning. Their strictly complementary nature is evident in the structure of the stories. They both involve familiar connection and conversation of God, and then the determinative role of desire and rivalry. In both instances God is responsible for the object of desire: the fruit in the first and his favor in the second. The role of the serpent suggesting rivalry with God in the first story is matched in the second story by the rivalry which God himself inexplicably sets up by preferring the animal sacrifice to vegetable offerings. (The attempt to argue that animal sacrifice shows more devotion on the part of Abel can only be an after-the-fact justification: nowhere in the text is this value suggested.) Following the crime there is a trial, then punishment, with a description of alienation. The stories are thus in fact saying the same thing from two sides, but always with the same basic drama and outcome—rivalry produces violence and death. The fact that God's warning that eating the fruit would result in death is only in fact fulfilled by the death of Abel shows clearly there is a single drama at work. However, the murder of Abel by Cain is followed by the paradoxical protection and flourishing of Cain as founder of the first city (and then of his successor, Lamech, and of his children as founders of culture). So it is easy also to see an intentional evolutionary account of the emergence of human order and culture: something that is apparently successful but based originally in murder and alienation. Reading it this way we can see the scriptural support for an anthropological account of violent origins. What contemporary science gives us is simply the material and structural basis of how the anthropoid arrived at this point and how the drama unfolds in primary groups of 'brothers' rather than between just two children of the same parents.

It seems then difficult to overstate the significance of this violent birth of human order and meaning. Few people would have trouble recognizing the way society operates on the sanction of violence, and so it should not be hard accepting very probably it depends on original violence. Arthur C. Clarke and Stanley Kubrick's movie, *2001*, illustrates this with panache. The primitive hominid group is visited by an extraterrestrial Monolith. The first thing that happens after this catalytic visit is for the group's leader to use an ox bone as a weapon, violently subduing a rival. He then tosses the bone in the air where it morphs gracefully into a stupendous space-station to the accompaniment of the Blue Danube. This does not seem problematic; it is even poetic. The first thing that intelligence does is kill. But if we go deeper into the Girardian hypothesis we see that the origin of intelligible meaning itself is from violence.

There is intuitively a world prior to language, and language has certainly enabled us to order that world intellectually so we know an immense amount about it. To speak today of 'quarks' and 'string theory' means we're talking about things we cannot see and which can only make full sense mathematically. And yet the language at once opens new dimensions of the universe to anyone who pays attention. At the same time, the whole scaffolding of words and the differentiation they make possible depends intrinsically on the founding murder. This is much more difficult to accept. It runs against our prejudice for what Girard calls 'the immaculate conception of thought'. Yet the fact that we are so close to the primates in neural mirroring means they have some degree of 'meaning' but then they lack the abstract processing of language to enshrine it. Something must have happened out of the neural motherboard but which would also produce the radical break of virtuality or words. The contenders so far have been some version of Plato's innate ideas (including its material version of 'hardwiring'), or indeed Clarke and Kubrick's extraterrestrial Monolith. A much more consistent evolutionary viewpoint is the founding event of the first crisis and murder which literally shocked the primary group into the articulation of an on / off switch: *this* rather than *that, here* rather than *there.*

What this means is that the basic device of articulate meaning is the killing of the victim. Without that original killing nothing would make sense, nothing would be differentiated. So, whatever we speak of, from cabbages to kings, there is always an echo of that primordial victim in our words, in our grammar. Every comma, so to speak, is made of blood. Again, obviously, this does not mean that there are no cabbages or there are no kings, nor any less is there no honor, no justice within such a world. Rather it says that to get to the name of 'cabbage' or the name of 'king', or to the concept of justice, depends on a string of differences (of *offs* and *ons*) which only language can put and hold in place. And these linguistic differences trace their source directly to the murder of the surrogate victim, the scapegoat, and to the on / off binary that grew out of her terrible death. It means something along the lines of what Augustine was proposing when he said 'the greatest virtues of the pagans are but vices.'

An appalling but entirely credible hypothesis, and one that gives birth finally to an equally gripping theological prospect. If meaning is rooted in the murder of the victim and our language cannot help but be complicit in that murder, then Christ, the one who entered willingly and forgivingly into the root structure of our human universe, is engaged in overturning the order of meaning itself. When John's gospel says 'In the beginning was the word / logos,' and the word / logos came into the world 'yet the world did not know him' (John 1:1,10), it is telling us that the divine principle of meaning arises in the midst of history and yet is not recognized. But then later in the same gospel we are told that when this principle is 'lifted up'(12:33), i.e. *as* the Crucified, he will in fact draw all humanity to himself. In other words the Crucified is the effective radical subversion of historical human meaning. The word / logos which has its beginning both in the gospel and 'in the beginning' with God can and will become the word / logos for human history.

But in what sense, compared to the original violence of the binary system? How can the Crucified change the root character of language? Paul gives us a hint when he says, 'For the Son of God, Jesus Christ, whom we proclaimed among you…was not 'Yes and No'; but in him it is always 'Yes'. For in him every one of God's promises is a 'Yes'.' (2 Cor. 1:20). Paul's words can suggest a massive creational affirmation present in Christ, and the consequences for the world would be a resounding 'Yes!' in answer to its deepest life questions. It is extremely difficult to imagine such a thing, to conceive of a situation where all the practical, moral and technical questions controlled by yes / no are swept up into a single 'Yes!' What would happen to nuclear fission, to computers, to genetic engineering, to law and prisons, to wealth and banks and politics and wars? The best paradigm, always, is falling into and making love, where everything in a person cries out to and for the beloved, without any sense of negation, only of fulfillment. But how is the whole world to become anything resembling one single great act of falling in love? And for ever and always?

Fortunately it is not my task to lay out any kind of analytic blueprint for this dream: first, because from the whole model of movement I have been pursuing this can only happen on an evolutionary pathway stretching into the future, something that can hardly be known in advance; second, and conclusively, because the nature of this evolution is always a willing embrace of the pathway by individuals and groups, and by its very nature this embrace is a leap into the void in the same manner as Christ's. To discover the gift of the Spirit and to bring about a world-in-love both require a mysterious surrender which cannot grasp in advance the things they seek. To try to do so undoes the absolute 'falling' which love requires. Indeed, reflectively, the overcoming of negation implies a leap which cannot be previewed: the moment the outcome is conceived in advance it becomes a kind of negation of the present order, and so back within the present order! The actual practice of a world-in-love has to be surrender through love and trust which indeed forfeits knowledge. I am thinking here of people like Dietrich Bonhoeffer or Mother Teresa who give themselves for a world of love without any guarantee of ultimate success. But paradoxically it is only by their not-knowing the outcome that an absolute act and affirmation of love is possible.

Revolution in Human Meaning

However, although I just very deliberately dropped the ball in respect of any attempt to visualize practically the transformation of the earth, this does not mean we do not have an adequate sign system to bring it about. If it is true that we can never program love on the level of the individual, it nevertheless remains possible and necessary to grasp the signifying effects of Christ's historical act of surrender on the cross: the way he has provided a core symbol for a world-in-love. There is in fact a knowledge of love in the world which inspires individuals like Bonhoeffer, Mother Teresa and others. To this extent no other person can be said to be in the identical situation as Jesus who did not have a pre-existing example to his own to benefit from. Although he clearly had many influences in his scripture there was no one before him who provided a concrete example of love in the remainderless, once-and-for-all manner that he did. (The prophecy of the Suffering Servant in Isaiah clearly points in this direction, but there is no story attached to this figure, no specific relationships to individuals or to God, no actual description of the manner of death. Although I believe there was an actual human figure what s/he has left behind is more a general template than an actual history.) Jesus can thus be said to have made the act of love in a truly contingent and elemental way and there is a real sense in which Jesus gave birth to love in the world. We will pursue this thought more thoroughly in the following two chapters. What is important now, at this point in our discussion of evolution, is that we are able to sketch a plan of human movement which points toward a merging of human meaning and the semiotics of the Galilean.

It can be stated as follows. The anthropoids began on the level of the raw phenomenon. They 'saw' the object mediated by the desire or acquisitive intention of the other. It was powerfully impressive but they had no word to name it or tame it. The situation erupted in terrifying crisis, ending in the catastrophe of murder but, through and because of that, there was the dawning of language. With language comes a world of difference, but also the symbolic, the artistic ability to construct a powerful image within that world, e.g. the picture of a bull, a stag, a fire or a person. In the second chapter I used the word 'symbol' inter-changeably with 'sign' because in the virtual world there is really no hierarchy between them. But we are describing things here from an evolutionary perspective and given that in primitive times images (paintings, statues) would have been the exception and held a considerable power of wonder, I will momentarily revert to the more traditional sense of symbol. In this sense a symbol is a figure sharing in and communicating the reality it points to. Symbols in this older sense have an integrating force, rather than a differentiating one. But what is that integrating reality which communicates in this powerful manner if it is not a relationship to ritual and the sacrificial? The world of meaning derives from the concentrating or systematizing force of the founding murder as much as from its differentiating capacity, and the symbol can be seen as tapping into this more 'holistic' level of meaning. We can conclude, therefore, that effective symbols have always communicated the world-gathering force of the sacred as it channels the violence of the group into collective agreement, producing established forms of divinity and authority. Think of the winged lions of Babylon, the solar disk of the Pharaohs, the statues and coins of the Caesars, and, in our own day, the Nazi swastika. Without a doubt the Mosaic ban on graven images derives from a sense of the sacred violence stored up in them and how this 'significantly' contradicts the liberating truth of YHWH. But then, as our story proceeds, something dramatically new happens! In the fullness of time, there erupts on the scene a figure able to communicate an entirely different power and depth than the sacred. With Jesus there is the absolute affirmation of love, and the figure of the cross introduces a sign to the world which (de)symbolizes (reveals) the original murder, while it resets creation toward a meaning of absolute giving.

The cross then becomes a symbol in a completely new sense. There is no mystique of violence suffusing the image. Instead there is a letting go, a letting be, an emptying of the sign in favor of the other, so that the other might live. This infinite self-surrender, this self-pouring-out, spells the end of the symbolic cover-up of violence, since it leaves no hidden depths, no sacredness of violence. It is also thus the beginning of the world of multiplied signs, of our actual world of virtuality, where each sign is as good as the next because none stands apart as especially 'holy'. But at the same time the cross continues quietly and humbly to realize the giving at the core of this world, something not a sign itself as much as a primordial movement which springs everything else into movement. At length, then, as the vortex of signs progressively spins into an infinite multiplicity, into a blur of confusion, the sense of the original movement is intimated behind it. Like the quietly counter-turning drive shaft of an enormous engine of signs our attention is slowly drawn toward it. As the vortex displaces itself continually, *ad nauseam*, the photon of compassion discloses itself as the astonishingly new yet original event of meaning, the endless 'Yes' at the heart of creation.

This is a revolution of incalculable significance in every sense; really, it is the only true cultural revolution. It has taken the original 'fiction' of human meaning and made it something wonderfully new, able to bring creation to its intended destiny of peace, life, love. De Chardin's evolution toward the Omega is now no longer simply a steadily increasing and unifying biological 'within' which somehow happens to coincide with the Christian message of love. It is the figure of Christ himself who slowly and steadily shifts human meaning in this direction by a re-creation of the construct that brought meaning about. It is the Christ who becomes the principle of human evolution after the principle of human violence has run its course. And the accent on 'human evolution' should be noted. This is not a deterministic mechanical sense of evolution, but the intensely human capacity to fabricate a universe out of signs and then to live in that universe. Essentially this can only happen twice, the first time in the violent and largely unconscious birth of culture, the second through the nonviolence of the gospel. Because human meaning is constructed and this has happened out of violence, then the human universe is, in and of itself, fragile, unstable, subject to a kind of radioactive decay. In the past the decay has taken the form of violent upheavals, wars and revolutions, in which the basic mechanism of violence is 'known' but not understood. Nowadays we are more and more helplessly aware that this is a human mechanism, that it is flawed, that it creates never-ending victims. Slowly, at the same time, the key factor producing this awareness comes to evidence, the sign of Christ. Humanity is then left progressively with a crisis and choice, and it is in the progressive crisis and choice that the singular meaning of human evolution is contained. From within the depth of our human experience we are pushed to re-fabricate our universe out of the sign of forgiveness, nonviolence and love. The progressive crisis is the evolution, the unavoidable choice is what might be called the 'unnatural selection' it is pushing us toward. The more the choice is avoided, the more the crisis grows, the more it grows, the more the choice is unavoidable.

All of this might seem a shock and a scandal, either to fundamentalists or to liberals. Fundamentalists expect violent judgment from God, not nonviolent transformation. Liberal Christians essentially see Christ as a metaphor for something else: a general principle of goodness floating somewhere in the universe available intellectually or spiritually to all. And yet they sit and listen Sundays to the intense particularism of the New Testament, they probably subscribe to the biological particularism of natural selection, and they fervently defend the concrete individual as an irreducible point of value. They are a mixture of historical individuality and the intellectually ideal and therefore, as it seems to me, hopelessly muddled. The scandal is really not the singular role of Christ but the failure to take history and humanity with absolute seriousness. Or, put another way, what fundamentalists and liberals have in common is they are scandalized by the absolute particularity of love: love can only enter the world case by case, individual by individual, and both the violent termination of history and the Olympian heights of idealism are ways of short-circuiting the crucial surrender to the particular required by love.

In anthropological terms human meaning and language arose crisis by crisis, victim by victim, and then, at a certain point in history, the theological subversion of meaning took place with one further yet final victim, the Christ. Christ thus opened the symbolic to love, to vision without rivalry and violence, and from then on the phenomenal world which the symbolic controls is always available to loving apprehension or contemplation without violence. The sign of the cross is therefore of transcendental importance. It is able to provide the necessary conditions of transformed meaning for a transformed world.

Philosophy Rules Maybe

To use a word like 'transcendental' moves the discussion directly into the field of philosophy. The word refers generally to something which has independent or superior status to the world, but it has also a more technical meaning derived from the philosopher Kant. The mention of Kant, the famous but famously-dry philosopher, sends up red warning flares of a shift to his type of discourse, and I feel I need to make a plea in self-defense. The way the argument has proceeded so far has been based in the concrete world of media and the theories of science which, although sometimes complex, depend on concrete evidence we can see and touch. Turning to philosophy makes one think of Voltaire's purported quip: 'When he who hears does not know what he who speaks means, and when he who speaks does not know what he himself means, that is philosophy.' In other terms, intelligibility gets lost in words which are capable of any or no meaning at all. But I would like to propose a dictum of my own: philosophy is like the weather; no matter what we think about it, it's going to be there, its sun is going to shine on us, its rain is going to make us wet.

Take, for example, the research data showing a large majority of North Americans believe in the immortal soul (e.g. 79% agree with the statement 'every person has a soul that will live forever, either in God's presence or absence'[6]). This is in itself a philosophical position inherited largely from the Greeks and passed on through Christianity. Or, another example: Hitler's admiration for Nietzsche and the way Nietzsche's writing was embraced by Nazism are well known and discussed. The very fact it is argued that Nietzsche himself could never have tolerated National Socialism and it was his sister, Elisabeth's distortion of his legacy that made him a favorite with the fascists, all confirm the power of thought, even and especially when its fumes are distilled for mass consumption. Others might respond that, of course, here is an illustration of the toxic effect of philosophical ideas, and they imply their own position is a 'natural' or default setting without need for further reflection. But in this case they are like fish in the ocean whose waters slowly turn different colors, and each time the fish find no cause for comment because as far as they can see 'things have always been this way'.

We are manifestly still under the influence of the classic Greek style of truth, as something eternal or out of time. Yet it is also obvious that our perceptions do and have changed, and that despite the enduring impact of some ideas others intrude and are able to alter the fundamental character of the world we are in. Christianity as a way of looking at the world is not immune to this process, and in fact is itself directly responsible for provoking change. This is the whole argument of the book and so it becomes crucial to examine the way philosophy has both impacted Christianity and been impacted by it. There is no way to avoid some inquiry into the progression of philosophical thought and how the curve of this thought—parallel to the argued curve of evolution—is bent relentlessly toward an encounter with Christ. In line with the theme of the chapter this shifting curve can be described as the infection of philosophy by movement. However, in the case of philosophy movement attains a much more directly relational or existential sense than the large-scale structural character of evolution. The relational sense of movement is the subject of the remainder of the chapter.

Time Out of Mind

Turning back to Kant (1724-1804), he is celebrated for having carried out a 'Copernican revolution' in respect of human knowledge (a branch of philosophy known as epistemology). Truth was no longer a flat earth and the heavens above, but an internal mental system. Kant claimed that the matter of philosophy was an innate structure of the mind by which human knowledge of the world is possible at all, rather than a naïve assumption of a real world imposing itself like an embossing stamp. He did not mean that there was no empirical world but there was no way of knowing it apart from what he called the 'a priori' principles of sensibility. In particular the concepts of space and time were something our minds 'did' for us rather than something external done to us. It was we who were the embossing stamp more than anything outside, independent of us.

One of the key reasons for the success of Kant's philosophy is that it does not dismiss the empirical world in idealism, but holds it as one pole together with the other one of the mind's architecture which places it in order for us. Exactly how the two poles are held together remains a puzzle for interpreters of Kant, but Kant certainly maintains this view. What is key for us is the way Kant stresses the essential proactive role of the mind in organizing our world, before we get to any kind of reflection or discursive thought. This generally coheres with Girard's perspective on the unconscious organization of thought through the victim, although of course we are dealing with two very different frames of reference. Kant is thinking of a pure mental architecture and Girard is thinking of a very messy prehistoric drama that puts thought in place. Kant is arguing for a kind of metaphysical hard-wiring that makes thought possible but, as we have seen with mirror neurons, that wiring can be very physical and fluid and dramatically open to the other. It would be a major undertaking to interface Kantian epistemology and Girardian anthropology and perhaps some thinker will take up the challenge, but it is of course not the scope of this study. The vital and only point here is how Kant powerfully established the supposition that there is an organizing mental structure before we even begin to think, and how his argument critically shifted philosophical attention from a static and flat world of the so-called real to the dynamic 'heliocentric' role of the human self or subject.

The placing of time within the human self is perhaps the most momentous part of this change. The naïve view of time as a kind of a cosmic clock wound up somewhere in the past and which we check with various external observations was countered by Kant's arguments that appearances of time and succession would be impossible unless the form or shape of time was already in us. And even apart from appearances time is central to our human experience, for we can remove all objects in time from our minds and yet time would still experientially be there. It is therefore, in Kant's words, an *a priori*. What this might mean is extraordinary. Augustine, as we have seen, discussed this, but Kant made it thematic. Time becomes with Kant something that human beings produce: it is a matter of a radical human orientation. It would not be too hard then to conclude that time could also be a matter of re-orientation.

The philosopher fully to realize this further possibility was Martin Heidegger. His thought powerfully developed the theme of time, and enormous credit is due to him for some of the most seminal thinking of the 20th century. And this despite the fact that he was a member of the Nazi party and, for a time, a fervent supporter of Hitler and his policies! There is a story attached to Heidegger's philosophy and it is more than his political pathway and responsibility within the horrors of German national socialism in the thirties and forties of the last century. His masterpiece, *Being and Time* (German *Sein und Zeit*), was published in 1927, and along with a series of philosophical influences the New Testament must be counted its core inspiration. Let me give a brief outline in order to make sense of this startling claim.

In *Being and Time* the human self (re-named *Dasein*, 'being-there' or existence) becomes the site of a continual revelation or disclosure of Being. Heidegger analyses the different moods or conditions of human existence, above all 'care', as ways in which Being is disclosed. He then reiterates the analysis under the heading of time or temporality, showing time or temporality as the basic condition of all disclosure and the basic structure of the human self or Dasein. The human self experiences the 'ek-stases' (standing-out) of time, past, present and future, but it is crucially the future which mobilizes all three, and specifically the future of Dasein's forthcoming death. Because human being knows itself as mortal and always at-the-point-of-death it experiences its existence as futural. Provoked by the inexorable future the present is a mode of Dasein's always anticipated absence (it is always slipping away), and the past is the consequence of its always knowing itself as having-been (because of the pull toward the future). Another simpler way of stating this perhaps is that because human being is a forward movement the actual present and past are opened up. Human existence is something like diving through water: the forward momentum creates the intense rushing of water which is the present (always just going by), and also the accompanying sense of having always irreversibly dived.

This extraordinary picture captivated at least two intellectual generations of the 20th century, first through existentialism, and then through deconstruction (the program of breaking through accumulated layers of philosophical misreadings). It also spread its effect into the fields of psychology, hermeneutics, literary theory, scripture and theology. Now a deeply intriguing feature of *Being and Time* is that it is intended as a philosophy of Being (ontology) but its actual pathway is a vivid portrayal of human existence. This led to the quite natural misunderstanding on the part of some—against which Heidegger forcefully protested—that existentialism was a 'humanism'. Heidegger did not live to see the triumph of the other major offshoot of his thought—deconstruction, but the same 'mistake' seems to have happened there too. The thought of its standard-bearer, Jacques Derrida, emerges little by little as a radical affirmation of 'the other' and specifically the possibility of forgiveness. Why did this humanist, and indeed Christian, twist on his best thoughts seem to keep happening?

Derrida himself remarked that 'Heideggerian thought was not simply a constant attempt to separate itself from Christianity (a gesture that always needs to be related . . . to the incredible unleashing of anti-Christian violence represented by Nazism's most official and explicit ideology, something that one tends to forget these days). The same Heideggerian thinking often consists, notably in *Sein und Zeit*, in repeating on an ontological level Christian themes and texts that have been 'de-Christianized.'[7] Derrida was Jewish so it was no small thing for him to recognize the intense anti-Christian violence of Nazism. Alongside this testimony, and having something of the same value, he is stating that Heidegger's thought both held an aversion to Christianity and—especially in *Being and Time*—a constant dependence on it. The list of borrowed Christian themes and texts is lengthy but the most striking is the sense of time.

Heidegger taught Christian temporality during his early Freiberg professorship (1915-1923), specifically a commentary on Thessalonians. John D. Caputo says that this New Testament sense of time—i.e. living into the future of Christ—was then 'recast in terms of a relationship to one's own death, and this analysis became a centerpiece of *Being & Time*.'[8] He also says: *Being and Time* amounted to the 'Hellenizing and secularizing [of] a fundamentally biblical conception of the history of salvation— a ruse both compounded and betrayed by the radicality with which he tries to exclude the biblical provenance of these operations.'[9] In more explicit terms what Heidegger took from the New Testament was the way the figure of Christ bent time—past, present, future—round to itself because it introduced an entirely new possibility to human experience.

Heidegger transferred this futural sense to the fact of death, but in my view Heidegger's fact of death is already a Christianized phenomenon. Pre-Christian death in the Mediterranean cultures seems at best to have been a passing across to a timeless version of this present world. But something without time cannot provide a future, only an endless past, i.e. an eternity. Christian faith in contrast impressed a forward-directed sense on death—death was always moving toward universal resurrection. It was this dynamic phenomenology of death that Heidegger incorporated into his thought, borrowing the tailwind of the meaning of death instilled by Christianity but isolating it to death alone. Accordingly in *Being and Time* there is a powerful undertow of Christian time and its meaning. Again Derrida points this out when he imagines a conversation of Christian theologians with Heidegger saying, '...we who would like to be authentic Christians think that you are going to the essence of what we want to think, revive, restore, in our faith...'[10]

Caputo and Derrida are not the only philosophers with this kind of comment, to say nothing of actual theologians directly indebted to Heidegger (Rudolf Bultmann, Karl Rahner, Hans Urs von Balthassar, to mention a few). So where does it leave us? What in fact can or should be thought, revived, restored to Christianity out of Heidegger? It seems to me that what Heidegger grasped and then secularized was something that standard Christianity had very largely lost, promulgating instead quite a pre-Christian version of death and the afterlife. Early Christianity lived in a concrete expectation of the in-breaking of a radically different human order. This changed their sense of time and everything in time. Paul expressed the changed sense in the words: 'The present form of this world is passing away' (1 Cor. 7:31b). Over the years the New Testament's shattered fabric of time was repaired and sown up by official Christianity, and instead Christians got used to displacing the radical change to a second world hereafter, not a transformed world here. The 'change' was thereby largely restored to the timeless, within an eternal heaven and eternal hell. In contrast Heidegger's grasp of time is intensely dynamic, rooted in the here and now and controlling the thought of Being itself. Time or temporality becomes the final horizon of interpretation and understanding. The very last two sentences of the *Being and Time* are: 'Is there a way leading from primordial *time* to the meaning of *being*? Does *time* itself reveal itself as the horizon of *being*?'[11]

With these two sentences Heidegger signaled his desire to continue the project in an investigation of Being itself under the rubric of time. He did not do so as planned with a 'second part' of the actual work of *Being and Time* but he did continue to inves-tigate the meaning of Being through an almost mystical theme of 'event' or happening. At this point (basically from the 1930's onwards) his thought becomes more complex, the meaning of 'event' doubling as 'appropriation' through a reading of the German word *Ereignis*. Essentially what is happening is that the figure of Being itself takes over from the human phenomenon as the focus of thought, closing the circle, or 'appropriating' the world of meaning into itself. It is not necessary that we pursue him down this road. Suffice to see that prior to this turn the dynamic of his thought was formidably Christian.

In summary of all this we might say that where Kant had brought time *into* the subject, Heidegger, at least initially, made the experience of time the leading quality *of* the human subject, producing the deepest sensations of existence. What this means ultimately is that forward movement becomes the determining quality of truth, rather than fixed entities mediated by concepts. Heidegger's later thinking after *Being and Time*, meant, I think, the abandonment of the human analytic characteristic of his great work and a shift to a more mythic sense of 'Being itself' or 'the mystery of Being'. It included a marked tone, even a celebration, of violence, and it is this later work which definitively shows Heidegger's intellectual separation from Christianity. But here is the point: if Heidegger had not first stolen the Christian DNA and then disfigured it he would feel no need continually to establish his distance, and it is essential that Christian theology understand the deviated but genuine debt he owes. As perhaps the greatest philosopher of the 20th century he recognized that Christian truth was time and movement, time as human movement, movement as human time. He saw deeper than the formalist and objectifying theology that has dominated Christian thought, but he did not pause to think this thought theologically; rather he quickly appropriated it for a neo-pagan project of an indifferent 'Being' which gives with one hand while taking with the other. This should in no way deflect us from his fundamental insight, one of enormous consequence for theology.

Alpha and Omega

What then does movement mean for Christian theology? Once again it means the intervention of the Christ drawing all history to himself. Rather than death or the faceless 'event' it is Christ who has set the world in motion — toward himself. The prevailing cultural motion before Christ was cyclical because it resolutely covered up the victim, continuing the eternal ritual of being, of the way *it is*. The city of Rome is the paradigm of ancient Western civilization and it pointedly saw itself as 'eternal Rome', the same thing again and again, the past for ever repeating itself in the present. Into this 'eternity' the Christian message leaped with an historical radicalism that earned itself a default state of persecution by Rome over the space of two hundred and fifty years. Ultimately Rome in the person of Constantine I understood that Christianity's historical sense could be harnessed to the needs of empire by subtly suggesting Christianity's future goal would, at least partly, be realized by the power of Rome. Soon after this toxic relationship was conceived the church learned to dissociate itself again from an integral connection with the state but in a different manner. Notably in Augustine's *City of God* it conceived instead its own independent existence in time, while emphasizing an other-worldly destiny. The result was a strange layering of eternal heavenly categories on the one hand with a continuing sense of forward movement through time on the other. It is probable the relationship then had a reciprocal effect on the state, provoking a secular parallel to the church's goal of ultimate perfection, and producing at length the peculiar restless imperialism of the West. The list of tragedy that resulted from this unhealthy imitation is long, but it does not undo the fact that the forward-directedness of the Christian gospel has at root shaped our culture. What is essential now for Christians is to understand and appropriate the generative depth in this shaping, in order perhaps to reverse and redeem the destructive results it has produced, or, positively speaking, to fulfill its purpose.

To be a Christian is to let yourself be pulled by Christ into a completely different quality of time and space, one produced by his infinitely loving death and its raising up by God to and as life. For a Christian time is relationship with Christ, because of Christ. It is never simply chronology, nor is it the alienating stretching out to an always receding horizon that characterizes Western culture. It is our deepest selves pulled along day by day, into the new creation that dwells in the midst of the world because of Jesus. To enter into this time *is* the new creation. It is a movement of the self to the absolutely new, perhaps almost imperceptible at first but gathering strength the more we let go of the displacement and anxiety of clock time. We might confirm this insight by reflecting that the foundational victim 'at the dawn of time' organized the sensations of the anthropoid into before / after, and progressively then the concepts of day and night, summer and winter, etc. In other words it was this core relationship in time that lay at the heart of what came to be called time. But time here was swallowed up in death, in the past, in eternity. It was an immemorial relationship, 'the past itself'—that which always has been and always already was.

The bursting of Christ onto the world scene revolutionized this sense of time. It set the world spinning in another plane, liberating time from the fixity of death and into a future of endless giving. However, because this change is cultural and semiotic it is possible that it co-exist with the old sense of time, and so various apparent hybrids have been developed. The Christian sense of 'eternity' is, I think, little different from the inherited pagan one: in other words the Christ-generated future has been grafted into schemes of timeless eternity. However, what is essential to stress is that, despite the grafting and the hybrids, the original interruption of the cross and resurrection continues to upend time and reverse the world's direction of spinning. The example of *Being and Time* is a compelling demonstration of this. But, again, the revolution I am arguing goes deeper than simply pointing us toward the future, something which can quickly dissolve into another version of clock time. The interruption of the cross is at the level of a foundational relationship which constitutes meaning. Therefore every time I relate to the new meaning brought by Christ I bring the future into the now, and every time the world is pulled toward the future of Christ the meaning of the world changes a little. Thus the gospel will continue to change time against its ancient self, even as that age-old meaning seeks to maintain its effect with all sorts of ruses. Christ brings a relationship of restless love into the world, something which, rather than abandon the victim in the past, institutes a willingness to give one's own life so that the victim might live. This willingness of itself opens time into its future, i.e. to resurrection, a life that can never die again. Thus absolute giving becomes an absolute way of 'being' at the heart of time. Better to say in fact it becomes a creation whose meaning is love. As it offers to change everything, it is necessarily the future in an ordinary sense, but as absolute giving it always provides life for the other (fore-giving) and so is the future here and now in a relational sense. My forgiveness is your future, just as my future is your forgiveness. The killing of the foundational victim always claims to be an absolute past—to found the world for ever—but it is now challenged by a future which can never die and must continue to change the world out of recognition.

What I have been describing in this chapter is a set of intellectual frames—essentially evolutionary theory and philosophy—which in their own ways have shown the profound impact of Christ on their respective worldviews. They have illustrated how the dynamic of movement is already a core element of Christian faith and one which may make the best claim to have provoked these cultural-intellectual frames in the first place. Christ is a transformative relationship of and to the future and because of this movement has become endemic to Western culture. In short movement is the gathering vector of the relationship he creates. Because he pours himself endlessly in the world as the absolute future, little by little he unlocks the icecap of human time, setting it underway in the same direction as himself. Intellectual forms, like evolution or philosophy, may not recognize the critical role of Christ in unleashing movement as an intellectual possibility but they are nevertheless formidably indebted to him. Here also is the meaning behind what we have already interpreted of the story of the Middle Ages and of the contemporary phenomenon of the virtual. The presence of Christ in the sign world of saints, poets and artists around the eleventh and twelfth centuries (and indeed onwards into the Renaissance) allowed the emergence of a positive desiring relationship to the object and so helped precipitate both romanticism and Western capitalism. It produced its own sign system of positive desire. More recently the system of signs has become frenetic within the overall dynamic of movement, but Christ is at its heart, the hidden turning point of compassion. All contemporary human movement derives from and presses toward the Christ, the Alpha and the Omega, as the seer of Revelation said.

Chapter Five

God Save Me from God!

Do we trust it when someone invokes the name of God? More and more we don't. We probably have to be in a specialized environment like a church or prayer meeting to relax our guard. And for a number of people even that doesn't work. Why is this? What has happened to the name of God? A rash of recent books in the English-speaking world makes a vigorous case for atheism. The heart of the argument is always the rolling violence to be found both in the scriptures and practice of religion, past and present.

Christopher Hitchens begins his assault on theism in *God Is Not Great: How Religion Poisons Everything* with a summary of 'the religiously inspired violence' he personally witnessed in six flash points of the world. Coincidentally they all begin with the letter B: Belfast, Beirut, Bombay, Belgrade, Bethlehem, Baghdad. For the seasoned journalist that he is these names form a banner headline for the unstaunched spilling of blood he believes intrinsic to religion. Richard Dawkins is not long into his book, *The God Delusion*, before he lets loose the following description of the God of the Old Testament. 'Arguably the most unpleasant character in all fiction: jealous and proud of it; a petty, unjust, unforgiving control-freak; a vindictive, blood-thirsty ethnic cleanser; a misogynistic, homophobic, racist, infanticidal, genocidal, filicidal, pestilential, megalomaniacal, sadomasochistic, capriciously malevolent bully.'[1] While having some comparatively nice things to say about Jesus he believes that this is because Jesus was not content to derive his ethics from the scriptures of his upbringing. What is good about Jesus' teaching does not come from religion. He then goes on to say that the doctrine of atonement for original sin (presumably he means what emerged much later in Christian history as a theory of penal substitution) 'lies at the heart of New Testament theology' and adds 'a new sadomasochism whose viciousness even the Old Testament barely exceeds.'[2]

I confess a lot of respect for people like Hitchens and Dawkins. Anyone who takes the argument to human and divine cruelty is on the right track. But the rub is there, in the order of the words: first human and then divine. Aside from a very two-dimensional reading of biblical scripture and tradition—ignoring the rich layers of historical development and tensions within and between them —these authors see the issue of actual humanity simply in moral and never in structural terms. In other words they do not consider the possibility that religion in fact derives from the deep structure of the human and that their protest against its violence is part of an astonishing sea change in that very structure. So we might say they are right about 'God' because they are part of the change in being human, and that change, as argued in this book, is itself a product of the gospel of Jesus.

But, still, as a matter of fact, that leaves us with a problem of speaking about God in general and the Christian God in particular. I already declared this problem in the first chapter with the thought experiment of 'No-Name.' We are now, however, in the full frame of Christian thought and we must address the question of the Christian God head on. That is, we must deal with it theologically.

How then do we begin to talk about the God of Jesus Christ in these circumstances? How do we speak about God when God is in crisis? It seems we must do so only by first talking about Jesus, and doing so with full recognition of the anthropo-theological revolution he brought about. If Jesus is responsible for a deep change in human culture then certainly we should pay close attention to him in talking about God. In the past we have worked very much in the opposite direction. We assumed we knew what God means and then proceeded to fit Jesus into that meaning. This is very much the order in which the Christian creed is written. But Jesus, in one of his most astonishing sayings in the synoptic gospels, said that no one knew the Father except him and those to whom he makes him known (Matt. 11: 27). A more outlandish idea, in the context of a people who had spent a thousand years plus getting to know their God, could hardly be imagined. But if Jesus has intervened in the profound structure of human meaning, if he has fundamentally shifted the human earth out of its plane of orbit, then of course all perspectives on everything— and especially the gravitational point of human existence called 'God'—will be altered. This is the reason why we pursue this topic in terms of signs rather than things. Signs are not a static system, but can shift and change their value. The system of signs in which we live is itself in flight, moving before us like the fleeing galaxies of space.

In this light we can say that we're at ground zero in the argument. In the last chapter I showed the way that movement as the governing theme of contemporary existence has been provoked by Christ. It is Christ who has unhooked the world from its moorings. He is a transformative relationship of and to the future, and because of this the theme of movement has become endemic to Western culture. Consequently our world of signs, mediating our relationships, is under the pressure of a forward vector, toward an absolute future of love. Conversely you could say our future is opened within our world of signs as it revolves and resolves, revealing the light source of compassion. Christians are those who live consciously within the shifting human cosmos and seek to conform to its deepest meaning. They are thus 'virtually Christian'. They do not listen to the drumbeat of inherited metaphysical Christianity as a definition of what it means to be 'Christian', but seek to follow the structural transformation that is underway, the biblical pathway of changing human signs and meaning. We shall arrive in the following chapter to this concrete meaning of Christianity in terms of 'church', but first we must think some more about what this means for theology. We cannot simply drop traditional Christian metaphysics. They are so deeply embedded they are intellectually identified with Christianity. And when they are grounded in the radical experience generated by the gospel we can see, in the framework of absolute thinking, a legitimate reason for their existence. But to talk meaningfully today about the question of God we must reverse the direction of thought and understand the metaphysics by placing them within the transforming universe of signs produced by Jesus. I shall approach the question in three stages, examining first the sign of Christ, then the sign of the human, and finally the sign of God.

The Sign of Christ

Jesus called sinners and the simple into direct relationship with him and doing so brought them forgiveness and love. His concrete connection with these people became a sign associated with him, known as 'open table fellowship'. This is one of the best established conclusions of contemporary New Testament scholarship, something we confidently associate with the historical Jesus. It had life and death consequences for him. It offended people who believed in the semiotics of purity boundaries and it was his calculated rebellion against the anthropological construct of clean / unclean, in / out, Sabbath / non-Sabbath, which probably first triggered the conviction that he had to die.[3] When he drove his rebellion to the heart of the purity system, to the temple, this conviction matured to a decision and he brought the sacred order crashing down on him (again a nexus of events strongly credited by historians). The temple was the gigawatt engine of purification, producing continuous atonement for ritual faults and guilt, and a daily solar flare of holiness through the offering of the holocaust. It is evident from the whole narrative of the gospel that Jesus did not simply act to 'cleanse' the temple. This is a language not in the text and still conceptually in thrall to the power of ritual sacrifice. Instead Jesus brought the business of the temple to a crashing halt, abolishing the institution for an hour or so of consciousness-forming symbolism. Some of the gospel story of Jesus will be taken up at the end of the book and there we will see how this action would be in continuity with the radicalism of his whole life and practice. For the moment, however, we are focusing on the general question of God. We must, therefore, set against this astonishingly powerful anthropological sign the doctrinal sign which has completely outranked it in importance. We have to look at and examine the sign that has come to dominate our understanding of Jesus, that of the eternally begotten Son of God.

Chalcedon

The strict doctrine of Jesus' divinity was evolved over the first centuries of the Church, reaching its conceptual peak in the Council of Chalcedon (451 CE). The definition given by that ecclesial body is an odyssey of nuances, like a tightrope walker adjusting his balance pole at every step as he makes a crossing of the Grand Canyon. On one side the precipice opens as the denial of the full humanity of Jesus. The tradition had already established that Jesus is of one substance (the very same thing) as God (Nicaea, 325 CE), but what use is that if that makes him essentially different from us, i.e. a divine being? He is estranged from our experience and cannot really communicate with us humans or give us anything of himself. But then, once you insist on the full humanity of Jesus, alongside his divinity, the other side of the chasm opens. Staring up at the tightrope walker is an extrinsic side-by-side association of divine and human, a kind of amalgam or sticky-tape bonding of the latter to the former, so again it can be said that God did not really enter and change human reality.

You might wonder at what looks like a very large hubris in the Christian tradition that it feels entitled—against such logical difficulties—to maintain the simultaneous full divinity and full humanity of this individual. There are plenty of stories, from just about every cultural tradition on earth, of gods appearing as humans, walking around and doing things among humans. But that was the way of it: they simply appeared as humans, in some evanescent fake flesh. They weren't really human. So why insist, against all odds, that Jesus was both *really* God and *really* human?

To move toward an answer I must first give the Chalcedon definition in full, not because we need to study every phrase, but to show where it ends up and how in some strange semi-verbal way it manages to get the tightrope walker clear across the canyon. After insisting on the full divinity and full humanity of Jesus it says the two 'natures' come together in a point of unity which it calls 'person and subsistence'. Everything hinges on these two words, which are intended to point to the crucial element: you could say it's the balancing weight of the pole itself. What do they mean? As a unifying category they cannot signify a simple 'something', for surely the whole area of definable *things* is taken care of by 'substance', the substance of God and the substance of humanity? And, necessarily, if we were dealing with a thing then God as God would already possess it first. Following from this Jesus would then have to have had his own separate human version, for if he had this 'thing' only from God he would not truly be like us. But if, in order to resolve this, you double up with a second, human example or version of the thing, you have lost the point and principle of unity! No, we have to be talking about something which is at once as authentically and integrally human as it is divine, and essentially outside the realm of 'things'. 'Person' or 'subsistence' is therefore a new concept, a shimmer in the field of reality, a phenomenon today we would characterize with the much more fuzzy-edged but very potent name of 'relationship'. Here then is the formula.

> Therefore, following the holy fathers, we all with one accord teach men to acknowledge one and the same Son, our Lord Jesus Christ, at once complete in Godhead and complete in manhood, truly God and truly man, consisting also of a reasonable soul and body; of one substance with the Father as regards his Godhead, and at the same time of one substance with us as regards his manhood; like us in all respects, apart from sin; as regards his Godhead, begotten of the Father before the ages, but yet as regards his manhood begotten, for us men and for our salvation, of Mary the Virgin, the God-bearer; one and the same Christ, Son, Lord, Only-begotten, recognized in two natures, without confusion, without change, without division, without separation, the distinction of natures being in no way annulled by the union, but rather the characteristics of each nature being preserved and coming together to form one person and subsistence [hupōstasis], not as parted or separated into two persons, but one and the same Son and Only-begotten God the Word, Lord Jesus Christ; even as the prophets from earliest times spoke of him, and our Lord Jesus Christ himself taught us, and the creed of the fathers has handed down to us.[4]

What is a person but a relationship...with other persons? The definition does not say this but simply asserts this other category in the text. It does so by the doubled expression—person and subsistence. The two words back each other up like two playing cards back to back—indicating the tenuous character of the new idea. In the eastern Mediterranean theologians had got used to calling the persons of the Trinity 'subsistences' (hupostasis in Greek), meaning something like *independent existences*. They did not readily use the word 'person' because it actually meant the face, the look or outward appearance, sometimes even 'mask', and so could hardly be applied to an eternal reality. However, when you're now talking about the concrete Jesus the word becomes more plausible—every human has a face! Furthermore, for the Latins in the west 'persona' had the same range of meaning but it had also taken on a legal significance, as 'a legal identity or individual'. So for Latin theology it was possible to apply the term to Jesus, the Son of God, with much more weight and confidence. Thus with all these influences coming together and using these two words for the divine / human identity of Jesus there was born the modern category of person, something other than a nature or thing but of truly infinite worth. It is this category, in all its glorious imprecision, that finally holds the definition of Chalcedon together. But the question at once arises, did the members of the Council just dream this up as a bit of desperate intellectual wizardry, or were there deep factors already in play that led them down that road? Answering this question allows us to rejoin the Jesus of open table fellowship. Here is an anthropological source of the Chalcedonian doctrine, rather than assuming it arrives ready-made out of a heaven of Greek essences!

Wisdom Jesus

The Jesus of the gospels has a relationship of profound intimacy and trust with the Father. I mentioned above the astounding claim by Jesus that 'No one knows the Father except the Son and anyone to whom the Son chooses to reveal him.' I advanced it as a critical principle of looking only to Jesus for the meaning of God, but it does not come simply as a principle for reflection. It acts as a working historical explanation for so much of the language and practice of Jesus that we read in the gospels. The statement appears in a collection of sayings in Matthew which belong to the category of Wisdom thought about Jesus. This is sometimes called Wisdom Christology and generally considered early, i.e. emerging in the first decades of the Christian movement. The new Testament scholar Ben Witheringon III believes it goes back to Jesus himself—that in some way he understood himself in the persona of Old Testament Wisdom.[5]

This to me seems highly plausible. We read in Proverbs that Wisdom invited all the simple and uneducated to a meal that she had prepared (9:1-6). Wisdom was also present at the beginning of creation, the delight of God and delighting in the human race (8:30b-31). In the deutero-canonical book known as Sirach we hear her inviting people to 'Come to me' (Sirach 24:19, 51:23) and the text invites these people to put their neck 'under her yoke' (51:26). The address to God as Father is typical only of Wisdom literature (Sirach 23:1 & 4, Wisdom 2:16, 14:3). In this connection we know that in moments of personal prayer Jesus cries out in his native Aramaic 'Abba!' (sounding so much like Papa!) and the immediacy and spontaneity of this prayer embedded itself so deeply in the primitive Jesus movement that its Aramaic form became common coin in Greek-speaking Christianity (Mark 14:36, Romans 8:15, Galatians 4:6). When his disciples asked him to teach them to pray in a way that was special to him he taught them of course in the same vein, 'Our Father.' When he was advocating the impossible love of enemies he backed it up simply but conclusively, by his vision of the non-violence of the Father. 'For he [the Father] makes his sun rise on the evil and on the good, and sends rain on the righteous and the unrighteous' (Matt. 5:45). In terms of general practice, the astonishing sign-making of eating with sinners and the subversion of the temple sacrifice necessarily depends on the appropriation of a serene and privileged relationship with God. What Old Testament frame of reference then has both the language and the supreme confidence of relationship that can make sense of this intimacy between Jesus and the Father?

At all events the authors of Chalcedon and the theologians before them had the four gospel record of continual vibrant relationship between Jesus and his Father. If we say, 'Of course he has this relationship, he was the eternal Son of God', then we a-historically ignore the order of discovery, the experience of the centuries before Chalcedon, especially the first. More feasibly we could agree that to one degree or another the gospel picture is an ideal one. There is certainly a progression in the gospels' account of the relationship (from Mark, through Matthew to John) but then nothing of Jesus' story in the New Testament makes sense—neither in terms of the key examples I have given nor the rule-breaching impact his movement so quickly deployed—unless there is an historical bedrock of exceptionality in Jesus' relationship with his God. Should we not, therefore, turn Chalcedon on its head and say that it's because of this real and remembered relationship in time that theology little by little had the confidence more or less to invent the category of eternal persons in relationship? Thus the actual historical relationship precedes the speculative one; the point of reference, chronologically and ontologically, is not some intellectual metaphysics of divine being but the living tradition of Jesus' relationship with the Father.

But can we say more? Apart from a personal claim on Jesus' part—which after all anyone could make—what was the lived tenor of the relationship that might warrant it? It's when we go deeper than the merely historical account and think anthropologically that everything falls into place in an astonishingly coherent way. In sum, if we remove the glassy forms of eternal ideas from our minds we are able to see the specific relational quality in Jesus able to warrant the doctrinal evolution. We are able to understand the root conditions of possibility in the person of Jesus which can make sense of the subsequent doctrine.

There was no shadow or hint of violence in Jesus' relationship with the Father. To say this seems obvious as to be trite and yet, very quickly, it can be claimed as false doctrinally, and it is this mind-bending contradiction in the Christian tradition that shows how pivotal the statement is. In terms of Jesus' own witness the evidence is all in favor of it. There was never any mention of God's wrath in Jesus' preaching. The examples I have repeatedly given, and others congruent with them, demand an immediate personal sense of God's non-retributive loving character: eating and drinking with sinners, personally forgiving sinners, actively healing on the Sabbath, and above all his action in the temple. Blocking the sacrificial traffic in the temple was to disable the archaic engine of violent holiness, known to all ancient society and in the case of second-temple Judaism one that concentrated in itself a thousand years of history. To do this could only be the action of a madman or, alternatively, someone of absolute religious integrity. The subsequent decision of the authorities that he had to be killed requires the latter—they could not dismiss him as a madman. And the fact that there was zero hint of following up his action with any kind of armed rebellion means that the religious integrity of Jesus was holistic and integrally nonviolent.

But what then of the doctrinal tradition that Jesus death was, in the final frame, a satisfaction for an outraged deity, a personal undergoing by Jesus of the wrath of God? Here is the point where all the nonviolence of Jesus gets transformed at a stroke into a fearful violence. The Father, rather than forgiving enemies, becomes a monster who demands the last drop of blood—and Jesus of course colludes with this grim demand, for it is his blood. It's hardly necessary to deal with this scenario here as it is so evidently a product of Christendom. Its massive mechanical form first emerged in the Middle Ages, displacing the previous plural and fluid metaphors and semi-mythical thinking about the meaning of Jesus' death. What is important, however, is precisely its cultural power, to have emerged in the tradition in the first place and then to have achieved default status, what Dawkins calls its 'ubiquitous familiarity'.[6] The 'familiar' doctrinal status of satisfaction or substitution doctrine demonstrates the generative force of violence in producing our thinking, against the evident teaching, practice and persona of Jesus. But then, conversely, we get a sense of the remarkable power of the latter slowly to hold this up to question, producing a sign system that begins to dissolve the archaic power of violence and tease us forward into something wonderfully new.

'Ah,' I hear the faithful believer exclaim, 'You cannot get away with it that easily. You have skipped over the event of the cross and the alienation of Jesus from the Father during that terrible experience, so that it must be said at that point he endured the wrath of God.'

The Cup

I am glad of the reminder! It would of course be impossible to leave out from an account of Jesus' nonviolent relationship with God a reckoning on the final climactic event of his life, one of unrestrained brutal violence. In the garden of Gethsemane Jesus says that what is facing him is the will of the Father and in doing so he uses the image of the cup. 'Abba, Father, for you all things are possible; remove this cup from me; yet, not what I want, but what you want' (Mark 14:36). The image of the cup has a history in the Old Testament: it starts as human violence—the way one nation will make another drink the cup of their wrath; then quickly it is administered by God, through other historical agents of violence, against the original perpetrators (Habakkuk 2:15-17). In Jeremiah it is seen as issuing directly from the hand of the Lord against the nations, but also including Judah (25:15-29). Finally the experience of the exile is interpreted retrospectively as the personal experience of God's wrath now finally come to an end in the circumstances of return (51:21-22). Undoubtedly this is a primitive form of justice in light of the ruthless violence of the nations. It is a cyclical violence under the rule of God—equalizing out the doing and the suffering of violence. But then when it falls on Judah the sense of a rupture in relationship makes it become doubly painful and threatening as a personal response by

God, 'God's wrath.' But Jesus never uses the expression of the cup with the descriptive genitive 'of wrath', let alone the subjective genitive 'of God'. He uses the term with symbolic economy, suggesting the original metaphor, the systemic sense of the cup. It is the phenomenon itself as it is passed around that he is talking about, the endless recycling of violence itself.

The will of the Father in this case could be exactly as Jesus understood the Father: one who wished to bring an end to violence in the world, to retribution and vengeance against the enemy. The way to do this was for Jesus to drink to its dregs the system of violence itself, precisely the endless passing on of the cup. It was before the desire on the part of his Father, that he should do *this*—drink up the totality of human violence, that Jesus' spirit quailed. It quailed in fact before us, before the endless history of our violent anthropology (as indeed any human would). The attribution of this desire to the Father would then be consistent for Jesus—the sense on Jesus' part that the Father willed a definitive and absolute nonviolence and it was Jesus' vocation to enact that. The fact that he never said this but used the phenomenon-metaphor, the cup, to signify it, is under-lined by a parallel remark in John. There Jesus uses the metaphor of the cup in direct relation to human violence and in terms of answering nonviolence. When Peter cuts off the ear of the high priest's servant Jesus says, 'Put your sword back into its sheath. Am I not to drink the cup that the Father has given me?' (John 18:11).

But still doesn't that seem an instrumental act on God's part, an act of willed violence against another, no matter its transcendent purpose? To look at it this way is again to exceed Jesus' consciousness and see the Father in a metaphysical mode, a deity we can envisage and capture intellectually as one willing this instrumental pathway. What we are given access to in these quotations is not the abstract instrumental will of God but rather the deep existential relationship of Jesus with his Father that formed his sense of mission. Beyond the quality of that relationship we cannot, and may not go. The question brings us to the threshold of the next sections, the sign of God and the sign of the human. In these sections we will look deeper into what's at stake here, but before we move to these areas, we need to bring to a focal point what all the foregoing means for the sign of Christ.

My Lord and My God

The New Testament itself went a good way down the road to naming Jesus as God. John's gospel ends with the classic confession of Thomas 'my lord and my god!' But what we can conclude from the above is that this was based in the direct experience of relationship that Jesus generated. As Raymond Brown says in his magisterial commentary on the gospel of John, it was a liturgical expression, something wrung from the heart in prayer, rather than a metaphysical declaration.[7] Calling Jesus 'god' is not then to be seen from a dogmatic perspective, but rather as a response to the character of his consciousness and person, and above all at a point—after the cross and the resurrection—when its revolutionary impact had become fully apparent and affirmed. Translated anthropologically this was the total absence of violence in Jesus' relationship either with God or his persecutors, and this absence then came to include the absence of the final violence of death itself. The Risen One becomes a pellucid window of a completely different, fore-giving mode of relating to everything, including the meaning of God in the earth.

The transformative anthropology of Jesus underpins then the meaning of Chalcedon, of the crucial concept of person and subsistence at the heart of the statement. Long before the intricate doctrine of two natures and one hypostasis was formulated there was the human relationship of Jesus with the Father and his disciples. The quality of this relationship prompted the movement toward naming him as God, because of the aston-ishing impact it had on the relationships of those around him. Here was a sign—really a complex of signs, from open table fellowship to resurrection from the dead—which changed absolutely everything in how people felt about themselves, others and what they called God. Put another way, Jesus' rebellion against the semiotics of exclusion brought his own life to the point of maximum exclusion; but his trusting refusal to collude with this final exclusion—either in despair or anger—was itself raised to deathless life and so became an infinite resource of inclusion for the world. It was in effect an explosion of love and forgiveness, the original *good news*. Then, in the aftermath of this explosion, there is progressively no other adequate linguistic response than 'my lord and my god'. Why? Because the explosion has become an irreducible source of an entirely new sense of God. The rest is metaphysical gymnastics—perhaps inevitable, but gymnastics just the same. Before Chalcedon, therefore, there is the seamless human harmony of Jesus and the new realization of God whom he called 'Father'.

The consequences are profound. The metaphysical priority of a God-to-whom-a-man-is-attached is inverted, offering instead a human-relationship-reconstituting-the-meaning-of-God. It means that the person and subsistence of the Son of God is understood exclusively from the history and anthropology of Jesus. There is no 'prior' philosophical knowledge of divinity to which we then somehow graft his humanity. Instead there is the intrinsic quality of a relationship, one characterized by infinite nonviolence. The doctrine of the two wills of Christ which evolved subsequent to Chalcedon—again intended to preserve the full divinity and full humanity of Jesus—does not override the common person or hypostasis but in fact makes it more prominent. Here is the crucial truth of a relationship of infinite nonviolence experienced and responded to by Jesus' human will. And it is the selfsame identical relationship experienced and responded to by the 'eternal Word', but this Word cannot be known via some eternal intellectual truth. Rather it is apprehensible immediately and only in the historical Jesus, the *person* of Jesus. To further understand this—really a kind of 'mystery' that can only be appreciated by a mystagogical path of understanding—we will come back to it again in the sections below. At the moment what is vital is to grasp the immense human import of this relationship. It has of course always been there in the story of Christianity, but it has been masked beneath both the 'two nature' essentialist thinking of Chalcedon and the appalling violence of substitutionary atonement. Now finally with the understanding given by transformative biblical anthropology its crucial role can be clearly understood. This relationship of Jesus, this hypostasis, is the most powerful relationship in the world. It is able to change everything, and is in the process of doing so. It arises at the deepest level of the imitative human self, changing the almost-inevitable foundation of human culture in violence to the humanly new creation of self-giving love. It is the single historical power that has mobilized the movement of the world toward its future. Should Christians begin seriously to think this as the meaning of the 'incarnation' what further wonderful acceleration of this movement would it mean? If speculative theology were displaced by this kind of anthropo-theology, if the sign of Christ as human were to fold within itself the sign of Christ as God, would that mean anything less than the descent of the New Jerusalem, the bride of the Lamb?

The Sign of the Human

Once we have seen how a true human being can be given the name of God it seems we should turn directly to how this impacts God's meaning. But we need to keep the rhythm of the beat here. If it's by the historical appearance of a relationship that the meaning of God has been changed, then the more we understand how that relationship has impacted human beings the better ultimate position we will be in to discuss the changed meaning. Moreover, we remember the point at which we came into the discussion: the crisis in the name of God itself, and the basis of this crisis was the human crisis of violence. The name of God, therefore, surely cannot be rediscovered in our time before the human situation begins to understand itself in a new way. And once again—completing a circle of interpretation—it is the figure of Jesus who provides this new way. The very figure who shifts the figure of God is the one who historically entered the depths of human violence in order to transform them.

Christianity has never supposed a simple moral or aesthetic perfectibility of humankind. It has always seen the problem as structural: something basic must alter before things can get better. In the past that has been seen in cruelly legal terms. Humankind stands in enormous deficit vis-à-vis God and Christ provides the payment or dissolution of the penalty. More spiritual aspects of the tradition have also emphasized affective relationship, holiness, transformation, but while these have been of immense value more often than not they have been framed within the philosophy of an other-worldly soul and a doctrine of the intellectually knowable eternal (and residually violent) God. Certainly an apophatic element has always been present on the sidelines, providing a vital corrective. Meister Eckhart famously said 'I pray to God to save me from God,' suggesting that the glib commonplace of 'God' was not only wrong-headed but dangerous. But what was missing from both the legal and spiritual traditions is an anthropology of violence and its transformation in Christ. This approach provides a truly organic understanding. As we shall see shortly, in this understanding Christianity becomes both humanly grounded and mystical!

Those Neurons Again
Our reflections in the last chapter on evolution help us here. We saw how humans and the higher primates are characterized by

the activity of 'mirror neurons'. These neurons have the effect of making someone else's intention an immediate 'personal' experience of my own. 'I *am* the other...I want (exactly) what you want.' As we have also seen this can escalate with unbelievable speed to a deadly conflict, for we both occupy the selfsame 'neural' space of desire. Or should we say the same hypostasis? There are two wills but only one intention, and only one possible outcome, the overwhelming and defeat of one desire by the other. The thought is surprising: that we can consider the intensity of mimetic desire as a form of shared hypostasis. It has crept up on us but it has done so naturally. Contemporary neurology and anthropology more and more show us that we already inhabit all sorts of common space so that it is impossible at certain points to distinguish one relationship to the object from the other. Now if this is the case where the identity of desires is negative and destructive is it not also possible that it have a benign, life-affirming form? Indeed it is.

We are used to it in a number of settings and in its most striking realization it's what we call compassion. Sympathy, empathy, compassion, these affective states have attracted the attention of moral philosophers because of their remarkable evidence of other-centered behavior. Perhaps the most basic form in the animal kingdom is what we call the love of the mother for her cub, her willingness to risk her own life for the sake of her offspring. We might hypothesize this as a mirroring not of intentionality or desire, but of weakness and vulnerability. The mother bear imitates or replicates internally the danger the cub is in or its condition of suffering, and so she does not hesitate to defend it, to stand for it, in its place. From an evolutionary perspective this of course makes a whole lot of sense. The neural mirroring of a threat of danger to the infant will provide the immediate, heedless protection for the next generation on which the survival of the species depends. But once the neural system mirroring weakness is in place it is easily conceivable how it could 'overflow' beyond its intra-specific goals. And so we have the many examples of one species taking the infant of another under its wing (sometimes literally), a duck caring for chicks, or a cat for a puppy, or a dog for a human. And it seems it can happen not just between an adult and an infant: what explanation, for example, can we give of traditional stories of dolphins shepherding shipwrecked men to shore?

It is when it comes to humans of course that fellow-feeling or compassion becomes a locus of meaning in its own right. It can suddenly erupt for any vulnerable member of our species, or the animal kingdom, or indeed anything that has a personal or hypostatic character. Once as a little boy my son burst into tears when he heard news that the Voyager spacecraft, sent on a mission to Mars, had been allowed to drift off into space after its tasks were completed. The hypostasis of my son identified with the hypostasis of the spacecraft! However, at the same time as recognizing the marvelous openness of compassion we also know it is an inconstant, uncertain thing. It's as if it has to appear in the cracks that violent cultural difference allows (i.e. where reasoning that 'those people' are nothing to do with us, or are to blame for their situation etc., does not obtain.) In other words what we might call neural compassion is unstable and occasional, easily reduced to sentimentality or overwhelmed by group hostility. The enormous thing about Jesus is that he took this neural pathway, and in the immense freedom and generosity the biblical journey had prepared for him, he committed himself body and life to it. What sets his action utterly apart is that he carried through compassion not just for the weak and vulnerable, for the excluded, but for the strong and armed, for his enemies. He thus did something that was based in the animal and human, but 'unnaturally' exceeded the animal and human, breaking entirely from the violent limits and constraints imposed either by biology or generative culture. The gospel of Luke gives it formal expression. As he hung on the cross he found a basis for compassion for his enemies: he prayed, 'Father forgive them, they know not what they do' (Luke 23:34). Of course this response fits integrally with the exclusion of any violence in Jesus' relationship with his Father. In his prayer he evacuated the reflux of revenge violence that would automatically be projected on God for this unjust suffering. He thus affirms definitively the nonviolence of God. And in exactly the same measure he drinks the cup, ending the world's relentless decanting of violence into its most enduring reservoir, God. Jesus' compassion, therefore, is a reconstitution of the divine and the human together. He re-invents compassion as infinite modality, making it boundless, without structural limit. And when this example is raised up in the deathlessness of resurrection it is stabilized ontologically, as a final truth of being. It thus becomes an enduring human possibility, able to embed itself in the neural pathways of humans who look to him in faith as a true and living realization of the human. It is something genuinely *super*natural, part of the natural repertoire, rooted in the neural self, but enhanced now to an astonishingly re-creative level.

Resurrection

We stand now at the beginning of the humanly grounded and yet mystical character of Christianity. To make it clearer I need to spend a few moments reflecting on the Resurrection. It is very difficult, if not impossible, to describe the resurrection physically. Paul's account and the gospel accounts are concerned to emphasize continuity in change, change in continuity. The essential thing for the overall New Testament is that Jesus did not rise into a separate and separable realm. Apart from how foreign this was to Jewish thinking this kind of resurrection would have taken the mainspring from the Christian movement. The exponential power of the Christian message in the first century could not possibly have depended on other-world speculation; it had to be immediate and visceral within the human realm. Only within this realm stood the profound sense of the overturning of condemnation and death which was the content of the message. Paul is the great witness: as a zealous Hebrew he would not have been angry about a claim to resurrection into a Platonic heaven or to some version of Mount Olympus. This would have been simply another story of a Greek hero, with no possible impact on the real world of the Messiah that he and so many Jews were awaiting. But the fact that he was so incensed meant he precisely understood the claim about the Risen Crucified. It meant an individual had somehow anticipated the end times: that Jesus had somehow brought the full physical restoration of the world in justice and life in the midst of unredeemed time, and he had done so via the abomination of the cross! Then, of course, something happened to Paul that convinced him this was indeed the case. As a result he became one of the greatest and most urgent exponents of this new meaning of Messiah. What is important for our purposes now is to understand clearly that the Christian message is based on a real experiential change in the human order. The human order remains the human order but it is experienced as changed from within. In this perspective actual human life is literally opened up to a new realization, a new configuration.

We might say, in an adventurous paraphrase of Paul, what was sown neurally conflictive has been raised neurally nonviolent, what was sown neurally deadly has been raised neurally life-giving, what was sown neurally compromised with killing has been raised neurally transformed in creative blessing. Therefore, by contact with the Risen One my own humanity is made nonviolent, life-giving, a creative blessing. The thing to do is to follow Jesus, to know him more clearly, love him more dearly, follow him more nearly. This is itself an alteration of my neural structure in imitation of him. The given world is constituted *ex principio* by conflictive desire and violence and its violent solutions of creating scapegoats and enemies. This given world does not mean a physical territory outside my front door, downtown Manhattan etc., but a complex of inherited and reinforced cultural relationships to which I am assimilated. The fact that I may have been brought up a Christian, or I am a church minster or a member of a religious order, none of this makes a difference. I am constituted by the world the same as anyone else. What makes a difference is my daily personal encounter with this new humanity, the way in which I allow myself to be transformed piece by piece by this style of infinite nonviolence in a living human being.

But I can sense the protest: 'Even though you just said it's impossible to describe the resurrection physically that's just what you've done. In fact you have made it grossly physical and unspiritual.' In answer to the 'unspiritual' I would argue anthropologically that a transformed relationship to human violence is precisely what constitutes the spiritual in the Christian tradition. The roots of violence go so deep that a change at this level forms the primary human experience of rebirth in the Spirit. Correlative to that the encounter with the divine has already been implied in all the foregoing and I will be returning to it directly below. But what of the charge that the description, from the side of Christ, is too physical in process, that it perhaps over-determines the meaning of resurrection with talk of neurology? Does it not give the impression that the Risen Christ acts as a kind of download into my nervous system, a direct transfer of electrical signals?

In answer I would return to the governing theme of 'sign' which has guided our discussion all along the way. I have constantly attempted to show that the human world consists of signs, that we have no world apart from our signs. Furthermore our system of signs, no matter their huge number and complexity, all goes back to the original crisis of desire and its resolution through the victim. The resurrection as I understand it here does not escape the character of sign. It is communicated as sign, along with all the other things that Jesus did. Christ is in the business of reconstituting our symbol system and it is this and only this that can finally act to restructure our responses. Looked at this way a 'download' of the Risen Christ would presumably completely overwhelm my nervous system, and that is why the gospel remains a sign system designed to reconstitute my human world through a mediation which allows for freedom. When I talk of the neural effect of the Risen One it must always be placed in that semiotic context. However, it is also easy to understand how a neural change could take place through a change in our system of signs.

Human Reconstitution

As we have seen before our given-world system of meaning is rooted primordially in the surrogate victim. The immense galaxy of signs I live within trace their singular origin to this point. It is then simply a shifting of one key element in the time-honored discharge of violence upon the victim that brings about the reformulation of meaning and at the same time of neural response. In Christ the victim goes from passivity to the supreme agency of self-giving love. Once this central component of the symbolic world is switched, from murky blameworthiness to open forgiveness, it is inevitable that the very movement of meaning is changed. For this is the point: meaning is movement as I have described—up / down, here / there, for / against—all based in the primary victim. Once this movement is revolutionized in the person of Christ the innermost density of our sign system goes with it, and sensitive contact with the signs of Christ will pull me in the direction of the new meaning. Subtly but inevitably it flows out of and away from violence into the astonishing new pathway of love. In other words, with the semiotic shift of the gospel based in the event of love my neural pathways are thrown into their other core possibility, of compassionate self-and-object-giving, otherwise known as love.

The sign of the Crucified helps reconstitute my neural

geography. Yet, as already suggested, I have to agree to it, to allow that geography to take hold. It is an act of surrender, because there is always a break in the move from generative violence to generative forgiveness. In the first it is death that forms the point of meaning, in the second it is the life and forgiveness of one who was dead and is so no more. The person who is responding to Christ is like an ice skater doing a one-hundred-eighty: it takes momentum but also a deliberate choice to pivot in entirely the opposite direction. The momentum is provided by the sign of the Risen Crucified, but the turn by the skater herself. Then, as she does turn, the more it becomes possible that there come a sudden flooding of the senses under the impression of the transformative sign. It's as if my neural pathways of desire suddenly come to a point of critical restructuring where the old paths collapse and new ones are literally burned into consciousness.

Many Christians can give examples of moments when the risen life of Christ has taken root in their bodies, in their lives. There is John Wesley's 'I felt my heart strangely warmed', and Blaise Pascal's famous *Memorial*. I was recently sent a book written by an Italian friend in which she tells the story of her own lifelong pilgrimage to what she calls 'the Source', the brimming sense of God in the world, wherever it may be found. As the story unfolds she speaks of the influence of her mother who was Jewish and converted to Christianity. Similar to Pascal, her mother's account of the dramatic change in her life was found after her death, hidden away in a drawer. It describes how she lived opposite the local church and one day a humble parish curate came to her door and, because he had frequently heard her playing the piano, asked her if she would consider forming a church choir. Supported by her family she agreed, and then one day as she was waiting for people to arrive the following happened. 'I was alone in the little church of the Roses and was waiting in silence. Suddenly an unforgettable experience was gifted me: it was without a shadow of doubt the living experience of Jesus.'[8] My friend's mother had already made a move by coming into the actual building of the church with all its semiotic impact. What happened after is consistent with both the well-known examples and countless others unremarked by history. There is a 'living experience' which speaks to our living neural selves. I was sent this book at the same time I was writing these same pages and the story at once underscored itself as an instance of the mystagogia I am proposing.

Mystagogy is what all this comes to—the possibility of a profound restructuring of the human person on a pathway of encounter with Christ. What is essential to stress is the human process. This is not an alien, other-worldly 'divine grace' which arbitrarily by God's good pleasure bridges a gap to the human earth. Instead it presupposes the signified reality of resurrection: it claims that through a pathway of signs associated with the Risen Crucified a genuine neural reconstitution can take place. It does not override choice, either in a possible single-moment condensation of experience, or in other more mundane situations of decisions for forgiveness and love. It does, however, claim that there is a genuine anthropo-ontological encounter underpinning Christian experience and relationship. The figure of the Risen Crucified brings us to the heart of (new) reality and by 'locking on' in faith (self-giving) to this figure our humanity is changed in an absolute way. The consequences for a doctrine of God are enormous. We have rooted our understanding of Christ in a concrete transformative anthropology not in a metaphysics of divinity. The point of reality we have come to (our ontological starting place) is the place where Christ touches and transforms humanity, not in some speculative vision of eternal verities, the supposed intellectual vision of the eternal God. With this starting point we are now therefore able to retrace the concrete pathway of Christian doctrine and so approach it with a new, less presumptuous, more nourishing respect. The Christian God is not first in our minds, she is in our nerves, and by recognizing this we have some chance of shaping our intellectual understanding by and toward the truth of love.

The Sign of God

Is 'God' a proper or a common noun? Does it have a single reference or multiple references? Everybody seems to understand what is meant by the word, but is that any kind of a guarantee? In the Richard Attenborough movie *Gandhi* the last words of its eponymous hero of nonviolence, as he falls before the assassin's gun, are 'O God!' The historical Gandhi's native tongue was not English. The words he said in fact were 'He Ram!' and they are engraved on his tomb in New Delhi. They refer to the Hindu God, Rama, who is an avatar or incarnation of the supreme God Vishnu, who is in turn a primary form of God alongside other gods like Shiva. There is actually disagreement whether Gandhi even said precisely this. I have seen it argued that he said 'Ram Rahim' which would invoke both Rama and one of the ninety nine Arabic names for Allah, i.e. the 'merciful' one.[9] When I last saw the movie, in a class I was teaching, I felt moved by these final words of the Mahatma. But I wondered why. What was it Gandhi actually intended, and did I mean the same thing as he did by the word 'god'? Certainly the huge masses of Hindu and Muslim refugees shown at the end of the movie fleeing in opposite directions did not mean the same thing. They turned murderously on each other because they meant entirely opposite things, and part of that opposed meaning was the respective homes and lands they were losing. In other words, cultural differences as to divine meaning are very often not simply metaphysical. They include such concrete references as the possession of territory and its undisturbed enjoyment under their 'God'. When liberal and transcendental thought claims a univocal meaning to the word, one that we all should somehow recognize, it's hard not to reflect that there is a territorial message there too. Just accept this univocal 'God' it seems to say and we will all inhabit the same cultural homeland, and, by the way, the borders the homeland occupies will politically and practically coincide with liberal capitalism. The point is not to negate the valid concern for security and peace but to show that the human purpose of deciding the meaning of God is an essential and common one, shared through all cultures. Liberalism does not sit Olympian above the fray.

The Greek System

Part of the viewpoint that makes us think perhaps we do sit above it is the Western philosophic tradition. The unique form of thinking that we received from the Greeks has had an enormous effect on our religious and cultural attitude in the West. Étienne Gilson is probably the premier 20th century author on medieval Christian philosophy and in his classic little book, *God And Philosophy*, he makes plain the trajectory.[10] He describes the organic evolution of Christian thought from the Greeks, through Augustine, to Thomas Aquinas. He shows most importantly how Greek philosophers were not themselves seeking a theology, an understanding in which relationship with god or gods played a role. Rather they were seeking the basic matter or principle by which to explain all things, including gods. It was a question of 'what is' in an ultimate sense, and god or gods came, subordinately, under that heading. For Plato the ultimate character of things, the real 'what is' of things, is Idea or Ideal Form: an eternal, unchangeable, immaterial Idea is the place where the buck stops in explaining everything. Aristotle went in another direction. He considered movement or change a key issue in the ultimate explanation of things. Thus he is led to a thought of an Unmoved Mover as the source of all motion in the universe, and therefore its supreme god. This god is also an eternal Mind, but thinking only itself; it cannot be dependent for knowledge on anything outside of itself. It is therefore impossible to have any kind of relationship with it. This Mind is in some way the most unconscious of all minds, and so hardly qualifies for the upper case 'g' when called 'god'. Thus, according to Gilson, the pinnacles of Greek thought are inherently non-religious. Stoicism as a popular quasi-religious strand of thought in late antiquity is the exception that proves the rule. It turned the non-religious condition into a virtue, making philosophical non-religion into a kind of grim religion. As Marcus Aurelius put it, 'The World Cause is a torrent, it sweeps everything along.'[11] Serenity is found by simply going with it.

For Gilson the coming of Christianity rescued Greek thought from its dead end, saving it in the clinch. Christianity provided a final cause which was both intelligent and dynamic and positively available for personal relationship with its creation. A pivotal text is Exodus 3:13-14 where the biblical God describes himself as 'I AM.' In the third century a Christian author declared that Plato had said almost exactly the same thing when he argued that ultimate philosophical explanation had to bring us to that which truly *is*. There was only one difference between the two: the personal or impersonal article. 'For Moses said: *He who is*, and Plato: *That which is*…either of the expressions seems to apply to the existence of God.'[12] Can't you hear the cosmic thud of eternal principles falling from a height on the trembling of human possibility? So it was that here, and in many other places, the spiritual union of Christianity and Greek philosophy was born. In the Middle Ages Thomas Aquinas would celebrate the millennial marriage by saying 'He who is' is the most proper name for God: it signifies being or existence itself, *ipsum esse*.[13] By now the holy union is so established by custom that it could not even qualify for Dawkins' 'ubiquitous familiarity', as in some theological viewpoint in our environment to which we have grown accustomed. Rather it would be the environment itself, something almost as total as the air we breathe and the ground we walk on.

But does the thought of 'what is', the claim correctly to

envision the ultimate nature of things, apply appropriately to biblical thought? There is no doubt the marriage has been incredibly successful. It has yielded an effective Christian universe and it has shifted the character of philosophy itself. To say that God is existence (as Gilson names it) moves existence toward relationship, and—as the previous chapter showed—philosophy has had *de facto* children out of this marriage. But in a world ruled by media stream, atomic weaponry and global warming what relevance have essences and first causes? Something much more horizontal, human and dangerous shapes our universe and the real question is 'Where is God in this?' not 'What is God?' or even 'Who is God?' The question is immediate and existential, not speculative or religious.

Where then is God to be found? Surely—in the popular phrase—where the rubber meets the road! Not in ideas of the infinite in our heads, but in the limitless desire humans experience in their bodies, in their neural pathways. Not in movement in any abstract or impersonal sense, but in the particular human events of movement that make up the world—individual movements of anger or peace, of killing or reconciliation, and the cumulative force of these movements in one direction or the other. In the evolutionary scheme I have presented humanity arises neither in the visualization of ideal forms, nor in a hard-wired language that forms ideas, but in a crisis of desire and violence. It is from these depths that the being of 'God' arises. Now if someone were to intervene in these depths of desire and violence and we were able to experience that intervention as a release into a new movement and a new meaning—a resurrection from the dead, exactly as the New Testament relates it—then we are on the track of a new truth and meaning of God. Eastern religions are much more familiar with both the question of desire as pivotal and the meditative immediacy of the divine. They have not had the background intellectual culture of the objective 'what is' of God, the *ipsum esse,* and this has to be a reason for their attractiveness to some people raised in the Western Christian tradition. For some Christians to integrate an Eastern sense of the divine can accent a truth intuitively felt to be compatible with Christian theology but lacking a ready Christian framework or language to express it. But neither do Eastern religions tend toward a scientific sense of the primary scene which has arisen from the biblical narrative. They seek rather to place the individual in a purely religious dimension over against the illusion of this world. They thus repeat in their own way the alienation from the actual human world that 'eternal' philosophical thinking produces in the West.

In contrast the biblical record is an extraordinarily concrete story of striving to find real human distance from the primary scene of violence and murder—beginning with Abraham leaving his native city, through his amazing interceding against the destruction of Sodom, to the Exodus, to the prophetic critique of royal power, to the Suffering Servant producing a revelatory sketch of the primary victim, to Jesus willingly re-entering the scene in order finally to expose and undo it. The Western tradition with its accent on 'what is' enables us to claim the veracity of this scene, and that is its enormous cultural contribution. But the religious response to its subversion cannot be to 'what is', but to the inconceivable movement of the heart of Jesus that brought it about. Here is something much more personal, overwhelming and transforming than an abstract concept of divine nature. Here is the dynamic hypostasis which is able to generate the same hypostasis over and over, bringing individuals to the human point where they respond not with further violence but with life and forgiveness. Here begins Christianity's religious truth.

Divine Hypostasis Now

The hypostasis of Jesus, his self-giving relationship to the other, brings us therefore to a stunning new sense of God. The human and divine transformation cannot be separated, and there is no way back. If Jesus relates to God in his human existence by a practice of infinite compassion then by the rules of relational imitation, of compassion itself (i.e. if Jesus truly imitates *God*), God has to be of the exact same character. And then even more radically, if Jesus practiced this infinite compassion all the way to his final breath, pouring himself out to his Father / Mother, even as 'God' abandoned him, then we are required to follow him all the way to the death of any meaning of God not consistent with this, his absolutely self-giving human hypostasis. This is the hypostasis that wrung from Thomas 'my lord and my god', and cognate with it the whole meditation of John continuously affirms the Christ-based meaning of the divine: 'Whoever has seen me has seen the Father' (14:9); 'The Father and I are one' (10:30); 'No one has ever seen God. It is God the only Son, who is close to the Father's heart, who has made him known' (1:18). But then at once you say this the priority of course flows back—through Christ—to the Father, the God of Jesus: 'The Son can do nothing on his own, but only what he sees the Father doing; for whatever the Father does, the Son does likewise' (5:19); 'I came from God and now I am here. I did not come on my own, but he sent me' (8:42). Jesus simply says that the God who is like him is in fact God.

What results in fact is an undecidable priority. From the anthropological side the priority is with Jesus—'Whoever has seen me has seen the Father...' From the side of Jesus' internal relationship the priority is with the Father, as indeed it would have to be in a self-giving relationship. To use a banal example it is like two polite people going through a door at the same time, first one says, 'After you,' and then the other says, 'No, after you.' The difference with Jesus and the Father is that even as they say 'After you' they go through the door, because the going through the door *is* the 'After you'! The only 'door' they have is the 'After you,' the absolute self-giving to the other, and they endlessly reiterate the absolute surrender to the other. Another, more pleasing, image would be the plunging of two torrents into the same void where the waters of the one mix with that of the other, so it is impossible to tell which one went first and opened the way. The early eastern-Mediterranean theological image and name for this was *perichoresis*, meaning a dance (related to 'choreography'), where two partners follow in each other's footsteps, back and forth, round and round. In the full doctrine of the Trinity, with the Spirit included, it became a three-person dance, a three-handed reel! This understanding has recently gained much more traction among theological writers.

> At the center of the universe, self-giving love is the dynamic currency of the trinitarian life of God. The persons within God exalt each other, commune with each other, defer to one another. Each person, so to speak, makes room for the other two.... After all, John's Gospel tells us that the Father is 'in' the Son and that the Son is 'in' the Father (17:21), and that each loves and glorifies the other. The fathers of the Greek church called this interchange the mystery of *perichoresis*...and added in the Holy Spirit—the Spirit of both the Father and the Son. When early Greek Christians spoke of *perichoresis* in God they mean that each divine person harbors the others at the center of his being. In a constant movement of overture and acceptance, each person envelops and encircles the others.[14]

In connection to this perspective it's worth hazarding that what is known as the Greek church was in some way less 'Greek' than the Latin church which emphasized the first-principle thinking of philosophy, rather than this intensely relational approach. Bishop Zizioulas in his book on the Trinity strongly contrasts the Eastern Orthodox understanding with the Western accent on essence or substance. He says the latter

... represents a misinterpretation of the Patristic theology of the Trinity. Among the Greek Fathers the unity of God, the one God, and the ontological 'principle' or 'cause' of the being and life of God does not consist in the one substance of God but in the *hypostasis*, that is, *the person of the Father*. The one God is not the one substance but the Father, who is the 'cause' both of the generation of the Son and the procession of the Spirit. Consequently, the ontological 'principle' of God is traced back, once again, to the person.'[15]

However, perhaps we still see here an eternal priority of the Father rather than the radicalism of the dance where all 'take turns' at being 'first'. What confirms this radicalism and makes it unavoidable is the anthropological priority of the Son, Jesus, which I have been outlining. Because, upon reflection, the priority of Jesus as human hypostasis becomes also fully theological. Early patristic theology did describe Jesus as eternally generated or begotten by the Father. This derives logically from the image of father and son and from the philosophical sense of eternity understood as 'preceding' Jesus' historical existence. The hypostasis of Jesus as a complete revelation of God entails for a Hellenized way of thinking that he was generated by the Father 'from all eternity'. If Jesus makes God present in a self-identical way then logically he must always have been God and the way this happened was that he was eternally generated by God the Father. Here is the famous theological theme of Jesus' *pre-existence* presumably affirmed in John, and the way it was worked out gave a priority as 'cause' to the Father. But, as already suggested, John's gospel points deeper than this. There is an undecidability in the priority of Father and Son and it occurs manifestly at the level of the human Jesus.

John's gospel does not talk of 'pre-existence' but of 'beginning'. There is the beautiful introduction to John's gospel: 'In the beginning was the Word, and the Word was with God, and the Word was God.' It is true, this is in the past tense. But it is also clear in that phrase that what in fact comes first, 'in the beginning', is the Word, not eternity, nor even God or the Father. And when we read the gospel attentively we can see that the 'beginning' has a rich repertoire of reference that overrides and diffuses what we think of as 'eternal' priority. The miracle at Cana is the 'beginning' of the signs (2:11); Jesus tells his disciples they are 'to testify because you have been with me from the beginning' (15:27); and shortly after this he says 'I did not say these things to you from the beginning, because I was with you' (16:4). In the first letter of John this open horizon of 'beginning' is brought front and center, perhaps in a deliberate attempt to contrast and balance the apparent 'eternalizing' account in the gospel: 'What was from the beginning, what we have heard, what we have seen with our eyes, what we beheld and touched with our hands, concerning the word of life...' (1:1) The succession of demonstrative pronouns shows there is no distinction from what was in some (perhaps) aboriginal beginning and what the writer has experienced directly in human relationship. The whole chain of usage in the literature tells us, therefore, that 'beginning' is absolute with Jesus, and if there is an 'eternal past' it is also contemporaneous with Jesus. So to take the beginning in a Greek way, as an immense forever preceding all historical life both reduces eternity to a backward prolongation of time, and, still more problematically, neglects the absolute beginning experienced in the gospels.

Through Jesus eternity enters time, and it gets stuck there. If the temporal hypostasis or person of Jesus is truly 'also' the divine hypostasis of the eternal Word, then surely this means that the gospel is itself an absolute beginning, just as God is. And before we again fall down the rabbit hole of a Greek eternity remember that our guiding principle is the infinite nonviolence of Jesus' relationship to the other. Here is the absolute beginning of the gospel and it pulls eternity into itself, into the historical moment of Jesus. I have called it the ontological starting point, using ontology in a general sense of ultimate reality. But I want to emphasize this is not an ontology of 'what is'. Here it has much more the character of an event, as in Heidegger's thought, an event in the midst of time, an event producing time. It is also very different from Heidegger's event because it is a personal event, one of unreserved self-giving, not an impersonal oscillation of Being. The really correct name for it, therefore, is one that has emerged in the course of the discussion: the beginning of the gospel is a hypostatic (relational) beginning, and it conclusively shows us that hypostasis is the first principle of reality and truth.

In this light, therefore, we can no longer affirm a priority of the Father generating the Son from a philosophical eternity. Rather the Son generates the Father right here on earth and does so in the eternity of infinite self-giving. And of course, reciprocally, the Father generates the Son in exactly the same eternal 'now' within the heart of Jesus each moment it beats. There is in fact a simultaneity of generation in the boundless 'beginning' of the gospel. Generation is not a work of patriarchal biology in an Olympian sky but the infinite power of the cross opening the abyssal space of love where God cannot help but follow: and, of course, the Father / Mother of Jesus has also, at the same time and first, opened that space for Jesus to follow. Generation is 'going first' in self-giving, shaping the infinite com-passion of the divine other in imitative self-surrender. In a strange way it is also simultaneously 'going second'! Because this self-giving is also always relational in deference to the giving of the other, so 'priority' is also always to follow, and so on for ever in a circle. Perichoresis therefore becomes the conclusive stepping out of the divine dance partners here on earth. Can't you hear the music? Can't you feel the rhythm of their feet making our own feet tap in time?

Contra And Response

But more likely in reaction we will hear three complaints contra! Perhaps there are more than three, but for the moment three sound clear. I will deal with them now in a straightforward fashion, not because they are not worth discussing in detail, but because I want to preserve the freshness of this vision as we have arrived at it and, again, not to be pulled down the 'eternal' rabbit hole.

First of all, it will be said, are you not making the Trinity unthinkable and so pastorally useless? Does not the criterion of the hypostasis of Jesus make everything too human and so the idea of a triune God get lost on that too-human horizon? In answer I would say, no, in fact, the contrary! Hypostasis is relationship and everyone knows relationship at first hand. It is the most vibrant and alive thing in the universe. People also know relationships can be described and explored but hardly defined or thought in a logical essence like chemical formulae or math. If God impinges on us by means of a singular human relationship it is because God cannot be thought, only encountered. And the encounter can only take place one person at a time, as in any true relationship. A relationship that is mediated by a general idea is not a relationship, rather a collective myth used to hold the world together. Accordingly the truth of Jesus' relationship with the Father must itself be encountered via relationship with Jesus. Through him and with him, in a very literal way, we encounter the Father of Jesus and this is the pathway of discovery I have already underlined and called 'mystagogia'. The evangelical and pastoral task therefore is to lead people to a transformative encounter with the God of Jesus through an authentic encounter with him, because that indeed is the point of the scripture. The Spirit is implied at every stage too, for neither the encounter with Jesus, nor the Father, can take place without the Spirit. The Spirit is the regenerative force within our neural humanity that first is prompted by Jesus and then connects us both to Jesus and the Father. At a further stage of reflection, the Spirit is felt as a person in its own right: for we have a relationship with Spirit too, praying 'Come Holy Spirit!' In a way the Spirit might be called 'relationship or hypostasis itself', for it communicates the very relationship of self-giving that is the heart of God. But then relationship cannot be an 'it' and so it has to be a 'she', a person, the third person of the Trinity. If we in fact embrace the hypostasis of self-giving so it becomes 'us', while still knowing it is also beyond us, this means that there has to be a 'third person' who is not Jesus or the Father. As Paul said, it is this Spirit that makes us cry out 'Abba!' i.e. the new meaning of God.

Relationship is therefore the basis of intelligibility of the Trinity and it is in fact a much simpler business to lead people into the heart of these relationships than explain to them in terms of 'substance' and 'subsistence' what they conceptually mean. But it may also be truthfully claimed that it is the first-hand communication of the hypostasis of Jesus that brings us to the radical source of all intelligibility: not the intellectual vision of essences but the living communication of loving relationship. Hypostasis in fact has become for us the new principle of human understanding—the true, radical transcendental—not the 'what is' of the metaphysical tradition.

The next objection says, well, what about creation? Haven't you lost Genesis chapter one, the actual biblical beginning, and the dependence on a pre-existent God it clearly displays? Must not a Christian see there the necessary conceptual space of a pre-existent Christ, moving from eternity into the act of creation? The answer is, 'Not unless you see it with Greek eyes!' The biblical writers were not interested in the concept of God prior to creation. What concerned them was the character or tenor of creation, the concrete way it took place itself, and the vital repercussions this had for relationship with God in history. Genesis chapter one is a theological strategy, written very likely in the context of exile or the decades after, and benefiting from a critical reflection on the history of God's people and the meaning of that history. What is absolutely striking about it is the way it excludes every hint of violence from the act of creation. Here there is no primeval battle, no conflict of gods giving rise to the universe. It could only have been written after the defeat of Israel's national and military identity, and the discovery of a sovereign God who can work with means other than violence, a viewpoint that emerges to prominence only at the end of the exile in the prophecy of 2nd Isaiah. To think here of a metaphysical God, and not God's historical character, is to mistake the biblical world for the Greek one.

This interpretation is reinforced when we see that the prophecy of 2nd Isaiah is itself not beyond invoking a primordial divine battle, but for the sake of historical liberation! 'Awake, awake, put on strength, O arm of the Lord! Awake as in the days of old…Was it not you who cut Rahab in pieces, who pierced the dragon? Was it not you who dried up the sea, the waters of the great deep; who made the depths of the sea a way for the redeemed to cross over? So the ransomed of the Lord shall return, and come to Zion with singing' (Is. 51:9-11a). We don't find this battle in Genesis one, but does that mean 2nd Isaiah is wrong? No, because the issue is not a metaphysical account of the 'beginning' before the dawn of time, but rather what God means for history. The image of a primordial battle is invoked for the sake of historical redemption now. We see in fact that the bible has multiple beginnings and they are always there in order to cut across the world's deadly continuity, their purpose to begin the world over and over in a continuing work of divine creation. When we see it in this way we gain a new understanding of biblical 'beginning'. It is not a flat linear scene we can picture to ourselves and so gain a mathematical account of everything and the sequences of hierarchy and power. Much rather the bible is a continual series of present tense interventions seeking to bring

God's creative project to final fulfillment.

In a world of relationship, of 'relativity', the beginning of things is thus never set from behind. Beginnings are flowing toward us all the time from the future, the endless torrents of God. In particular the gospel 'in the beginning' is not a matter of providing knowledge of the eternal spheres and circuits of the gods, but a way of stopping us and the world in our tracks, of saying something utterly new is happening, now! We therefore have no business imaging any kind of divine 'pre-existence'—a stretching back which is always a covert matter of time—rather than the inconceivable endlessness of beginning. Only this (and then with all due hesitance) has any claim to being named 'eternity'. A relationship with God through Jesus is really our only certain way into the divine 'beginning'.

The final objection I hear is from the perspective of diversity, the respect to be offered to other cultures and religions. When I say that a relationship with God can only be found in a relationship with Jesus then surely this discounts the separate value of all other religions and cultural viewpoints? From one point of view there seems no way round this. By insisting on hypostasis as the principle of truth, and not idea, we are unable to create an ideal 'divine' in our minds to which we can then approximate all cultural forms as true in one aspect or another. Relationship with a human person can presumably only take place one-on-one with that person, leaving no other pathway. However, what I am claiming is a primordial quality to this relationship. Exactly because its character is that of utterly re-creative self-giving it was interpreted by the primitive Jesus movement as the one true divine relationship. For that same reason this relationship should be able to occur any time anywhere in the mystery of time and the universe. As I stated it, it is the radical transcendental, the hypostatic principle of every-thing. It should always be possible for a sensitive, generous human being to attune to it at some level. We can therefore easily believe that this relationship lies somehow at the heart of very many religious expressions. Moreover, as all human experience testifies, regardless of religion, it seems possible to meet God in other human beings anytime, anywhere in the world. Whenever one human helps another for no reason but to help then the divine relationship is present. Thus the hypostatic truth is the truth of the universe and any universal relationship will find it in some way.

But the universe is one thing and human history is another. And for every time a stranger has been helped a thousand have been slaughtered. As the whole background argument of the present study maintains religion is indelibly compromised with the violence of human culture, of nations and empire, of politics and society. One of the functions of religion is to create a safe area where peace is experienced but, at the same time, through the backdoor, by a subterfuge intrinsic to its being, war is continually declared. The singular thing about the story of Jesus is the way he enters deliberately into the crosshairs of that backdoor. He stands in the frame where religion, empire and the mob unload their cumulative violence upon him. So it is that the relationship we find in Jesus has an intensely historical realization: he is on the wrong side of religion, of empire, of the crowd in a particular time and place. He is the one excluded by all these forces in concert; and yet his compassion flows back to all the historical agents in forgiveness. The hypostasis that Jesus offers, therefore, is not in this sense universal, poetic, timeless. It occurs at a particular moment and situation where the confluence of forces gather and reach an historically singular mass. There would be no way of again bringing those forces together with the intensity of the passions and meaning involved—the millennial crisis of Judaism (embracing temple, Pharisees, the potential for apocalyptic revolt), the millennial violence of the Romans (approaching the peak of their power against which Judaism was helpless), the volatile cruelty of the city mob subject to these forces, and finally the development of the Hebrew scriptures to the point where a response like Jesus' could emerge. The hypostasis of Jesus, therefore, has one historical vortex wherein we can discover all the forces of violence in paradigmatic form, and it is these that he forgives and transforms through love. His own response, as explained before, has no violence in it, because his relationship with God has no violence. He is therefore able to offer paradigmatic violence a qualitatively different alternative. *De facto* these forces piled on one individual are encountered nowhere else prior to Jesus, and any similar scene of martyrdom subsequent to Jesus is imitatively dependent on him. For this reason the name of Jesus becomes unique from an anthropological and semiotic standpoint. It is not a matter of talking metaphysically, but of an historical drama where an absolute crisis is emerging and a genuine human newness emerges in fact.

The hypostasis or relationship of Jesus has the quality of an unrepeatable model—unrepeatable, that is, in its quality of the 'first time'. It is a moment of unrepeatable surrender, of abyssal descent, of trust and creativity. In fact there would be no other way to produce such a human singularity except in contingent circumstances: Jesus in a very real way has to make his best guess about his course of action. But because he did launch himself into the historical void something immense and irreversible was set in motion. He became the dynamic point of a confluence of conditions able to set the world flowing toward it. It is the whorl in a chaotic system that pulls the whole tempest into itself. For this reason Jesus has historically changed the meaning of God, i.e. both in and through history and as an effect within history. It is no wonder, certainly, that metaphysical categories became attached to the event. And in some respects those categories are inescapable. The Nicaean creed may be seen as an inevitable development when the requirement was made to define the Christian experience from an eternal perspective. But what I have done is pay attention to the essentially human roots of that development and thus seek to redirect Christian practice to an appropriation of those roots. Jesus represents a novum in the cultural and semiotic order, challenging the very construction of meaning itself. But that is such an astounding thing to do the traditional name of 'God' is irresistibly attached to him. The crucial thing is always to return to the process by which that happened in order to grasp its transformative anthropological value, and, because of that, the way it transforms metaphysics itself. Because of Jesus metaphysics starts not with ideas but relationships, and only in repeating the pathway of those relationships can you in any way grasp Christian metaphysics. There is now one absolute beginning in human history, and every little beginning flows out of it and toward it. We now turn to the question of the conscious human gathering around this beginning, the social movement that has been called 'the church'.

Chapter Six

A Virtual Church

I have been so longing to get to this chapter! Because it is the heart of everything, dealing with the practical ways in which all this can impact in actual human life. It seeks to answer the question of how the thought of human meaning radically transfigured by divine nonviolence would play itself out as community, as organization, as church. How indeed does it play out in relation to the multiple organizations that already name themselves as 'church' but without the inspiration of this anthropological thinking?

The word 'church' derives from the Greek *kyrios*, meaning 'lord', and then *kyriakon* 'the place of the lord'. It has an imposing ring to it, and around it has swirled so much of the power and politics of the West. How easy has it been to mistake 'the lord's place' for the palace of an imperial lord, or at least the headquarters of some supernatural captain of business who conducted his transactions there. The church spires and cupolas of the world each with their lightning rod atop speak both physically and metaphorically of negotiation between a horizontal earth and a vertical power-charged sky. As I travel from place to place, in cities or on the highway, it always strikes me how incredibly important the vertical motif is in church architecture...

On the other hand, the romance languages' word for church (for example, *église, iglesia*) comes from another Greek term, *ekklesia*, meaning an assembly, a group called out of their houses to deal with some matter of public concern in the city. And so at once there comes also the sense of the anthropological, of humanity gathered around some theme of importance to its existence. Here is the opposite connotation, the one we have been dealing with throughout this book which tells of the entry of the gospel into the structure and movement of human life. These two words then give some sense of the acute ambivalence of the human organizations claiming to represent the figure of Jesus, of not just the lightning but the potential earthquakes associated with them. (Naturally I am not implying that there is a division along the lines of national languages! An *église* can as easily be lordly as a *church* can be open to human transformation.) I am aware, therefore, that this topic is about as charged as you can get and my entry into it will focus on itself powerful and time-tested forces. My hope is that all the preparation given to this point in terms of history, anthropology, popular culture, philosophy and theology will enable these forces to be engaged not in a superficially conflictual way but in a deeply creative one.

Dinner with the Pastors

Just recently I was at a dinner party where all these issues were the topic of discussion (no kidding!) and in something of a classic style. It would be entertaining to give it in dialogue form, but brevity demands summary. I hope all the same my account captures some of the drama of the churches at this moment in time. The hosts, wife and husband, were both pastors in a mainline Protestant denomination. As the evening wore on everyone relaxed and they felt more confident to express their more intimate thoughts. One of them declared that in twenty years time half the congregations of their denomination would be gone and so would half the seminaries. This person also described the experience of working in various parishes, telling how in one case the local congregation was wedded to an ethnic identity and the maintenance of that identity was more or less the congregation's raison d'être In another case the wealth and position of the local church members made it impossible to broach any challenging social or political matters in the Sunday sermons. Part of this pastor's analysis was the unavoidability of the church-as-institution, and so the near impossibility of doing anything serious in these instances. What was essentially meant was the pastor was directly employed by the congregation and would lose job and livelihood should the congregation's toes be seriously trodden on.

In gloomy counterpoint it was recognized by everyone that two forms of Christian churches were actually on the rise, viz. fundamentalism and the mega-church movement. Fundamentalism covered the waterfront from traditional biblical literalists, through Christian Zionists, to ultra-orthodox Roman Catholics. The overall Roman Catholic situation was marked by the trauma of the pedophile scandal and the closure of viable congregations because of the lack of priests. In this context a convulsion of hyper-orthodoxy seemed the only convinced direction that church could muster. The mega-church movement referred to the rise of single Protestant congregations with numbers in the thousands, featuring arena sanctuaries, rock bands, projection screens, fitness centers, coffee shops, schools, and a theology that has been dubbed as Jesus-lite. The number of these churches in the U.S. has leaped from just 50 in 1970 to 1300 today.[1] Against this the inherited mainline congregations find less and less cultural traction. Based as they are on a traditional Christian worldview of sin-in-need-of-forgiveness they find it hard to compete with the up-beat success-oriented message that refuses to look at the negative and seems to be the latest mutation of God's blessing on the American dream. I will return to the topic of the mega-church later, but first to continue with the dinner party.

The other pastor at the table did not have so bleak a view. This one agreed with all the problems but saw the consoling existence of 'disciples'. In every place there were a few real Christians prepared to serve the gospel and get involved in churches as the most important thing in their lives. It seemed a dubious consolation. It was almost as if the churches had become the world and a few genuine Christians scattered among them were prepared to give them legitimacy.

My wife then moved the discussion forward with the contemporary idea of small groups. She said that the 20th century had been characterized by large scale popular movements that brought civil rights, forced an end to the Vietnam war, produced revolution and took down the Soviet Union. Instead the 21st century would be the era of the small group, the cell of political activists, the close network of researchers, the team developing software and web applications, the members of intentional community. Everyone at table agreed with the aptness of this idea for the renewed growth of the church, but the first pastor pointed out the problem of education for these cells. Without theological preparation of some kind how can you be sure these groups would not relapse into fundamentalism? In reply I suggested that during the first 300 years of Christianity there were no seminaries or formal structures of education and yet all the classic theology of the contemporary churches traced its roots to that period. By this time it was late and the discussion began to fade on that rather idealized point. We soon said our goodnights.

That point, however, is where this book and this particular chapter pick up the trail. I did not tell our table partners that I had a manuscript in preparation and it certainly would not have been polite to suggest the answer to the whole topic was on my computer. But I am sure that there are any number of similar dinner conversations happening across the societies and countries traditionally called Christian and I am hopeful that the ideas here would at least be welcome. So I feel good about continuing the conversation, at least for the moment, on my own, while interjecting remarks of others I am pretty certain would occur. And the first remark I can easily imagine would be in response to my own talk about the early centuries. It would come from a convinced Roman Catholic who would say, yes, during the first 300 years orthodoxy was shaped and articulated, and the source of that process was the role and rule of bishops. Ergo, that is what's needed now.

Back to Scripture (and the Future)

In reply I have to say—and in a somewhat animated fashion—that among Catholics the hierarchical episcopate is a wildly overpriced and over-stretched theme. In other words far too much meaning and weight are attached to it, which the evidence does not bear out and which is counter-productive to the vitality of the gospel. I trained and worked as a Roman Catholic priest for twenty years and I can honestly say that my personal life in Christ was ninety nine times out of a hundred discovered in areas marginal to officialdom. So allow me to examine these claims more closely by taking a trip into the New Testament. I do so with a sense of solidarity with my Catholic sisters and brothers. So many things, I believe, in that tradition are awakened and energized by what I am saying here. Meanwhile if for some this discussion seems redundant I would ask them to be patient. I would also point out that pursuing the topic in the New Testament will have an important bearing on the central content of the argument, so it is worthwhile in its own right.

To begin with there is no doubt that the figure of Peter and the Twelve have real significance in the writings of the New Testament. However, that does not amount to legal institutional authority, let alone 'apostolic succession'. The figure of James, the brother of the Lord, is almost completely absent from the gospels and he is certainly never present as a disciple of Jesus, but he turns up very early as leader of the primitive church in Jerusalem. In the crucial Council of Jerusalem which decided on admission of Gentiles into the new movement he is shown as having the final word over Peter. Peter makes an argument largely from the facts of the mission but James makes the theological argument from scripture and then says 'I have reached the decision' (Acts 15:7-19). From where did James get his authority? Certainly not from Peter.[2] The same thing applies to Paul. The hero of the Gentile mission is at pains to point out that he did not receive his commission from any man (see Galatians 1:1 and 15-17).

Paul (along with James) has been subtly merged with Peter and the Twelve but he is the greatest exemplar of the free operation of the Holy Spirit and the direct personal authority of the Risen Jesus. He never gives any hint of getting his authority from an 'apostolic college', but rather goes out of his way to assert himself independently from the apostles in Jerusalem (Galatians 1:17). At the same time he *is* concerned to stay in communion with Peter, John and James (and with the Jerusalem community generally). He says of these three that they are 'reputed to be pillars' (Galatians 2:9 R.S.V.) and this provides a pathway for understanding his attitude. He recognizes that these people *represent* something, they have emblematic importance. Possibly the 'pillars' are symbolic of a messianic Jerusalem and its temple, promised by the prophets, to which the Gentiles will turn for teaching and worship. But Paul does not see this in any literal or institutional kind of way. He never preaches that converts need to worship with these people in mind or submit to their juris-diction. The community in Jerusalem, particularly its leaders, simply possess this sign value. They have a significant concrete quality rather than an official or legal one. Moreover, this value as sign fits with Jesus' typical way of communication and making meaning. We shall examine Jesus' specific practice in this regard in the next and final chapter, but for the moment we should allow that if Jesus were in some way to provide for the situation after his death it would be in a manner consistent with his life and manner of teaching. Just as he did with healings, stories and symbolic actions during his life he would have provided signs for the time after his life. These signs would create a changed field of meaning around themselves which would bring people into connection, rather than forming an institution with legal and coercive power. In an institutional setting this might seem a fatuous distinction, but if you pay attention to the open manner of operation both by Jesus and the Spirit it becomes critical.

As far as Jesus was concerned I would personally guess that the sign of Peter /rock had nothing to do with vertical authority but everything to do with the storm of death and violence (symbolized by the sea) that was bound to come upon the movement. It meant the ability for Peter and the community around him to witness 'rocklike', i.e. with nonretaliatory trust, in its midst. 'The gates of the underworld [Sheol, the depths] shall not prevail against you!' The tradition that tells us Peter went to Rome and ended his life as a martyr in Nero's persecution suggests that he allowed himself to be pitched into the depths of the violent world in faithfulness to that name. In the meantime the fact that the primitive community knew that Jesus had given Peter a personal sign value would have automatically earned for him considerable respect and concern for relationship with him, exactly as the accounts in Acts and Paul show. But that clearly did not amount to a chain of command. For Paul, the greatest New Testament witness of free charismatic authority, the meaning of Peter and the Twelve (and, by association, James too) was almost certainly continuity with physical messianic Israel which was the necessary source of salvation for the world.[3]

This link with the physical also leads us to probably the most instructive illustration in the New Testament on the role of Peter in relation to non-institutional Christianity. It shows us both how easily that role could become interpreted as vertical power, and how, even as that occurred, the emerging status of Peter was subtly debunked by a parallel theology of the immediacy of Christ. Raymond Brown is the premier Roman Catholic New Testament scholar of the end of the 20th century and his studies of the literature attached to the name of John are at the head of the field. Brown follows the history of the community gathered round the anonymous 'Beloved Disciple' as it produced the gospel of John and the three Johannine letters.[4] The distinctive teaching of this community seems to have been the immediate communication of Christ through word, vision and Spirit arising in the witness of one who was first in such direct relation. The original and paradigm figure in the line of communication was the Beloved Disciple. This remarkably structure-free style of Christianity, characterized by intense relationship with Christ impressed through the testimony of another disciple, seems to have entered a crisis round about the end of the first century. As may easily be imagined a teaching dependent on immediate personal knowledge could, against the background of the Greek dualist worldview, fall prey to a doctrine of a heavenly truth given in an entirely 'spiritual' way. And this is what seems to have happened. Paradoxically what depended on relationship with the Word-made-flesh was thought of happening without the flesh. In reaction the writers of the first and second letters of John protest about people who deny that Jesus Christ 'has come in the flesh' (1 John 4:2-3, 2 John 7).

According to Brown so serious was the impact of this spiritualizing group that at the end of the first century it caused the dissolution of the Beloved Disciple community. The only way to preserve the insights and teaching of that community was in fact to come under the shelter of an emerging institutional church with its structure of bishops. This body derived its authority from the physical and societal signs of Peter and the Twelve which betokened an earthly reality to the message of Jesus. It seems a straightforward matter to see how these signs were progressively translated into a foundational authority, almost inevitable in the contextual cultural order of that time. For the community of the Beloved Disciple it became an unavoidable historical compromise, and at that point of joining the 'Petrine' church a redactor of the gospel wrote chapter 21 to concede the pastoral role and responsibility of Peter.

Peter is told three times by Jesus to care for the sheep. At the same time, however—and this is the real point here—the author privileges the relationship of the Beloved Disciple with Jesus. This disciple believes before Peter does (20:8) and, at the end, has the startling quality, as Jesus says it, of 'remain(ing) until I come.' The meaning of this is enigmatic, but it surely implies a quality of relationship over against Peter's more official position. Peter has asked, rather lamely, about the Beloved Disciple, 'What about him?' Jesus answers 'If it is my will that he remain until I come, what is that to you? Follow me!' (21:22) When we connect 'remain' in its Greek form with the extensive Johannine theme of 'abiding' in Christ (the same verb) then it is strongly hinted that the intense relational quality of the Beloved Disciple would endure until the end. The Disciple and all those who continue in his / her pattern will 'remain in Christ' until Christ draws all to himself (a key expression of the Second Coming in John). By contrast, the role of Peter is limited to its functional character and seems to conclude its pathway with his personal witness as a martyr. There is an unmistakable one-upmanship at the end of John's gospel, suggesting that even as some kind of compromise with an authority structure was accepted the relationship of loving discipleship would always outstrip that structure, just as the Beloved Disciple outran Peter on Easter Sunday morning.

The actual history of the Johannine community as Brown presents it shows the role of Peter is accepted out of historical and cultural necessity rather than theological principle. And that reinforces the conclusion I come to here. Leadership and authority in the New Testament have multiple independent sources and meanings, through James, Paul, Peter, the Beloved Disciple and presumably many others, and they were only merged into a single hierarchy by a gradual historical revisionism. Slowly the generative sign-value of Peter and the Twelve was turned into a juridical structure. In the meantime the actual experience of the first three or four centuries, without the benefit of hindsight, would have been much more akin to multiple local centers of Christianity rather than a united institution. With the benefit of hindsight I will readily grant the crucial role of the early episcopacy in maintaining the rootedness of the gospel message in human history, but this can never imply a necessary connection between rootedness and hierarchy. The construct of a single authority structure is always capable of a sundering back to it its original multiplicity if only because hierarchy creates itself a distancing from actual humanity. Moreover, while the message continues to inscribe itself in the concrete meaning of the world the splitting away from a single structure can and must include the spontaneous appearance of small Christian groups deeply incarnated in human reality.

In other words what chapter 21 of John's gospel means is not that in some long-distant Second Coming the deep relationship of the Beloved Disciple would triumph, but that its effect would progressively establish itself in real time. 'Remain until I come' means endure with vigor and life until this relationship revives and realizes itself with its own strength in the world, without the protective shell of Petrine law. This is nothing more or less than the thesis of the present book, showing in many different concrete ways how that relationship has in fact established itself. What I am seeking now is that we as Christians should catch up with the general human shift toward a Johannine style immediacy of Christ, and away from big institutional form. Which brings me back again to the topic at the conclusion of our dinner party, the small group.

A Matrix of Christ

We left the question of the small group for a glance back to the leadership of the first centuries. Aside from the somewhat fuzzy role of bishops the first three centuries clearly lacked other institutional forms. They did not have seminaries, libraries of the fathers, or standard ordination procedures. So the question remains, how did Christians at that time ensure good theological education? In answer we have to accept they relied on the vigor of Christological relationship as it grew of its own power. Local churches would have pressed forward in the spiritual urgency of the message of the crucified and risen Christ, and leadership emerged organically from that urgency. The communities would have felt naturally related to other communities with the same experience and, after that, it was only through the slow process of debates among intellectual leaders that a theological corpus emerged. What these communities lacked in books or formalized doctrine they made up a hundred-fold in the existential matrix of the gospel message.

We now seem to be in almost the exactly opposite situation. We have had seminaries and libraries for centuries, but where is the existential matrix? Well, as everything I am saying has worked to show, there is indeed a matrix. Its character is much more implicit than before, but every bit as vibrant as that of the first centuries. Christians have only to realize it! When we come now to examine the nature of church we must begin then with a description of the contemporary sense of Christ in the world, this new matrix. I want now to describe it from a subjective side under a heading of the mystical, because I think that is the best approach to give to its character both of human depth and spiritual vibrancy. It corresponds to the theme of mystagogia proposed in the last chapter, but looking beyond the development of a personal relationship to the wider cultural context where Christ is present literally everywhere. After laying out this characteristic as the spiritual basis for a new sense of church we will then be in a position to outline practically the small group church or 'virtual church', as it comes to birth in our time.

When we talk of the existential matrix in the first centuries it invokes a sense of liberating truth communicated from person to person, one of forgiveness, love and Holy Spirit. This plainly still exists today but it comes laced in a body of doctrine and academic theology that sometimes makes it hard to taste the brandy in the cake! I can hardly imagine the directness and rawness of the message in those first centuries before the doctrinal edifice developed. Evangelical and Pentecostal Christians often look for 'revivals' that reawaken the direct experience of those early days, but my guess is that when these revivals happen—for all their genuine impact—they still do not carry the shock of the new that the gospel would have had back then. The gospel message and the edifice around it are today part of the fabric of our existence and there is no unpicking it. But that brings itself something decisively new and this is potentially the really exciting thing for our time. In the second and third chapters I identified this new and exciting thing as the photon of compassion and in the fourth as the sense of movement in the world provoked by Christ. These insights mean that the gospel is not simply communicated one to one, along the frequencies of personal forgiveness and freedom, but that the whole world has been set in motion toward the new humanity of Christ. As the world is unlocked from its archaic orbit around death and violence the sense of instability is immense and dangerous, but at the same time for those with eyes to see the new center of gravity is experienced—an intense inner well of compassion, nonviolence and life, even to the overcoming of death itself. This sense rooted at the heart of our collective human universe has been put there by two thousand years of Christian history, but the wonderful thing is that as it comes to focus we understand that it has been at the core of all things all along. There is, naturally, a feedback loop from what we perceive as 'nature' or 'creation' and the eyes of violence or the eyes of love that we bring to it. The more we sense the well of life-giving compassion the more we see it as the true original meaning of the universe, but we had to be brought by a world spinning off its axis of violence to see the well of love as if for the first time. As if the world of love began today and not before! Which is also true, because the day of love is always the very first day of creation.

Here then is the mystical. We can call it mystical because it is holistic, involving both the human and the divine in an inseparable union. Mysticism in its classic sense is a change in human perception whereby a quality of the divine is directly experienced in this present life. Paul expressed this in all its strangeness. 'I know a person in Christ who fourteen years ago was caught up to the third heaven—whether in the body or out of the body I do not know; God knows' (2 Cor. 12:2). The experience was so amazing that Paul could not be sure if it belonged to bodily sensation, and yet Paul didn't say that it didn't or, on the contrary, that it was an experience of his 'soul' or 'spirit'. It is very significant that Paul refused to make a concession to the dualism of his cultural context, but stayed within the orbit of the body. Thus the phrase 'whether in the body or out of the body' speaks to a dramatically changed state of human perception which is still very much bodily perception, for it revolves around the body. What I have been proposing throughout this book is a much more contemporary collective sense of how our perception or meaning is constructed and how 'the body' must also be understood in terms of deep interconnectedness. Our bodies are mirrors of other bodies and our signs or meanings are put together out of intense crises of interconnectedness. Paul indeed says that all this happened to him 'in Christ', in other words through the new world of meaning produced in and through another body, that of Christ. Today the whole old world has been deeply impacted by this new human body and so to some degree therefore we are all caught up in the 'third heaven' of Christ.

This is not individual private mysticism. It is historical. And it is not mysterious. It is practical. The re-creative Christ is embedded in the neural pathways that link humanity, through the effect of the transforming cultural signs arising from the gospel. It belongs therefore to the true character of the one-to-one immediate discipleship of John: not some spirit-world gnosis, but the neural impact of one human being modeling intimately the humanity of another. Heart speaks to heart, or neural chain to neural chain, even in remote tangential ways. Therefore, if we believe an experience of changed bodily perception is possible for Paul, why not for the rest of us and after two thousand years soaking in the new meaning brought by Christ? The only way we would exclude this is by imposing the traditional metaphysics of split levels, earthly and heavenly, bodily and spiritual, and not taking Paul at his word that he experienced the heavenly in the orbit of his human body.

If, however, we accept the holistic anthropological meaning of Christ we can see Christ at the heart of our contemporary human system calling us to a new creation. As I described in chapter two the figure of Christ brought nonviolent other-centered desire into the world, which was a critical platform for the launch of capitalism along its slow century-by-century development in the West. Now we have an infinite proliferation of the signs of desire. But these are not at root opposed to Christ; on the contrary as I have continued to argue their artery of life rises in the story of the gospel itself. I want to focus on this aspect of desire rather than the upwelling of compassion perceived in movies in chapter three. The two themes are obviously not separated but our daily immersion in signs of desire is much greater than visits to the cinema. So to trace the presence of Christ in this aspect will perhaps make the case of an anthropological Christian mysticism most forcefully. And the story of Christ in the movies can be kept in our minds as a parallel, if more thorough-going, instance of the same thing.

While I was a young man in Rome there appeared a giant billboard which was selling, I think, jeans. It showed a scantily clothed and provocative woman's rear and bore the legend 'He who loves me follows me' (*chi mi ama mi segue*). The fairly obvious echo of John's gospel was reported to have alerted Vatican officials who, suitably scandalized, got it taken down. Scandal aside, there was a smart guess on the part of some copywriter that following Christ and following an image of worldly desire were not entirely contradictory phenomena. A purely discordant message would have sold nothing. The kingdom of desire somehow knows about Jesus even if Christians following Jesus try to avoid desire. The successful U.S. boutique clothing line called 'Imitation of Christ' makes the same point in a condensed and compelling fashion. Every time a model struts the catwalk with the huge letters 'Imitation of Christ' behind her the clothes she is wearing get a jolt of transcendence and sexiness so merged together you cannot tell where one begins and the other ends. Jesus is 'cool', he is desirable. He belongs to the real world and offers the fulfillment of desire not its negation. That is why advertisers and fashion leaders are able to fuse Jesus and images of worldly desire, placing the ultimate cachet on their objects for sale even as they also turn us only toward those objects.

As a child I used to find God 'in nature' as it was said. I would find the dynamic growth of things, their green density and invisible energy, to be a presence that was personal and kind as well as mysterious and exciting. I also found great open spaces to be filled with longing and wonder. Today these things do not mean so much, perhaps because I have learned a scientific viewpoint, but also because I know 'nature' can be highly ambiguous, unleashing enormous destruction by geophysical forces or by one life form on another. But, more important even than this, I have a much greater consciousness of the human sign-filled world as just as organically connected and alive as any forest or seascape. Our understanding of 'nature' is itself communicated by signs that give meaning and which are derived from the cultural tradition of the West, especially romanticism. It is only by finally transforming our world of signs through nonviolence and love that the world of nature has any chance of its life being cared for and ultimately finding peace.

So-called creation theology or ecological spirituality are in fact shaped at a more primary stage by images and signs and these signs are obliquely the product of nonviolent desire brought into the world by Christ. Christ drags the natural world along with him, in the order of the human and, consequently, in reality. In this light Christian ecology gains a much greater human consistency and strength. 'Imitation of Christ' is just as green as it is cool! Or, put the other way, to be either green or cool is to imitate Christ!

So, in order now to make the point about our sign world as forcefully as possible, let us bring the conversation into that world's backyard. Let us now take a kind of field trip with our imaginatively prolonged dinner party. We will go to the local shopping mall, to take a bite and a drink in the food court and just look around. There is really so much to chose from. There is Sbarro, Arbys, Wendys, Subway, and then there are Chinese, Japanese and Cajun specialty cafes. There is of course Starbucks, and in the great emporium itself there is Gap and Best Buy and Radio Shack and Aerospatiale and Abercrombie and Bon Ton. There is also a multiplex with theatres screening at least a dozen movies. And here at the edge of the food court there is an electronic games area for kids, with pin ball and video racers and dancing machines. Next to it there is even a fairground ride with carved painted horses. Then there are the people, thousands and thousands of them. Troops of children with balloons, teenagers everywhere with their bags of brand name clothes, families, with mothers and fathers and infants, and over there a group of developmentally challenged adults with their care staff. People wander round in a strange semi-dazed state, neither unhappy nor fully alive. They are like fish swimming in a sea saturated with nutrients, their hunger at once activated and filled-up.

I used to hate shopping malls. I used to see shadows of the poor behind the store fronts, their faces refracted in the glaze of the windows, their lifeblood woven in the threads of the garments. The labor of the poor and the earth's resources were needed to produce this fish tank stuffed with the world's riches. And that remains true, but where can you go with the anger and alienation that arises from this sense of exploitation? The corporate world is not going to disappear just because of fair-trade protest or alternative activism, even though we might support so many of the ideals of these movements. What is required is something much deeper, something systemic which can change the very roots themselves, without simply being in opposition. For this it takes the eyes of an anthropologically rooted faith which can gaze deeper even than the shadowy forms of the poor and see the Crucified and Risen One transforming the primal conditions of our desire. In Christ everything is mediated to us as good, communicated as sheer and absolute gift without a hint of violence. And this is not an abstract truth, derived somehow from a speculative thought of Christ as universal Logos. It is now endemic in our cultural sign system and because of that it continually works upon our vast collective neural inter-changes, slowly separating itself out as the truth of desire beneath and beyond greed and conflict.

Why, we might ask, is Christmas such a huge consumer bean-feast? Again, I used to dislike Christmas for that kind of reason. But now I understand that the absolute nonviolence and self-giving of the Nativity scene, and the whole earth pulled into its orbit, generate a great surge of true desire, of desire for giving itself. Of course the stores and the businesses get hold of it. If people need gifts to give they will readily supply them! The angels who appeared to the shepherds proclaiming the dawn of grace have had their message outsourced to a billion busy elves laboring for a dollar. But, no matter the so-called materialism, and no matter how it might get repackaged as 'holidays' and remixed in a farrago of symbols, with Santa and Fir Trees and Candles, the whole thing still has Bethlehem at its core. Trade has always ridden on the back of the festival and this one, which sets the world so definitively in motion toward the other, is in every sense the high holy day of buying-and-selling. Evidently, what is so true at Christmas is true at a less visible but structural level throughout the year. Every day in the post-gospel universe is a kind of mini-Christmas. The authenticity of desire as love has set loose the possibility of desire in general, and buying and selling bound forward on the literally sterling value communicated to everything by Jesus Christ.

Once again this includes the factual increase of desire as selfish and destructive. I am in no way minimizing the paradox. If anything I am accenting it. In one sense it is no different from the traditional religious viewpoint that says we fall in love with the created thing and forget the love of the Creator, that we take God's gifts as items to possess rather than discovering the divine giving behind them. But this time it shows the paradox to be historically critical, not some timeless spiritual truth. It is Christ who has anthropologically released the possibility of the two loves into the world, and the historical and dynamic reality of this cannot be ignored, either as the possibility of increased destruction and violence, or the possibility of increased self-giving love. And it is of course the latter that becomes imperative for the Christian, once she understands that in the crisis of desire there is no middle way, there is no heavenly other-world on which to displace the solution. There is only the intensity of the human situation provoked by Jesus. Once this historical truth is seen she can only seek to be faithful to the radical character of desire as love.

Thus a Christian looking at the whole world of capitalism and consumerism, does not stay on the surface, either to indulge or to oppose, but looks with the eyes of an anthropological mystic and sees the gift of heaven at its heart. And she plunges headlong toward that gift! A Christian who sees human reality this way cannot help but begin to live deeply in the present world, in the present moment, in committed, loving anticipation of infinite love!

Beloved Disciples

I recognize that this approach would need a great increase of recognition and conscious practice among Christians. It's not going to happen easily on the reflective level, given the various default theologies which separate Christians from the world and from the work of Christ in the world. However, if what I am saying about a Christ-grounded shift in human meaning is true then there should already be some sensitivity to this among Christians who are, for one reason or another, closer to contemporary changes in culture. The largely evangelical movement called 'emerging church' fits the bill here. It is perhaps too undefined and diverse to be called a movement but various church groups that see themselves under this heading have shown a much more flexible way of locating themselves in culture. They are open both to modern and ancient practice, to the Internet and multi-media, yet also to historic church practices of icons, candles, lectio divina, etc., while maintaining traditional study of the bible. The ability to embrace a variety of cultural languages extends also to location, to use of settings other than traditional church buildings, bringing study and worship to halls, unused stores, people's homes. The theology associated with these groups also shows much greater concern and involvement in the world and its contemporary crisis.[5] A lot of what I will go on to say now in more practical terms runs parallel to these insights of an emerging church, while coming at it from the overall anthropo-theological basis I have presented. For the moment the sense of an emerging new format underlines a migration away from the institutional complacency of the churches toward a more organic connection to the world and its deep travail. The perspective I bring is an understanding of why this move is happening and a way of bringing it greater depth and coherence. Looked at from a scriptural point of view we have seen that a theology of the immediacy of Christ is central in the gospel of John and that free-standing communities gathered in the strength of that immediacy existed before and would be sure to come again. What this book has done has simply added a contemporary understanding of Christ's long-term effect in the dynamics of desire, bringing a cultural crisis of open-ended desire and open-ended love. I am therefore advocating communities of Beloved Discipleship which find a vibrant presence of Christ in this contemporary crisis. The more members of these communities practice the transformation of contemporary desire through Jesus the more they will be communities of beloved discipleship, and the more they are communities of loving discipleship the more they will model the transformation of contemporary desire.

They will also necessarily be communities of new human possibility for the world. We remember how over the space of some five hundred years the monastic communities of Europe provided the foundation for medieval culture. They were an essential source of its economic, educational and spiritual development. In their time and place the monasteries did not offer any anthropological criticism of militarism (although they did seek to curtail the more outrageous aspects of violence in the Middle Ages). We might say perhaps that Europe (and consequently the whole world) has suffered repeatedly from this anthropological blind spot on their part. However, if these communities nevertheless provided a crucial human resource for the emergence of Europe, how much greater would the impact be of new Christian communities of nonviolent desire in an era of global human crisis? I would emphasize that something else is being talked about here than simple ethical or political pacifism. This goes deeper into the roots of who and what we are as human beings, as Jesus always intended, and the issue of an ethical 'ism' is entirely secondary.

A church that understood itself in this way—finding its work as recreation of the human— has no destiny beyond the earth. This of course is always the final question, what is the destiny of church and humanity, here or hereafter? The enormous fact of death has always skewed the answer to the latter, but concentrating on that has left the actual creation exposed to ultimate violence; while, if we give an answer in favor of the former, the issue of the latter is fully resolved also. A creation that overcomes violence and death *is* the hereafter, as the New Testament teaching on resurrection, and Revelation's vision of the final restored state of the earth testify. It would seem that the overcoming of death is more of a technical question, while the issue of violence goes to the very core of who we are and the purpose of humanity in the first place. If Christ is pressing on history for humanity to solve that question then surely we can trust the problem of death may be solved also. Thus the church is moved by the relentless questions of contemporary humanity to shift its perspective to the here and now. What follows then is an outline of some of the key aspects, as I see them, of a church that decisively takes that position. What I have done up to here is to provide the necessary spiritual depth or mystical perspective to these more practical themes. So before I turn to them let us rejoin our dinner party one last time, and where we left it at its field trip to the mall. Let's take one last glance around in this place, and let us look deeper than its business function.

What is present here is people, and at the heart of each person floating in this fish tank of systemic desire is the Spirit of infinite love which brought life to these human waters in the first place. Let us plunge to the depths with them and for them, so that the life in those waters will come to birth as God our Father / Mother always intended. Is this not what Paul understood, telling us there first must be the emergence of new humanity before the physical order itself can be set free? That creation cannot be changed until human meaning is?

The creation waits with eager longing for the revealing of the children of God; for the creation was subjected to futility not of its own will but by the will of the one who subjected it, in hope that the creation itself will be set free from its bondage to decay and will obtain the freedom of the glory of the children of God. We know that the whole creation has been groaning in labor pains until now; and not only creation, but we ourselves, who have the first fruits of the Spirit, groan inwardly while we wait for adoption, the redemption of our bodies. (Romans 8:19-23)

Paul is saying the children of God and creation are joined in an organic process of giving birth but it is the children's life in the Spirit which is the guarantee the process will one day bear fruit.

There follows now six key practical elements for a form of church emerging out of the contemporary matrix of Christ, from the mysticism of Christ working at the roots of our desire. They are: 1. Informal structures; 2. Inclusive boundaries; 3. Local and networked grouping; 4. Non-rivalrous relationship with established churches; 5. Bible study as reprogramming our sign system; 6. Signs and Sacraments. They are not all given the same length of treatment. Some are discussions, others not much more than notes, but each one constitutes a vital component of what we can now begin to call a 'virtual church'.

Informal Structures
We are used to understanding the various churches in terms of their forms of government or what is called their polity. Do they have bishops or superintendents, elders or clergy, covenants or conventions, assemblies or synods, etc., etc., etc.? There is often minor doctrinal difference between groups which are forcibly separated by structure, suggesting how important these differing methods of organizing the churches have become in the story of Christianity. The array gets bewildering but it comes down basically to forms of hierarchical or parliamentary control on one side, and complete local autonomy or charismatic leadership on

the other. What I am suggesting tends at first blush toward the latter but there are substantive differences.

The vital thing to bear in mind is the primary role of relationships within the small group. They are shaped by the Christ who is working at the core of the human system to restructure desire as love, violence as nonviolence. So they are understood as transformational rather than formal. The transformational character takes front and center stage rather than legal constructions like 'salvation', 'baptized membership', 'confirmation', etc. The small group of this kind is meant as a workshop of new humanity, and why should that be so hard or absurd to accept as the meaning of church? If church is the practice of the gospel and we take the Jesus of the gospel at his word then this meaning is incontestable. A potent New Testament word for human relationships in Christ is the Greek *koinonía*, weakly translated as fellowship. There is no really good word to use but perhaps we can recapture some of the Greek's active quality by using the phrase 'common life'. The 'common life' as I am presenting it here is not primarily one we create or produce out of rules of practice but is more radically the life of Christ at the heart of the human system which the small group plugs into and makes its own. It is the transformed humanity that Jesus is bringing about by slow pressure on our human structure, which because of human resistance is normally manifest as crisis. The small group instead embraces this radical change with all its heart, making it the meaning of its existence. From this, yes, there flow group practice and structure, but the identifying thing is not one practice or another, but the constant relationship to Christ's generative life at the heart of the world.

I already highlighted the model of the New Testament community of the Beloved Disciple and how it sets the pattern for the style of Christianity I am proposing. Probably the greatest single passage outlining the transformative relationship is from the first letter of John and it includes the key concept of *koinonía* or common life.

> We declare to you what was from the beginning, what we
> have heard, what we have seen with our eyes, what we have
> looked at and touched with our hands, concerning the word of
> life—this life was revealed, and we have seen it and testify to
> it, and declare to you the eternal life that was with the Father
> and revealed to us—we declare to you what we have seen and
> heard so that you also may have fellowship [common life]
> with us; and truly our fellowship [common life] is with the
> Father and with his Son Jesus Christ. (1 John 1:1-3)

It is all here, the stress on the human reality of the Word rather
than some fleshless spirit. It is also indeed Word, i.e. sign, but
through the sign the flesh of Jesus is real, something impinging
the sense apparatus of hearing, sight, attention, touch. This is
precisely the apparatus which produces the intimate mirroring of
the other, which allows the neural pathways to take on the being
and meaning of the human other. First John's prologue, therefore,
serves as a kind of manifesto for the transformative meaning
reaching up through Christ from the depths of human history. In
the letter's narrative world it means a direct, almost visceral
communication with the human person of Jesus through what
Brown calls a 'chain reaction' continuing from the original
disciple through subsequent disciples who knew the first and so
on.[6] Such closeness to a first disciple is of course no longer
possible. What is—and what makes the prologue still immediate
to readers two thousand years later—is the visceral quality of
Christ arising in the fabric of the human system of signs and
meaning, subverting its original violence with compassion. What
initially came from the flesh through the sign, has now so
permeated our signs that it begins to shape our flesh.

If this reality is at the core of the small group then leadership
will not be a matter of an ordained figure receiving sacramental

power or doctrinal authority, but of two, three, four individuals who together share a sense of the transforming immediacy of Christ. Together they constitute a sign-value of Christ's nonviolence and compassion in the earth. How they arrived at this sense and how they came together will be a story every time anew of the contemporary matrix of Christ freely captivating people's lives. I would hope that this present book would help clarify that experience a little but the whole argument is that it is self-generating and immediate. Given that experience and the coming together, these two or three individuals may then act as the core of a larger group. In the story of the contemporary matrix of Christ and its mystical awakening in individuals there cannot be any hard and fast rules about how it plays out in social fact. The question already overlaps to the next topic below, but for the moment I would very much guess that the extended group that gathers would not exceed the number of people who can fit with comfort in an average sitting room. The reason is that the mirroring of new humanity can only take place at a level of face-to-face proximity where real conversation, accountability, forgiveness and love can happen. Exceeding that you inevitably enter a more formal level of human organization. This should not be ruled out in principle, but the obvious human grouping where this dynamic can occur has to number a dozen or so. Is that not a much more vibrant meaning to the Twelve than a foundational hierarchy?

The unofficial character of the small group speaks, then, to the virtual nature of the church it builds. It has no recognizable structure beyond the core of disciples. For this reason it largely escapes financial burdens, like salary, permanent rents, utilities or ownership. The closest historical parallel to this unofficial structure is early monasticism. What ordination or resources did it take for two or three individuals to move to an isolated spot, build a cabin and begin a routine of shared life, work and prayer? Initially these men and women understood their lives as a flight away from the world toward God, away from the brutality of everyday human existence and toward a full-time contemplation and service of the divine. They moved in the opposite direction from the world but even in their own time the world caught up with them. Nowadays there are fewer and fewer isolated spots to escape to, but much more importantly the world of signs and communication has shifted into such a high gear that it constitutes a permanent sphere of human existence. It is effectively impossible to escape it. Today monasteries have websites, post blogs and receive comments and answer questions directed to them! But, as I continue to argue, Christ himself is at the heart of the world of media and image, re-tuning the frequencies of desire toward love. In this changed human condition it is not a matter of finding God in deserted empty spaces (although there remains, I'm sure, a role for that) but of discovering the new humanity of Christ in the web of the human system he has begun to unwind and then weave anew. In the matrix of Christ we are all now in the desert of immediacy. The world has itself been changed into the realm of contemplation. In this transformed human setting—remember the gospel has already been preached for two thousand years so some qualitative impact must surely be expected!—monasticism does not flee the world. It enters more deeply into it through communities of the matrix of Christ and the common life to which it gives birth.

These communities echo the unofficial structure of monasticism but also its original obscurity. At least for the moment they fly under the world's radar and that is how it should be. Obscurity and hiddenness are the place where organic change and genuine new growth can take place. As Jesus said the kingdom of God is the treasure hidden in the field. Or it is like a woman who hides yeast in a batch of dough until the whole batch is leavened. Anything too visible, too evident, the old world of greed and violence will want to get hold of for its own purposes. In contrast, hiddenness fosters newness and freshness of relationship, seeking to grow its life away from the shaping and control of the world. Here then are the key reasons why these communities make up a virtual church: they find the matrix of Christ in the world of signs and they largely avoid the physical and legal structures associated with traditional church organization.

Inclusive Boundaries

You could say the whole of the New Testament revolves around questions of inclusion. The gospel story of Jesus stakes its meaning on open invitation to the table, and Paul's theology is a fire consuming the boundary marks of Judaism in favor of embracing the Gentiles. A community based in the matrix of Christ thoroughly fulfills this original instinct of the gospel in the modern situation. It experiences a situation of near indiscriminate openness, imitating the sense and shape of Jesus' feasts with their welcome of the sinner, the enemy, the outcast. But its welcome is now pitched at a new and even more radical level than Jesus' historical crossing of the boundaries of ritual and national purity. Those were questions peculiar to the crisis in which Judaism found itself in the first century. Now, as I have sought to demonstrate, the theme of absolute goodness communicated to the world by the love of the Risen Crucified has not only continued to erase boundaries but in step has provoked a storm of desire. More and more the 'nature' of human beings is not body and soul, or various constructed identities, but universal desire.

In this situation not only is the Christ-based human community open to those who sit low on the hierarchies of worldly privilege but it explicitly recognizes and affirms the changed human situation brought about by the gospel. I myself do not see much value in arguments from biology and genetics supporting gays and lesbians. In fact I find the arguments vaguely dangerous, as biology has been and can be used against people just as much to support them. Rather I believe what is most properly and reliably human nature is precisely the lack of fixed nature, i.e. the open-endedness of desire. It is only the relentlessly open horizon of the human that has the possibility of transforming itself fully into love. Any other starting point makes deep human change little more than the effect of a magic wand. As I continue to point out, the gospel has served itself to render boundaries ineffective, precisely because it seeks the goal of love. In the absence of a decision for love the historical result is exacerbated desire which is destructive and plainly not the purpose of the gospel. But conversely the condition of desire is progressively the side-effect of a half-assimilated gospel and it provides the shifted anthropology—a kind of *preparatio evangelii* of crisis— which continually prompts and presses the choice for love.

In this framework the social emergence of gay rights is a consistent accompaniment of the gospel in the world. The welcome of LGBT people into Christian community becomes then a statement of the true situation and goal of humanity as love rather than law (whether physical or moral). Sexuality on its own, whether gay or straight, is no solution to any human life. What provides the ultimate and endless solution is relationship, and that is precisely what gays and lesbians turn to the Christian community to find. A mystical vision of Christ at the root of our desire will then offer a specific emphasis on this transformation, turning the quest for admission and recognition into the celebration of a core value of Christ in the world. A gay couple can and should be a testimony of the transformation of desire into committed love which is the question for all contemporary existence, straight as much as gay. Far from being threatened by gay and lesbian relationships in the Christian community the critical accent on relationship and love they bring supports the sanctity of Christian marriage. Straight sexuality just as much as gay exists in the contemporary storm of desire and feels its effect in the breakdown of so many marriages. Seeing gay relationship arising out of this storm and then finding truth in committed married love points the way for contemporary heterosexual marriage, rather than proving something to break it down.

This hot-button discussion can help us, therefore, with a more general and ordinary vision. What is important is not so much the issue someone brings as the end point the community is moving toward. The small core of disciples seeking to live in the transforming immediacy of Christ provides the momentum of the community. Because they are turning in this orbit and the point of gravity is objective and real then those who chose to associate with them must by virtue of this deeply human gravity also find themselves slowly pulled into the same great attraction. That is why in principle no one can be excluded. No password is required, no certificate of membership, no test of doctrine. The movement of the group toward nonviolence, compassion and forgiveness will itself decide whether people stay or leave, continue to attend or are not seen again. And this is not insignificant in a Christian universe broadly dominated by the three big forces of traditional evangelicalism, Roman Catholicism and liberalism. All of these have specific ideological agendas. The first two of a strict doctrinal kind, the other of an ideal intellectual nature. The notion that Christ could be working immediately in and for the world is going to be in some way counterintuitive to all of them. So naturally there will be a self-selection away from the group by anyone committed rigidly to these worldviews. But there will be a self-selection in favor on the part of those seeking a holistic solution to a world of chaotic desire and violence. I am not of course claiming that this latter is not its own type of agenda, but I am saying that because it is rooted in the crisis of our time the sense of movement it brings will be much more real and urgent than shibboleths of doctrine or intellectualism.

Strangely this brings us back to the idea of the mega-churches mentioned above, and it is worth thinking it again for the sake of the present discussion. With their numbers sometimes in the ten thousands these churches exercise a Woodstock festival type of inclusiveness. Their unfenced approach can look as if they mean less than nothing in terms of real commitment. The General Secretary of the World Council of Churches, Samuel Kobia, reportedly criticized these churches as 'being organized on corporate logic. That can be quite dangerous if we are not very careful, because this may become a Christianity which I describe as 'two miles long and one inch deep'.'[7] Perhaps the WCC stance is a case of thinking 'Those who are not with us are against us.' Could not these churches just as easily provide an instance of Jesus' inverse saying, 'Whoever is not against you is for you?' (Luke 9:50) Do not these huge churches reflect the general impact of Christ in culture and the broad affirmative sense that Jesus brings to the world, one that may even be celebrated in a pep-rally atmosphere? The inch-deep of these gatherings is at least touching the surface of Christ's matrix of love affirming the goodness of everyone's world. From this point of view I wonder what the WCC official would think of the feeding of the five thousand? On the other hand, if there is lacking at the heart of the feast a disciple group prepared to witness with their lives to the transformation of desire into compassion and nonviolence, then Kobia is entirely right: the leadership does have a corporate logic, and is simply making money out of the Christ matrix.

The conundrum is at the core of the gospel story itself: as I just pointed out Jesus fed bread to a multitude, but then he had to escape when they then wanted to make him king (John 6:15). Because there is a tension between universal accessibility and radical commitment there will always be a painful shifting along this fault line. Meanwhile, just as it seems in the gospels to be possible at least for a while to span the divide, there will surely be examples today of large churches with a mystical heart. One place whose story seems to fit the bill is Mars Hill Bible Church in Grandville, Michigan. At the time of writing it meets in the anchor store of a former mall and attracts big crowds to its two Sunday services. On the history page of their website they say in so many words their initiating dream was that 'the church could be about desire, longing, and connection....' And under theology they say, 'When we put into words what we believe about God, we discover that he has been writing a story of hope and redemption for all the world. His story is a movement from creation to new creation, and he has given us a role to play in that story, in the restoration of our relationships with God, each other, ourselves, and creation.'[8] Sounds very much like what this book has been all about.

Cedar Ridge Community Church which Brian McLaren helped found at Spencerville, Maryland, shares much the same thinking. These two examples signal a remarkable and very hopeful move in evangelical Christianity. Both a progressive shift in the surrounding culture and a deeper attention to the bible and its narrative structure have brought about this new sense of church. These larger organizations stand somewhere between a virtual church and what a virtual church might look like if it were to morph into a big visible one! Here is Cedar Ridge's Vision Statement as at least a gesture in this direction.

Cedar Ridge is a community of hope and transformation dedicated to following Jesus.

Imagine a community that dares to dream of heaven on earth; a community where everyone is accepted and respected and their journey cherished, regardless of their background, beliefs or place in society; where everyone looks out for the concerns of others and no one is alone. Imagine a community of peace and safety where it's possible to shelter from the frenzied pace of life, in order to slow down and explore the mystery and meaning of our existence; where we can take time to address the roots of our anxieties and pain; a place of hope where we can find help and healing and the power to change, no matter how desperate our situation. Imagine a community of people devoted to following Jesus together, learning to live like him and helping one another grow in their relationship with God; where we are gradually transformed to become better people: better friends, better family members, better workers, better neighbors; becoming people who enjoy life to the full and who can also deal with adversity well, learning to grow through failure and suffering. Imagine that community scattered throughout the region around Washington, Baltimore and beyond working as agents of love, peace and hope wherever they are; serving our neighbors, caring for the poor, helping the oppressed. Imagine a community of people who live simply and ethically, who share their land and resources with their neighbors; a community that treasures the Earth and reaches out beyond global, cultural and political barriers to offer friendship and practical support.

Imagine a community of people who make the world a better place.[9]

Local and Networked

The churches of Mars Hill and Cedar Ridge are organized as small community groups as well as the large Sunday gatherings. They could hardly fulfill their dream of transformed relationships if they were not. But in talking about virtual church we are looking at something purposely and systemically small and this should be underlined. A small group is not distracted by allegiance to the big group with its dangers of accumulated status or too dilute a message. In particular it is free to take on the critical issue of violence. A large structure will find itself embroiled inevitably in questions of legitimate violence, the police, guns, war, etc. This is the trap that had bedeviled the church since the emperor Constantine's highly convenient fourth century 'vision' and the potent battle symbol given him invoking the figure of Christ for his military struggles. He claimed he was shown a sign and heard the words 'by this sign you shall conquer...' (*in hoc signo vinces*). The sign was then copied on his soldiers' shields and standards as the first two letters in Greek of Christ's name. Apparently his rival for the imperial throne had a superstitious dread of these letters. Did his opponent fear the blood of martyrs that the letters evoked—i.e. did the letters on the shields in one stroke twist the nonviolent death of Christians back to an archaic meaning of revenge-in-waiting? At any rate Constantine indeed went on to conquer and this enormously effective piece of revisionist anthropology has skewed the meaning of Christianity ever since, up to and including the dropping of the atomic bomb on two Japanese cities by a majority Christian nation.

In contrast a small group will not have to defend or explain itself politically and will be able to pursue the anthropology of nonviolence freely without getting bogged down in the cultural sensitivities of past or present Christian military activity. Violence is indivisible—today more and more so, with war coming home as PTSD and kids experiencing the environment of combat in the enhanced graphics of video games. To deal with the roots and tentacles of violence within me I have to be free of a default culture of 'justifiable violence'. This latter is not the true Christian situation. It is not the situation the gospels place us in when Jesus teaches 'turn the other cheek' and tells us to love and forgive our enemy, no exceptions. The evolved Christian sophistry of spiritual forgiveness and politically necessary killing makes it impossible truly to explore that transformative anthropology of Jesus. In particular it makes it impossible for a group to respond to Christ's matrix in our contemporary world. Instead a small group is free to plug in directly.

It is the existence of the Christ matrix that moves us toward the virtual church where the new humanity of the gospels can be sought and experienced. The small group opts for the hiddenness of the gospel for the sake of the transforming movement the matrix realizes and allows. Now I know—and I hear the objection at once— that in life there are no perfect solutions. There are dangers in the small group too, risks of isolation, or elitism, or too much control by self-appointed individuals. In answer we can say it should always be possible to walk away from a small group, but the really crucial factor is one I have already described. The virtual church is always somehow in the public domain because its inclusive boundaries demand that it be welcoming, open to visitors, neighbors, strangers. This puts the group in the public eye and allows for transparency and humility. The small group is at the same time a public group. It behaves something like a pilot fish, always in the same big shoal but with a different DNA from the other, more dangerous species!

Beyond that, and as frequently repeated here, the contemporary world of communication creates its own imperative to stay in contact with others. The life of the small group is nurtured and deepened in direct relationship but it may also be shared electronically. Websites, blogs and social networking sites are a fruitful medium for the small group church in addition to direct encounter. And as its life is shared in this way it intensifies the refracted light of Christ within our world of signs. The words of forgiveness, compassion and peace take their place on the Internet as of right, and the more the small group gives expression to this new humanity the more the Christ matrix moves to authentic recognition.

There is always a universal dimension implied in the existence of the small group. The work of the gospel is aimed at 'all nations' and so there is inevitably a trans-local dimension to any Christian community. The Internet with its amazing global reach allows that, but the dimension is not limited to cyberspace. I would certainly expect the time to come when there will be a council or conference of virtual churches meeting physically for encouragement, study and common life. These occasions of general gathering are among the most exhilarating and joyful times for small Christian community. They are moments when we can sense the fullness and freedom of humanity to which all existence is moving. When this happens for virtual churches it will be especially intense and fulfilling. It will be the physical realization of a new reading of Christianity, one that belongs to our time and promises hope and transformation for our world's long-suffered story.

Nonrivalrous Relationship

Protestantism began as a protest against Catholicism and ended as a different version of the Christian religion. Today bible-based Christians pride themselves on the difference and regard many aspects of Catholicism as corruptions of biblical revelation. Protestantism, however, did not overcome the inherited violence of the Catholic tradition, either in doctrine or practice. If anything it exacerbated it. The more subtle violence of Anselm of Canterbury's eleventh century satisfaction theory of atonement became the straightforward violence of penal substitution. The sixteenth and seventeenth century wars of religion in Europe left a permanent wound in the soul of European nations which continued to fester, erupting again in the multiple trauma of the 20th century.

In this sense, therefore, the Reformation never truly happened. It is still waiting to happen. The question of violence goes to the very core of who we are as human beings. It is the easiest thing in the world to define something, to give it meaning, by the use of violence. In *Cross Purposes* I showed how atonement theory arose basically from a human mechanism effecting change of status and meaning through violence toward the other. The Christian use of this mechanism to explain Christ's death evolved slowly over fifteen hundred years to attain the form we have now, so second-nature as to seem beyond question.

But what is second nature is not the theory but the violence behind it. When we say that God required Jesus' death in order to forgive us, this is violence talking not God. It is not the supremacy of grace or forgiveness, because at the level of essential function there is only absolute murderous reciprocity. And when fundamentalists, of whatever stripe, express a harsh certainty over biblical interpretation, or over the invincible claims of hierarchy, at root what they are invoking is this selfsame act of enormous violence that sets up text and world in an unanswerable way. What Protestants do in terms of biblical inter-pretation Catholics do at their high altars. In the meantime the actual work of Christ's death is the undoing of the age-old mechanism itself, a self-giving so profound that it penetrates the world and is the life by which the world lives. To be in the world is to be profoundly touched by the new meaning that the self-giving has brought. To be Christian is to dwell consciously and fully in that meaning. But to grasp this change is itself a process of gentleness and nonviolence, so those who are locked in a scheme of foundational violence will find what is said here almost incomprehensible. But it is the greatest and only test set before humanity, to see if we can make this change in ourselves through the change brought about by Christ.

When it comes, therefore, to talk of virtual church the issue surprisingly is not that the traditional churches got it wrong and so are to be rejected—because that would simply repeat the gesture of change of status and meaning through violence. And we only have to check the story of the Reformation to see the effect of that when disputing ownership of Christian truth. Rather the question is how to continue to explore and assimilate the new meaning of Christ in the world. This is where the Christ matrix is of supreme importance; it gives us a positive dynamic to refer to, rather than simply rehearsing the age-old claims of disputed ownership.

Small groups of a virtual church, therefore, will not see

themselves in opposition to traditional churches. Rather there is a parallel existence. The great churches of Christian history are bearers of the tradition. They have passed down the new humanity of Christ day after day, year after year, whenever they have read aloud the gospels and reflected the actual conduct and response of Jesus as he moved in the abyss of human violence. At the same time these churches do not possess the tradition by title, no more than the actual written gospels do. The Risen One is an agency in his own right and it is this astonishing factual presence of Christ in the world that is turning it slowly toward the change that God has always desired for it.

Reprogramming Our Signs

How do Christians catch up with the change that God is making? In the fifth chapter I spelled out the impact of the crucial sign of Christ, how it works to reconstitute our symbol system and this produces an effect on our actual neural responses to others. I described it on a general abstract level but how would this work in practice? Such a thoroughgoing reorientation of our humanity is not going to happen all at once or without constant reversals. It needs a practical pathway which can help us to reprogram our meaning day by day, year by year. The bible is the record of the long historical journey in which a people lived in constant company of a God of new meaning and through many reversals on the route. It was this journey which ultimately produced the astonishing figure of Jesus. The study of the bible record is a purpose-built means to reprogram the crucial signs by which we think and live.

Putting things this way at once raises the question of biblical interpretation. The thoroughly obvious historical character of biblical revelation has led commentators, at least from the time of Augustine, to suggest different periods or stages in God's dealing with humanity. So you have divisions like Creation, Fall, Covenant with Noah, Covenant with Abraham, Covenant with

Moses, Exile and Return, Jesus, etc. In this picture it is assumed that God has step-by-step plans or purposes, so that everything comes on line progressively at the moment God has decided. However, although God's purposes are revealed in stages, the character of the main actors, God and human beings, never changes. On the one hand you have a God of justice and on the other a sinful humanity. In vivid contrast, when you begin to talk about God changing the meaning by which we live you suddenly illuminate a very different thought of interpretation. The character of both main actors changes as the story unfolds, humanity because that is the whole point, and God because *de facto* there cannot be any idea about God outside actually existing human meaning. God does not change in principle, but in human thought s/he does because human thought does.

Let us consider for a moment the way in which we build structures linking two unlinkable points. There are some spectacular examples of this around the world, from the Akashi-Kiakyo bridge in Japan to the Bosphorus bridge in Istanbul which links Europe and Asia. The engineering requires building piers and pylons from below, then masts above from which to suspend the great steel cables holding the spans. Finally the structure becomes free-standing. A similar painstaking process is necessary to build a space-station. This floats in space without support, but each piece has to be ferried up laboriously from earth against the pull of gravity. After immense efforts you might end up with something resembling the breathtaking spaceport of the movie *2001*. If this is what it takes for human beings to reach out and connect to a point which seems at first beyond them, would it not take something similar for God to produce an authentic human being capable of connecting to God? If God were to do it all at once then the human being would be unrecognizable to herself, an android without memories or history by which to know her freedom. Or, if her relationship with God were to arrive over the centuries by purely formal stages you'd have to wonder why God took so long over it, rather than moving to term at once. No, the bible shows us very much a God working through human history over a long arc of time, building the initial pylons of support, then the masts and cables, and finally completing the spans to connect what is impossibly connected. The difference is that instead of mindless pieces of concrete and steel the pylons and spans are human beings with thoughts and signs related to their partial and provisional place in the structure. And it is only when someone gets to drive in one continuous movement across the bridge that that person has any clear and full sign of what the structure is.

When in 1974 the daredevil Philippe Petit walked out illegally between the tops of the Twin Towers in New York the team supporting him had first rigged the high wire by shooting an arrow attached to a fishing line across the chasm between. Rope of greater and greater grade was then pulled across until finally they had one strong enough to hold and drag the steel wire itself. At the beginning of the biblical experience what tightrope was going to be able to bear the weight of God in the world? Not the fibers and threads which wove meaning for human thoughts! But these strings were necessary to pull to themselves a steel wire of arm-buckling weight, forged in fires of immense suffering and contradiction. It was the experience of Babylonian exile that brought the minds of four great prophets, Jeremiah, Ezekiel, Second Isaiah and Daniel, to begin to see something impossibly new and to set forth in writing signs and symbols of this new thing. But the steel cable they anchored was still not the high-wire walk itself. Philippe Petit had to step out into the abyss and he did so for forty five minutes, crossing back and forth again and again, dancing and kneeling and laying flat out upon the cable with his balancing rod across him in a perfect image of a cross. It was this dance in the light with 450 meters of emptiness between him and the concrete below that was different, that captivated people and had them thanking and fêting him for the rest of his life.[10]

Understanding the bible with this metaphor we can see that upon the high-wire of post-exilic writing Jesus was able to step out into nothingness and be suspended literally between heaven and earth. Then in a mystery only intelligible in and through this single man he dispensed with the wire itself. On the cross at a certain moment there were no 'visible means of support', i.e. there were no spiritual means of support. Jesus was absolutely alone and yet still giving. This really is the challenge of the new sign system of Jesus—a high-wire dancer who somehow manages to dispense with the wire! It is such a stretch that interpreters have preferred to see only hellish punishment on the part of the sadistic impresario god who set up the whole scene. They want to see Jesus in fact as one pushed off the wire into the abyss rather than one dancing in infinity, rather than one leaping into thin air as unconditioned and boundless love which finally changed the meaning of God itself. It is the latter which has inspired people, while the former has only enabled the power of churches.

A key of interpretation that shows progressively changed meaning may be called an anthropological reading of the text. By its means we see the bible as a developing register of signs and symbols, moving from the ones more easily understood to the wonderfully new ones the first would draw behind them. Let us think for a moment how this might work in practice. For example, the God of Exodus brings down the plagues on the Egyptians, culminating in the slaughter of their firstborn. What this succession of events enabled was a huge reversal of meaning for a group of Hebrew slaves. They were at constant risk of their lives in a world history which would never give their deaths a second thought. In contrast, the death of the firstborn said plainly that they were of equal value to all Egyptians, up to and including the divine son of Pharaoh himself. For another more powerful god was prepared to prove it! Was the God of the bible then responsible for the death of the firstborn? Not in any sense beyond allowing death in the world in the first place. What God was responsible for was the first stage in a shift of meaning within the minds of his people. What God intended and brought about was a critical new perspective that saw the marginal, the dispossessed, those abandoned by fate or the gods, as a group who were central, blessed and loved. At the point of origin of the tradition, even on the most literalist reading, it's hard to miss the literary and constructed character of the narrative. The steadily mounting crisis, the hardening of the Pharaoh's heart, the supremely countable number of plagues, the dramatic finale, all suggests a rehearsed liturgical format. Here is meaning arising as a story and the story is the most potent of signs. Essentially, therefore, a bunch of escapee Hebrews were theologically inspired to read a series of catastrophic events as a story of meaning, one in which God sides with the weak and oppressed.

The writing of the tradition explicitly understood the whole thing in terms of sign. The word is used frequently in both Exodus and Deuteronomy, referring to God's deeds: for example 'I will multiply my signs and wonders in the land of Egypt' (Ex.7:3). The events are never simply a brute exercise of power but are embedded *as* meaning in a framework of meaning. They point to the law and the covenant, constructing an on-going dynamic of relationship, one which entailed that if the Hebrews were liberated from oppression it was so that they would not oppress each other. Thus any purported act of violence on the part of God already means much more than that; it means in fact the overturning of the rule of violence!

By the time then Second Isaiah came to write his prophecy the tradition of sign is understood and valued for itself and the overturning of meaning is enacted consciously from within. The prophet saw a second Exodus about to take place, returning the Jews from exile. This time, however, instead of a charismatic prophet leader, or a king or priest, it would be the Lord himself who would lead them, and the relationship that before had appeared contractual and violent would appear as compassionate and without violence. 'I, I am he who comforts you' (Isaiah 51:12). Then in the absence of the classic agents of violence, the king and national army, another figure comes to focus, the Servant, marked explicitly by nonviolence ('I gave my back to those who struck me', 50:6). It was through this figure that God's will would be done and 'many' (an indefinite number) be made righteous (53:11). The overturning of meaning has become exponential, while in the process losing its anthropological residue of violence. With this sign of the Servant, the high wire of the humanly new had been strung, between the oppression of Babylon and the miraculous powerless return. And so, finally, upon this thin-air narrow wire, it becomes possible for Jesus to walk out, moving toward his definitive forgiving encounter with the combined agencies of human violence: empire, temple, crowd and faithless friends.

This then is a way of reading the main narrative thread of the bible—as construction of new meaning. But it is possible to read just about everything in the bible in this mode of progressive strands or signs. You could call it an ophthalmic approach, a bit like the optician slipping different lenses in front of your eyes until you get twenty-twenty vision. The lucid eyesight we're looking for is that of Jesus, he who said six times 'You have heard that it was said…but I say to you,' the so-called antitheses of the Sermon on the Mount. Especially relevant in this sustained claim to a new perspective is the last one: 'You have heard that it was said, 'You shall love your neighbor and hate your enemy.' But I say to you, 'Love your enemies and pray for those who persecute you…'' (Matt. 5: 43-44). In this one saying Jesus undid the great violent arc of his own scriptures, from the military defeat of peoples who stood in the way of Israel's entry to the land, through the conquest itself, through the multiple wars of the various kings, all the way to the brewing rebellion against the

Romans happening in his own time. With these words his message becomes truly universal. For the mission to the Gentiles is surely implied here, and if bible believers see that the gospel reaches beyond national boundaries they must also see the radical human implication of nonviolence. Really the formal gospel proclamation deeply affirms nonviolence. For once Jesus had challenged and changed all human parameters by non-exclusion and nonviolence, and fulfilled his own teaching with the witness of his own life, there could only be two conse-quences—calamitous failure or astonishing resurrection! If, therefore, the disciples actually had the courage to go out and proclaim a risen Jesus it must be because something had in fact affirmed Jesus' impossible message. Indeed who, if anyone, could conceivably be the firstborn from the dead if not the one who defined and produced in himself truly new humanity, the one who taught a love that makes forgiveness of the enemy as holy as any contemplation?

The biblical trajectory of transforming human meaning leads step by step to resurrection and any small group reading the scriptures as reprogramming of the human sign system points unwaveringly in that direction. Reading the bible in this way the small group will find itself confronted again and again with the ancient sign value of violence and then be prompted by its pivotal place in the overall biblical journey to see how it has been overturned and made into something amazingly, totally new. Steeping itself in this reading can lead only to the Crucified Risen One, the truly new human, the first born of many sisters and brothers.[11]

Signs and Sacraments

After the key role of the bible the obvious elephant in the room in a book with a stress on signs is the traditional topic of sacra-ments. The importance of sacraments in Christianity points to the whole theme of signs and shows it has always been a core feature. Keeping the topic here to last underlines it has always been with us and is not to be taken as a subject separate from everything else. Baptism and the Lord's Supper, the great sacraments recognized by all Christian churches, are not semi-magical events cut off from the rest of the known world. They are rooted in the entire meaning-changing enterprise we are studying. In fact when Christ is changing human meaning everything is sacramental! All signs at some level find the effect of Christ in them.

The word 'sacrament' is traced to the sacred oath taken by a Roman soldier swearing allegiance to his commander. The oath-taking or *sacramentum* transformed his status from civilian to soldier. He was now completely under his commander's authority whose will was his will. The 'sacrament' in this context is therefore a new meaning or condition which the solider has entered and which binds his entire existence. As a vivid illustration the soldier exchanged the white toga of the citizen for the blood-red dress of the legionary. It was a highly visible emblem of the business he was now in, one no longer under the civil prohibition against the spilling of blood. The *sacramentum*, therefore, both stood for and brought into living effect the entire bloody lifestyle of the solider.

It is really of exceptional interest that Latin Christianity of the third and fourth centuries began to use this word for its special rites. The word had a wider usage than the military oath but this is clearly a primary everyday meaning. Against the background of our study we could say that the matrix of soldiering and bloodshed gave urgent sacred meaning to the oath of the soldier. The oath, rooted in that matrix, reciprocally set that person apart for the business of killing and so became a symbol of his whole life. Applying the word to Christian practice suggests equally that baptism or the Eucharist generated an entirely new meaning for the individual, binding them to the new humanity of Christ. It is an inverse meaning from being bound to a military officer. But what the two situations have in common is the powerful change of life-meaning and the fact that it is around the issue of violence that meaning is generated, permitted for soldiers, renounced by Christians.

Where would this leave us today if we suddenly came to realize that the sacrament of baptism was not simply a 'spiritual regeneration', a ticket to heaven or a washing of legal sin, but the taking on of a whole new human life based in a new human meaning? What if the Eucharist should no longer be purely a ritual recalling the Lord's death, but the handing over to us of an entirely new way of being human based in the cataclysmic events of Jesus' death and resurrection? What if sharing the bread and wine, the body and the blood, were not some inhuman sacrificial mystery, but precisely the communicative flesh of a new humanity based in infinite giving rather than endless violence?

These thoughts have huge ramifications but at least we can begin to see the sacraments in a deeper context than the legal and sacrificial ones in which they have been defined. As I said above, if Christ is changing human meaning then everything is sacramental. Our little trip to the mall showed that, in the dynamic sense that the sea of desire is stirred in its depths by the gift of love. It is also true at the movies, where the photon of Christ's compassion is seeking to break through, movie after movie. These situations are parables of a universal presence of Christ in day to day life, and they tell us that members of a virtual church will seek constantly to see and find the Christ of forgiveness and love at the heart of their common world.

They will do so also by turning times and spaces to occasions for meditation, contemplation, common prayer, and common life in the sharing of food and resources. These are the practices perennially associated with intentional Christian community and there is no substitute for them in nurturing that community. The point now is they take place in the midst of the world whose root meaning is being transformed. They are not done in view of another, *doppelganger* universe as may have been the case in the past. Thus there is no amazing new practice or method to be associated with the virtual church if it is not this awareness. There is no new technique but there *is* a vastly increased attentiveness to the Christ-filled here and now.

The use of prayer icons is both a specific example and general illustration of this aspect. The icon is a traditional Eastern Orthodox aid to prayer which is increasingly adopted in the West. Part of its power—its ability to invite people into prayer—is its strange two dimensional style of painting, lacking normal perspective. What depth there is moves the eye to play across the surface without finding a single relationship of objects to settle on. In other words the eye sees but doesn't see. Rather the observer is invited to surrender to the movement itself and, as she does, she suddenly finds herself gazing with her soul into the infinite depth of the icon rather than at its representational content. The mode of painting (or 'writing' as it is called) invites a nonpossessive, self-giving relationship and so the soul becomes part of the story of the new which it is beholding. As I say, this cultural form is increasingly part of our repertoire of spiritual practice. What I am calling the virtual church would of course value the icon, but it can also derive a more general lesson from it.

Everything should be iconic for the virtual church, and by that I mean two-dimensional until the infinite dimension can appear! The normal possessive mode of relationship toward things is the usual third dimension and this becomes forfeit. Love, however, does not lose a relationship toward things, evaporating them in a Zen-like meditation, rather it intensifies the relationship in the self-giving of Christ that underlies and informs them. In Christ the universe flows back toward me and I in turn pour it out to and for the other. Here is the sacramental character of the virtual church, a great affirmation of the world because of, and for the sake of love. Love in this case is no means to any end. It is not to make God happy, so I can go to heaven, or a display of virtue to make converts. It is the goal itself, in the here and now. It is the change in human meaning even as we speak.

The change of meaning even as we speak returns us in a final circle to the sacrament where, above all, meaning is changed when and as we speak. When I left the official priesthood the question of the Eucharist weighed on me. Was I still entitled to celebrate the Lord's meal, the occasion when the priest repeats those astonishing words, 'This is my body'? Of course the church said no, but was I to deprive myself for that reason? Then, on the one or two occasions I tried an unofficial 'mass' I quickly understood that it was impossible because the sign value of the event could not be untangled from that institution. It was only after years of growing in an alternative Christian community and finding the meaning of Christ diffuse through the world that a new sense of the Eucharist would emerge. The ancient churches of Christianity represent a temporal continuity with the pivotal moment in time which is the life and death of Jesus. I personally feel the power of that moment so I also know the sense of a temporal tradition from that primitive period. But to lock that moment up in a body of legal ownership goes against its borderless giving in principle and, as everything written here has shown, is impossible anyway. The importance of the tradition was to preserve the temporal rootedness, but now that temporal effect is so endemic in our culture the tradition takes a less imposing role. Time has grown young again around these ancient monuments, leaving them perhaps as simply and only that. In the present context the Eucharist emerges with a freshness and vigor that makes the old altars look dead and weed-strewn. It really is the greatest sacrament, embracing the depth and drama of the Jesus story and melding the most vivid human signs—bread and wine—to that story. By the simple acts of eating and drinking it embraces anyone and everything to the absolute newness of Jesus' humanity, to the wonderful different sacred he created. The only condition for its celebration—an appropriate word!—is, as Paul said, that it be recognized for what it is. That it not be understood in any way as some transaction with a violent God, but the amazing synthesis of signs that refigures our core humanity into absolute gift. As celebrated in the virtual church the Eucharist does not focus on so-called 'words of institution' with their freight of hierarchical privilege. Rather it retells the whole story of Jesus with his many feasts and friendships, his healings and teachings, bridging through to the prophetic shutting down of the temple and the final acts of surrender to and overcoming of all violence. The bread and wine passed round become indeed his body and blood, his whole life and his very life of self-giving. He signaled all this in his final meal, but it was 'all this', not a separate magical-sacrificial act. And now, because 'all this' has infused itself more and more in our world, it arises spontaneously out of the world as a universal birth of new meaning, not some thin line of priestly transmission. The sacrament of the Eucharist becomes the sacrament of sacraments, the sign that discloses the Christological leaven in every other sign. Every time we do this the earth itself is iconic, stripped of its third dimension of greed and violence and opened to the infinite dimension of love. Every time we do it the cash registers in the mall tremble and the triggers of guns begin to jam. Every time we do it we feel the shock of a new creation growing under our feet.

The whole life of the virtual church is sacramental, bound to Christ's transformed humanity. In the traditional language a sacrament signifies what it effects and effects what it signifies. But in this study the 'effects' part is not a separate magical parallel to the 'signifies'. Sign, signification, meaning are everything. To signify is to make a world and to do so at the core level of the forgiving victim is to change the central dynamics of human relations and with that the mainspring of the world itself. When we unfold the signs of bread and wine within the historical intention and action of Jesus we connect in a great arc of humanity to this dramatic change. It is this which is the 'real presence', the real human event of transformation in and through Jesus. 'Take, eat, and do this in memory of me!' Even so the earth and the heavens are made anew, as if for the very first time.

Chapter Seven

What Signs Did He Give?

To try to paint a picture of Jesus from the gospels as he might have been in real life is what I imagine painting out in space would be like. Getting the paint to stay on the canvas is a problem. It floats off in blobs. The light shifts in disconcerting patterns. Applying the right pressure to get a clear line seems almost impossible.

All this comes from over two hundred years of critical scholarship focused on the New Testament, devoting to the topic exponentially more pages than the last chapter of a general study can allow. Some of those countless pages are among the huge blobs, the many imposing works with their own astringent effect. The long years of scholarship also produce the problem of getting a clear line. Their immense labor has raised a host of questions and nuances which must always be borne in mind as interpretations are made. Nevertheless, I feel a portrait has to be attempted if my overall argument of the world-changing work of Christ is to be rounded out. If what I am claiming is true, if the change in meaning brought by Christ is anthropological rather than metaphysical, it has to start in a real human being. If it can be boiled down to a pretty story narrating only imaginary change, then change is only in our heads and it will come and go as a passing fashion. Then the violent construction of humanity and its endless permutations will remain fixed within us and all else is sorrow and wishful thinking. No, if there is real human transformation then it has to arise in a real human life and in the signs that communicate that life.

There is at first blush good evidence this is indeed the case. The very fact of prolonged scholarship without drawing a term to the discussion suggests that there is something here of substance. If some of the best critical minds of Europe and North America cannot conclude the question over two centuries then on the surface at least that indicates a seam of truth which is difficult if not impossible to exhaust. On the strength of this, and against the background both of the present study and of wider New Testament studies, I am encouraged to present the figure of Christ as someone who creatively and decisively orchestrated meaning and did so in reference to his own person and activity. I will try to show this by first presenting as a matter of credible history that Jesus broke from his mentor, John the Baptist, and on what grounds. And I will indicate the crucial signs he gave that spoke to those grounds and that continue to carry their deep meaning to us.

One of the really influential portraits of Jesus from the past presented him as a deluded visionary who anticipated a direct in-breaking of God in his own time. It came from the pen of Albert Schweitzer who brought the whole nineteenth century study of the historical Jesus to a crashing halt with *The Quest of the Historical Jesus: A Critical Study of its Progress from Reimarus to Wrede* (1906). Schweitzer gave us an apocalyptic Jesus who seemed so badly mistaken as not to be trusted, although he remained both an enigma and a challenge for the modern world. Because of the impact of Schweitzer much of subsequent twentieth century New Testament criticism shied away from any emphasis on the historical Jesus. Rudolf Bultmann is the colossus of this approach and generally of New Testament scholarship at the middle point of the 20th century. He led the way in stripping so much of the New Testament record from the actual Jesus, claiming it was the product of post-Easter community reflection and theology. There was not a lot we could know about Jesus the man apart from the fact he lived, died and preached the kingdom of God. What made Bultmann's approach doubly effective was his accompanying stress on the existential meaning of the gospel independent of its first century context. Jesus summons us to a decision of faith in the present moment, to live an authentic human life freed from the effects of our concrete fallenness in the world. Thus even as the historical Jesus disappeared something human and vital seemed to remain.

It would be hard at this point not to recognize the success of Bultmann's method to be linked to the anthropological shift Christ has brought. We know that Bultmann was a disciple of Heidegger whom I already argued owes the dynamic of his philosophy to the movement produced by the gospel. Bultmann himself said that Heidegger's existentialist analysis 'seems to be only a profane philosophical presentation of the New Testament view of who we are...'[1] Bultmann's existential theology is thus from his own admission a product of a Christ-meaning now embedded in human existence. He could dispense largely with the historical Jesus because the message of Jesus had by now become part of our human fabric. But existentialism although it promotes a human decision does not uncover the roots of violence and, deeper still, the human possibility of compassion and life. For this we have to return to the full anthropological dynamic of the New Testament, to the still astonishing story of the gospel.

Bultmann's New Testament technique is particularly responsible for the problem of keeping a smooth line. Sayings and stories about Jesus get sliced away and the arguments for or against any particular passage so refined that the image gets impossibly fuzzy. In the last decades of the 20th century a decisive reaction set in against this method. Scholars began putting together more cohesive accounts, based in the known first century circumstances, while supplying overall intelligible hypotheses about the content of Jesus' life. What marks these accounts off is their broad agreement with Schweitzer placing Jesus in the context of apocalyptic Jewish eschatology. This does not mean that they understand Jesus as expecting the stars literally to fall and the skies vanish but that he used such striking language to convey the end of the present human cultural order. Speaking within an apocalyptic context means that Jesus anticipated and worked for a constitutive change in the world system, one promised by the prophets and purposed by God. It seems that the increasingly unsettled character of the 20th and 21st centuries made it more acceptable to see Jesus in this light, and whether he apparently succeeded or failed in his project didn't matter so much as his intention to carry through something of that nature.

A formidable exponent of the changed approach is N.T. Wright and the new critical departure is called by him the 'Third Quest for the Historical Jesus' (the second being an inconclusive flurry around the middle of the century still under the shadow of Bultmann). It is Wright's characterization of the new movement as agreement around the core relevance of Jewish apocalyptic that I have referenced.[2] But everything in this present study has been about a dramatic and real change in human history brought by Christ. So it suddenly becomes the case that New Testament historical criticism connects vitally with a contemporary understanding of deep human change. First-century New Testament history meets twenty centuries of human history and there seems to be a possible lock between them. It is this gravitational touchdown—a bit like our artist's spacecraft coming back to earth—that provides the sudden ability to draw a persuasive portrait. We are empowered to speak about Jesus with confidence because his contemporary human meaning coincides with historical tools available. Suddenly Jesus stands up as a credible and realistic historical agent because the approach and purpose he had in his historical life meshes with his contemporary impact. The fact that this meshing is recognized as what is called a hermeneutic circle—we see what our vision first shapes for us to see—does not count against it; it simply reinforces the urgent and timely character of the interpretation.

Teacher to the Teacher

Wright believes that any history of Jesus has to answer at least four key questions: how does Jesus fit into Judaism, what were his aims, why was he crucified, and how and why did a movement dedicated to him arise after his death? A convincing hypothesis has to answer these questions and tie the answers into a whole. Obviously there is not the space here to embark on any kind of thorough-going discussion. Wright's own answers run to multiple volumes of several hundred pages each. It must suffice, therefore, to throw the light of anthropological criticism on the matter and begin by saying that an answer to the fourth question has to explain how the defeated nonviolent anthropology of Jesus changed into a victory—for at least a key group of disciples. At various points in the study so far I have commented on the anthropological conditions required for the primitive gospel. So at this juncture we can put it in thesis form: Jesus' message of turn-the-other-cheek and of the Father's welcome to all would have been drowned at birth in the age-old anthropology of guilt, anger and retaliation if he had been experienced as dead. It's very difficult to conceive of a gospel of open forgiveness if its original author was seen as 'dead and murdered'. And the fact of the empty tomb, important as it was, would not have been enough to provoke the message: just as reported of Mary Magdalene in John's gospel, the natural deduction would be that someone had taken the body and the offense against Jesus had simply been compounded. So, for the whole phenomenon to be humanly explicable there had to be an experience of death transformed and overcome. The New Testament is explicit again and again on the resurrection as the core condition for the proclamation of good news: we need to take it at its word that this extraordinary event was an authentic perception by its first preachers.

However, the sheer experience of resurrection is still not enough. We need come at the question also from the other way round, from the side of Jesus' historical life. The resurrection on its own, without the preparation of Jesus' actual teaching, would have made little inner sense. It would have been nothing more than a weird, uncanny miracle. (Incidentally this is the way that many Christians treat it today; deprived of its inner content of transformed anthropology that is just about what it amounts to.) Instead, for the integral message of resurrection and forgiveness to be proclaimed so quickly and centrally by the primitive community it would have to have been backed by the consistent tenor of Jesus' historical life and teaching. So, in answer to the fourth question, we can suggest there had to be *both* some transcendent event overcoming death *and* a radical teaching of forgiveness underpinning it from Jesus' actual life. Once we say this it then loops us back again to Jesus' own practice and teaching and to Wright's second question. It's on this point I want to reflect at some length. Jesus sets up the meaning of the final message about him by a compelling parade of signs and teaching-by-signs given in his ordinary life. As someone working to bring apocalyptic change, but without violence, he needed to intervene consistently at the level of human meaning and we can see that this in fact is what he did.

How does someone become a teacher unless he or she is first taught by a teacher? There is a certain aptitude in those we call 'born teachers' but what if the subject matter is not learning to read or making origami but resides in the deepest part of the soul? How is that set in motion if there is not someone who opens the way, who indicates the concrete pathway for an art or a truth which till now has been dumb? We might even say that the greater the art or the truth the more its bearer is paralyzed without that essential opening. In the case of Jesus we are blinded to the obvious facts by dogmatic considerations. The Son of God certainly did not need anyone to teach him and his relationship with John the Baptist was just theatre, providing him a stage on which to appear. John was the producer of a first century 'Judea's Got Talent!' with Jesus as its divine star. This downgrading of John is already happening in the gospels. We can see it in Matthew and Luke and—with some counter-hints—powerfully in John. But the very pattern of playing down the Baptist shows his importance.

John's crucial role in the gospels has come to steadily greater prominence in recent scholarship but the facts speak for themselves.[3] When Jesus came to be baptized by John the simple public impression would have been he came as a follower of John. And the gospels all in one way or another show they recognize that. The nature of the progression through Mark to Matthew's baptism account demonstrates it, seeking to play down the human character of the event. First, in Mark 1:11, Jesus hears a voice from heaven addressing him personally, and then in Matthew 3:17 the address is made third-person, suggesting a grand announcement from above. In John's gospel the tendency is carried to an extreme: we would not know from this gospel that Jesus had been actually baptized—John the Baptist simply functions here as someone who gives testimony to Jesus. Nevertheless the extended role that the Baptist has in this gospel demonstrates what an important figure he was. And then in the same gospel we actually see Jesus carrying out John's ministry of baptism (3:22, 26, 4:1), underlining the memory of him as a disciple of the Baptist. For how could anyone have distinguished their ministries at this point? The synoptic gospels provide no record of this because for them Jesus' independent ministry had simply not yet begun. So it is we must see Jesus effectively and willingly entering John's very effective prophetic sign—baptism in the Jordan—and only on this route opening his own career as a spinner of signs. Jesus came first to his meaning via John and then progressively broke from him to evolve his own.

And not only do the facts speak. There is a significant cluster of sayings in common to Matthew and Luke which records Jesus' own response to John and the character of that break (Luke 7:18-35, par. Matt. 11:2-19). The sayings can be analyzed each for their own sake and diced down to molecular meaninglessness. The fact that these passages are concentrated together, however, shows that John was an issue for these gospels and their sources. And the nature of the case brings the issue back from the early church to the life-situation of Jesus himself. John is never shown as an actual disciple of Jesus, but, as I say, Jesus was a disciple of John, so John could be claimed to have a spiritual priority. In particular if John made the first move in establishing a belief in God's imminent intervention, in what way did Jesus differ or improve on that? The passages I am talking about represent a sustained discourse, way beyond any comments Jesus made about any other human being including his disciples. It would make perfect sense that there would be a memory of moments like this in which Jesus publicly stated his difference from his mentor and how to understand that. Here is Aristotle rejecting Plato, Siddharta abandoning the ascetics, Bohr breaking with Einstein, but playing out not in philosophy, enlightenment or physics. It comes rather in a relationship of prophets and, within that, in terms of the most basic anthropology by which they shape and know their message.

Taking this approach shows us something vital. Following the verbal expression of the torn seam between Jesus and John allows us to understand almost the exact threads which Jesus broke and the striking new ones he wove. We can therefore call this discourse on John Jesus' 'personal manifesto' in which he frames his own meaning over against his teacher. If we now observe his pattern of verbal sign-making in this discourse, seeing its vital connection to other gospel texts, we can perhaps work our way toward the core of his meaning. Doing so certainly allows us to see Jesus not as the necessary victim of a pre-ordained plan, something beyond his control and understanding, but one who is articulating his own truth in respect of human violence and at a world-changing depth.

Elijah's Fire is not Jesus'

The first step in understanding is to place the manifesto in its broader textual setting.

The 'Q' tradition (from the first letter of the German word meaning 'well' or 'source') is New Testament studies shorthand for the large amount of material, almost all of a 'sayings' nature, which the gospels of Matthew and Luke have in common and which is not present in Mark. This material is exceptionally important for understanding the teaching of Jesus and without it Matthew and Luke could not have constructed their gospels. Its existence is one of the major reasons most scholars think Mark was written before Matthew and was copied by him in writing his gospel—if it was the other way round why would Mark have left out so much important material? The contents of Q give a striking confirmation of Jesus' verbal skill. They include such characteristic sayings as the beatitudes, the Lord's prayer, sayings on care, on wealth, love of enemies, judging others, signs of the times, the narrow gate, the cost of discipleship, etc. The quality of these sayings warrants recognizing Jesus as one of the great oral teachers of all time. Even in translation his words retain vividness and compression, and hints of an immense natural authority: 'Look at the birds of the sky; they do not sow or reap, they gather nothing into barns, yet your heavenly Father feeds them;' 'Let the dead bury the dead;' 'Ask and you will receive, seek and you will find; knock and the door will be opened to you;' 'You are the light of the world; a city set on a mountain cannot be hidden.' Along with the parables this kind of language justifies seeing Jesus specifically as a 'wisdom' figure, a first-hand exponent of a style of address which uses imagery from nature and pithy, easily remembered phrases. Moreover, the content of his teaching shows him as a figure who shifted the normal way of looking at things. He didn't teach an eternal perspective, rather a very earthly, pressing one, another way of living in the here and now. Rightly he has been called a 'subversive sage', a speaker who is able to turn our mental and actual world upside down.

To recognize Jesus in this way is a great deal. It says there was something arresting enough about Jesus' speech to provide the starting point for all the subsequent fuss about him. Here was a real man in real circumstances equipped with a language to set the world on fire. The problem then becomes the content of the speech and language. If there is something truly subversive about Jesus what was it? If it was violent rebellion this surely disqualifies it as life-giving wisdom. This is underlined both in Jesus' explicit teaching and in the scriptural tradition which seems to have influenced him: in the Book of Daniel 'the wise' are not seen to retaliate even though they fall by sword and fire (11:33-35). And it is the wise who have so fallen who shall rise from the dead to transformed life (12:2-3). But what then qualifies a non-retaliatory wisdom as subversive, as able to upset the order of things? The answer can be found articulated in Jesus' manifesto. Here Jesus' wisdom powerfully rejects the option for violence and then draws upon himself a choice for a completely new way of being human. He insists that he represents the concrete human presence of God's Wisdom in the world and is thus an unavoidable decision point for humanity. He does this in his manifesto by a coherent discourse which leads us step by step down the road to his dramatic claim of new human meaning centered in himself. (When I capitalize 'Wisdom' it refers first and foremost to a personalized identity spoken of in the Old Testament—but then Jesus takes on this identity as a living human being! Meanwhile the lower case 'wisdom' refers always to a genre of thought, speaking and writing.)

In Luke's version of the manifesto we hear first that John the Baptist's disciples reported 'all these things' to John who was in prison. The summary 'all' includes the immediately preceding events of the healing of the centurion's slave and the raising of the widow's son. It suggests that at least for Luke the doubt that John then expresses has something to do with the non-exclusive

and compassionate character of Jesus' work. In Matthew's introduction to the piece the accent is not so much on Jesus' actions as
his status as 'Messiah' ('When John heard in prison what the
Messiah was doing...') and so we immediately get a sense of
Matthew's doctrinal concern. Matthew's introduction is in fact
responsible for miscuing the interpretation of a vital bit of
content in John's question. John sent word to Jesus inquiring, 'Are
you the one who is to come, or are we to wait for another?' (7:19)
By far the most likely background to these words is the prophet
Malachi 4:5. 'Lo, I will send you the prophet Elijah before the
great and terrible day of the Lord comes.' Earlier the same
prophet had said: 'See, I am sending my messenger to prepare
the way before me, and the Lord whom you seek will suddenly
come to his temple. The messenger of the covenant in whom you
delight—indeed, he is coming, says the Lord of hosts' (3:1). There
is no mention here of the Messiah, rather of a coming messenger
who in the later passage given from Malachi is named explicitly
as Elijah.

The gospel tradition at Mark 9:11-12 shows an urgent
consciousness of the need for this coming of Elijah prior to any
other apocalyptic event. Returning from the mount of
Transfiguration Jesus is talking about the apocalyptic themes of
the Son of Man and rising from the dead. The disciples ask, 'Why
do the scribes say that Elijah must come first?' Jesus responds,
'Elijah is indeed coming first to restore all things...', indicating
that Jesus accepted the timetable and content of the Malachi
prophecy. In which case John's conversation with him from
prison is not about a vague figure of 'Messiah' but much more
likely to the effect of 'Are you or are you not Elijah?' with the
specific subtext of 'God's endgame for the cause of righteousness
cannot have begun if you are not...'

Matthew has smudged this sense with the much more recognizable figure of the Messiah in order to make the dialogue work
smoothly for the early Christian church—and that has been the

case ever since. What is obscured thereby is the primitive gospel environment dominated by the expectation of the coming of Elijah with the violent destruction of unrighteousness it would entail. It was with this expectation that Jesus was dialoguing and it was his self-differentiation from it which marked his unique identity, not formal titles. John's shadow falls long over the gospel and it is a measure of its weight that the tradition presents Jesus agreeing that Elijah had to come and according the role to John himself. As we shall see in the passage we are examining Jesus explicitly links John to the Malachi prophecy, and in Matthew states bluntly it is John who is Elijah. But in the last analysis why was it necessary to introduce the confusing role of Elijah at all? For Jesus it was not central and for the early church it would quickly be redundant. It had to be rooted in the earliest levels of the tradition and going back to the prophet of the Jordan himself. John is never simply 'a voice in the wilderness'; his memory revolves around the question of Elijah.

But who was Elijah and how was he going to act? In the Q tradition of his preaching at Luke 3:16-17 the Baptist says: 'I baptize you with water, but one who is more powerful than I is coming; I am not worthy to untie the thong of his sandals. He will baptize you with the Holy Spirit and fire. His winnowing fork is in his hand, to clear his threshing floor and to gather the wheat into his granary, but the chaff he will burn with unquenchable fire.' This can be related to another passage in the prophecy of Malachi. At 4:1 we see that the 'day of the Lord' which the coming of Elijah will presage will be 'burning like an oven, when all the arrogant and all evildoers will be stubble; the day that comes shall burn them up, says the Lord of hosts, so that it will leave them neither root nor branch.' The continuity of imagery is clear, and while Elijah is not the direct agent of the fire in the prophecy it is fire which sets the tone of his ministry. In this light the Coming One would set consuming fire to the useless husks of wheat in a final harvest of righteous and unrighteous Israel.

But mention of Holy Spirit shifts the accent to the post-Easter experience, the core early Christian experience of a new life-giving spirit from God. It seems probable that John, at the time of the written gospel, is made a witness to a very different meaning of 'fire', one associated with Pentecost and which is characteristi-cally nonviolent or 'holy'. But John looks to the Coming One as the agent of destroying fire and we may therefore see his words in tune with the zealous model of Elijah and a token of something more archaic, more fearsome than 'holy spirit'. In the Old Testament narrative Elijah gave his successor, Elisha, a double portion of his spirit (1 Kings 2:9-12) and in confirmation of this overflowing share Elisha saw 'a flaming chariot and flaming horses' which intervened between him and Elijah. We know that this is a heavenly war engine both by its literal sense and because we see that afterward Elisha had personally on hand an invisible force of these chariots to defeat the enemies of Israel (2 Kings 6:17). It was almost certainly this kind of 'spirit and fire' that John was predicting of the one to come after him. John was looking toward a violent supernatural intervention by the Coming One which would purify the people of Israel, returning the nation to righteousness in a division defined by fire.

The gospel tradition of Jesus' words shows him also warning of fire and on more than one occasion—he certainly used this apocalyptic image (for example, Mark 9:42-48). But, first, Jesus' standard use is 'Gehenna' as a place of unquenchable fire. This is a term with a rich Old Testament background referring to an actual valley, on the south of the hill of Zion, with a cursed reputation as a site of human sacrifice. It is a powerful concrete image or sign of destruction and is open-ended and existential in meaning, rather than metaphysically defined. It is clearly possible to read it in anthropological terms, as the endless self-consuming violence at the heart of the present human order. Secondly, there is always a consequential sense in Jesus' usage—

fire is conditional on choices people make in the here and now, rather than understood as a destiny already released at a cosmic level. He doesn't use language like John the Baptist's from Matthew, 'Even now the ax is lying at the root of the trees; every tree therefore that does not bear good fruit is cut down and thrown into the fire...' (3:10). The sense of these words is present-tense indicative, i.e. violence is released in the spoken moment, rather than conditional and self-actuated as Jesus sees it. In other words the way Jesus uses the image points to the final, real possibilities of unredeemed human existence not to a divine act of final violence now overtaking history.

There is, however, one saying of Jesus that switches the whole meaning of fire and it gives an indication of how he was changing John's entire symbolic scheme. He said, 'I have come to set the earth on fire, and how I wish it were already blazing! There is a baptism with which I must be baptized, and how great is my anguish until it is accomplished' (Luke 12:49-50). The image of setting fire to the whole earth is very different from burning the separated chaff. It is also connected to a baptism that Jesus has yet to undergo, and so is diverse from John's meaning. John's promise of a baptism with 'spirit and fire' refers to the final cataclysm of God's in-breaking in history. The water baptism at the Jordan that he offered stood as a powerful symbolic alternative to fire, the possibility of entering into a repentance and purification that pre-empted this fearsome eventuality. Jesus' putting together of 'fire' and 'baptism' in respect of something he had still to undergo suggests that he accepted John's symbols but at a deeper and decisive level he opted to bring the crisis down on himself in a totally exceptional sense. He would thereby release fire on earth, but in a trans-formed, generative sense. Here we have the absolutely character-istic gesture of Jesus that unites an apocalyptic viewpoint with something else, something that changes the orientation and content of apocalyptic itself. It returns us again to his otherwise-than-John manifesto.

The Scandal of the New

Jesus gives his reply to John's question and it makes a striking contrast to the scenario of violence. He rehearses a laundry list of healings, one we can find threaded throughout the text of Isaiah (26:19, 29:18-19, 35:5-6, 42:7, 61:1-2a). At once Jesus demonstrates his fulfillment of a very alternative program to that of final judgment. Rather it was an Isaianic vision of healing and helping. 'Go and tell John what you have seen and heard: the blind regain their sight, the lame walk, lepers are cleansed, the deaf hear, the dead are raised, the poor have the good news proclaimed to them' (7:22). And then Jesus adds a phrase that in one form or another is a signature line throughout the gospels, one that is absolutely typical of his thinking and action, and that here turns the discussion toward himself in a more crucial way than even an identification with Elijah could. In this phrase Jesus refers his activity and meaning to himself as himself and it is in this shocking personal turn that all the subversive power of his speech is contained: 'And blessed is the one who takes no offense at me.' The word translated here as 'to take offense' is *skandalizō*. It is the same word used of the people of Nazareth who 'took offense at him' at Mark 6:3, and at Mark 14:27 the word is used of the disciples when Jesus predicts that all the Twelve will be offended by him and desert him.

The verb is related to the noun, *skandalon*, meaning stumbling block or a trap laid in someone's path. It tells us that Jesus could become something as difficult as an object to make one fall, headlong, and therefore to be carefully avoided. It suggests that the list of actions he has just rehearsed, all so apparently good, constitute a frame of meaning, a series of signs which shape the world powerfully in a new way. That way is in dramatic contrast to the way it has been shaped so far and is one which could in fact make us stumble. Reflecting more on the thought of 'scandal' allows us to enter Jesus' world of radically changed significance.

Jesus uses the word also in respect of the power of others to cause his followers to fall, 'the little ones' who have very little power to defend themselves. Matthew has him deliver the severest warning in this regard: 'If any of you put a stumbling block before one of these little ones who believe in me, it would be better for you if a great millstone were fastened around your neck and you were drowned in the depth of the sea. Woe to the world because of stumbling blocks! Occasions for stumbling are bound to come, but woe to the one by whom the stumbling block comes' (Matt. 18:6-7). Therefore the stumbling block can work two ways, from Jesus to others but also from others to his followers. It can even occur to Jesus himself; he tells Peter who is seeking to prevent him going to Jerusalem where he will suffer: 'Get behind me, Satan! You are a stumbling block to me; for you are setting your mind not on divine things but on human things' (Matt. 16:23).

It seems then that mutually between Jesus and the world around him there is the possibility of one making the other fall headlong. By his use of this word Jesus expresses the profound dissonance between himself and the world constructed to this point. It is not simply a matter of rival political goals, as for example between the Pharisees and Herodians. If it were simply that then it's hard to see how John could or would be scandalized by Jesus. Both he and Jesus preached the imminence of God's reign on earth. In Jesus' case, however, the reign of God was connected to an unwavering practice of healing and forgiveness, and his preaching must surely, therefore, be understood not strictly in terms of end goals but the means by which they are achieved. To be scandalized in Jesus was to be shocked and offended by the apparent weakness of the means he had chosen, and to such an extent that he could not be the one he was thought to be. John's lifeworld of violence, including a necessary final violence by God, came crashing down when confronted by Jesus and his actions, and consequently his trust in Jesus was threatened by a similar collapse. It was not primarily a question of theology but rather fundamental anthropology, a new way of relating to others without the sanction of violence. With Jesus what was at stake was not a particular rival and the power of that rival to take the object of our desire from us—in the case of Herod, the righteousness of the nation before God. In this framework the response is old-fashioned theology (i.e. old anthropology)—God will act to defend and restore what is his. With Jesus, on the other hand, there is the offer of an entirely different model that stands against all violent desire and desire for violence. Jesus, therefore, was inviting John to cross the impossible bridge to where he stood as an agent of God whose agency was not violence, and yet was still agency. And he stood there alone! That is the point. It was and is so easy to be scandalized in Jesus because he is one against the vast crowd of humanity and its meaning as constructed to this point. How can he possibly be right?

So Who or What is John?

After the saying on scandal Jesus then turns to a prolonged third-person reflection on John. He and John are very close and yet very distant, and Jesus must spend time laying out the paradox. As he does so he separates the threads of meaning between him and John and continues to weave the astonishingly new ones which he alone knows.

First Jesus sketches John's concrete witness, forming a word picture of his ministry in bold strokes given in negative form: a reed shaken by the wind, like those on the banks of the river Jordan; someone dressed in the fancy clothes of palaces, most probably referring to the lifestyle of Herod's court: John is not to be found in either of these scenes. He is no mere desert ascetic, a reed of the river, and he is not a hanger-on at court, a supporter of Herod's fraudulent kingdom. He is a prophet, and 'more than a prophet'. The images situate John in his ministry at the Jordan and, by implication, in opposition to Herod. Jesus then references the prophecy we have already looked at from Malachi 3:1, about the messenger to be sent before the day of the Lord and associated with Elijah. John 'is the one about whom it is written, 'See, I am sending my messenger ahead of you, who will prepare your way before you.''(Luke 7:27) The Lukan wording places John in clear relation to someone else, someone for whom he is preparing, and in the tradition this is certainly Jesus. (The messenger 'will prepare *your* way before you,' a change from Malachi's first person prophecy — 'before me' — to second person.) But we should not forget John's concrete context which Jesus has clearly announced and which is interpreted at the outset of all the gospels with the Isaiah prophecy of 'a voice crying in the wilderness, 'prepare the way...''

This other reference for 'preparing' would have been a very natural connection, especially if Jesus had once been a disciple of John and shared with him the Jordan ministry with its powerful symbolism. What was intended in Isaiah's vision was God's triumphant return to Zion, and it was for this that the way was to be prepared (Isaiah 40:5-11). John's immersion ritual at the Jordan offered to all Israel would have been sensed as a purified re-entry of the people to the land and it is highly probable it was intended to enact symbolically the fulfillment at last of Second Isaiah's return of God at the head of the exiles. If we place together the consistent association of John with the Isaiah prophecy and his praxis of immersion at the Jordan it seems very likely that John himself made the connection. In this light John produced a prophetic sign of enormous daring and creativity. Rather than something small scale as other prophets had done (like carrying a yoke or making a model of a besieged Jerusalem) he employed an entire geographical feature, a river. The Jordan running down the eastern border and the point of access for the Exodus tribes would function as a living metonym for the whole land and its history. How focused and compelling this would have been! It's easy to imagine the impression it would have made on the sensibility of someone like Jesus. In one stroke John picked up the entire history of the people and got them to recommit to it, and in the process created something of equal or greater significance than Jerusalem and its temple, priests and scribes. Such an outrageous symbolism would have to be either the work of a crackpot or the authentic first shock of the Reign of God. Jesus clearly took it as the latter.

Jesus can therefore be seen as learning from John—learning the possibility of the compelling sign that overturns all significance to the present, together with the actual moment in which it could and should be brought to light. But how after John could you do anything of greater significance than what he did? It would seem impossible. Nevertheless for John there was in fact one thing greater. In a biblically consistent scenario the symbolic preparation at the Jordan needed the coming of Elijah to be fully realized. Elijah was a concrete individual who would in person provide the whole meaning of Israel and bring a definitive gathering around him of true Israelites: and he thought Jesus was that person. Jesus, on the other hand, gave the persona of Elijah to John and then proceeded to take the in-person role or meaning to an unprecedented level. This is where John's confusion lay: how could there be any other in-person role than that of Elijah? Jesus thought there was, and there was furthermore something about the Elijah role which he definitively rejected. The remainder of the discourse sets out the nature of that rejection.

Jesus produces a characteristic twist of thought that fixes two antithetical images in your mind, plunging it into a kind of free-fall. He declares, 'Among those born of women, no one is greater than John; yet the least in the kingdom of God is greater than he.' 'Born of woman' stands in contrast to those in the kingdom of God who are born of Wisdom ('Wisdom's children') whom we meet at 7:35. I would take this form of the tradition to be the more original version rather than Matthew's expression of Wisdom's 'works' (11:19) which forms an inclusion with his doctrinal expression 'works of the Messiah' at 11:2. Moreover, the crucial theme of children is reinforced both by Wisdom's standard biblical instruction to children and by the wisdom parable of children at 7:31-32. It is through this parable and its interpretation that we will get to the heart of the distinction between Jesus and John. We will return to this shortly but in the meantime we can anticipate that the conclusion at 7:35 does not warrant the usual pious reading of a common identity of Jesus and John as children of Wisdom. Rather in the context of the whole discourse it provides the uniqueness of Jesus-Wisdom giving birth to children of the kingdom. This is what distinguishes Jesus from John and gives content to Jesus' gentle but uncompromising contrast to the anthropology represented by John.

Jesus declares that the least in the kingdom is greater than John. In Matthew's version we hear also: 'All the prophets and the law prophesied up to the time of John' (11:13). What is suggested is that the whole prophetic Mosaic tradition reached its term in John; but now something qualitatively new had emerged that went beyond prophecy. This could only be the actuality of God's reign on earth. Anyone, therefore, who was a member of that kingdom was in a human situation that all others, no matter how great, could only have looked forward to. But what truly constitutes this reign? What makes this claim anything more than a rival rhetoric of power? It has to be the contrast of 'born of woman' and 'born of Wisdom'. For in the latter we have an entirely new matrix of human existence. It is not the age-old human shaping of humanity, one that includes even the prophets and the law of Israel. The new mothering of humanity does not draw a line at the family or the race but includes and nourishes precisely those who are left out, those who are not *our* children.

This change is illustrated in Jesus' healing practice, as he had earlier signaled to John, and above all it is demonstrated in his association with sinners. At the conclusion of the discourse, just before the statement about Wisdom, Jesus describes himself in the third person as the one who 'has come eating and drinking...a friend of tax-collectors and sinners' (7:34). Luke then underlines this with the shocking episode of the woman who was a sinner given directly after this discourse: she multiplied the breaking of purity boundaries by bathing Jesus' feet with tears, wiping them with her hair, kissing them and anointing them (7:38). Matthew does not have this scene but goes quickly to a mysterious wisdom saying which we cannot analyze in detail but is noteworthy for being directed to 'infants.' 'You have hidden these things from the wise and the intelligent and have revealed them to infants' (11:25). The term 'infants' signifies those not fully socialized, basically those like children who can hardly speak, who cannot read or follow difficult instructions and for these reasons cannot be exact in law-keeping. Jesus is revealed precisely to these people because they can never fully belong to the cultural boundary systems. Jesus stepped over the purity lines to be among them and in that act demonstrated a totally different generation of humanity, otherwise than the exercise of boundaries. Rather than John's Jordan river and its implicit border associations he, in and of himself, became the scene of forgiveness and healing, a mother by definition without boundaries.

The Precise Issue of Violence

The specific issue of violence is lurking in all of this and is brought to the surface by a powerful saying contained in Matthew's version of Jesus' discourse. Luke has it elsewhere (16:16) without this context and in an apparently more benign sense. The saying is almost always viewed as 'difficult' because it seems to set out what looks like a systemic relationship between the kingdom of God and violence, and without an anthropology of violence it is very hard to evaluate. But the meaning is straightforward once we grasp it in this light. 'From the days of John the Baptist until now, the kingdom of heaven has suffered violence, and the violent take it by force' (Matt. 11:12). The first half seems reasonably easy: the kingdom and those in it are made to suffer violence. John the Baptist can easily be included in this statement, as he is in prison at the moment Jesus is speaking. And the future suffering and death of Jesus quickly come to mind as confirmation of this reading. But what does it then mean that the violent (men of violence) take it by force? The verb translated 'take it by force' can be rendered seize, grasp, overpower (*harpadzousin*). It is the verb used of Jesus when men wanted to 'take' him in order to make him king at John 6:15; and of Paul at Acts 23:10 when the tribune orders the soldiers to take him in charge lest the mob tear him to pieces. Essentially it means to get hold of, grab, control, for one's own purposes, and thus immediately it suggests the kingdom of God is liable to being hijacked by the violent for their violent purposes. How does this fit with the first verb 'suffer violence' (*biadzetai*) if this is understood simply in terms of persecution? The mismatch between the two halves results in having to chose between them for the meaning—either the kingdom is suffering violence or it's the object of a power-grab. With an anthropology of generative violence, however, we can see how the whole saying becomes coherent. We can read the first verb as plainly the passive aspect or converse of the second (*harpadzousin*): the saying is not about the kingdom suffering externally through its representatives but how it is systemically affected by violence through the violent. It is 'violenced' or violated.

There is the potential for the kingdom to be misread and misconstrued in any number of ways. Where movement has been generated, where people are brought together by the action of Jesus, there is always the possibility of not recognizing the new source and meaning of that movement. It can at once be re-acculturated according to all the old concepts and moral forms based in violence, while the new source and meaning must remain obscure. The kingdom is therefore forced or violated (*biadzetai*) every time the violent (*biastai*) take it in their hands (*harpadzousin*) in the mistaken opinion that they are carrying through its project. It is very possible on this reading that Jesus is including John in this assessment, that he felt John had got part of the thing horribly wrong by invoking the agency of violence in his preaching. We should, therefore, read the statement as: 'From the days of John the Baptist until now the kingdom of heaven has been violated by violence and the violent have taken it over.' John was himself someone who hijacked the kingdom and sought to establish it in and through the anthropology of violence, after the fashion of Elijah. It was no trivial matter for Jesus to ask John not to be scandalized against him.

The Generation of Wisdom

Jesus finally develops the question of himself and John by asking what kind of comparison or *mashal* (Hebrew for a likeness or signified meaning) can he find for the people of 'this generation'. What is the character of the current culture or way of being human? He replies to his own question, saying they are like children playing a game of catcalling. 'They are like children who sit in the marketplace and call to one another, 'We played the flute for you, but you did not dance. We sang a dirge, but you did not weep" (7:32). Many commentators say that the calling back and forth goes on between children of 'this generation' and other children who are in fact John and Jesus. In this case the first group of children refuse to respond to the calling of the children of Wisdom. But the parable is about *this generation* which is 'like the children'; i.e. it is described in terms of the whole scene and what takes place there. Jesus is saying that everything takes place in the crowd where all is mimetic commentary and conflict, and the intervention of John, and then of himself, become invariably a matter of offense, of the *skandalon*. The children bat everything back and forth, never coming to a conclusion: that is the point of the game. There is also high probability that the disciples themselves, of both John and Jesus, were involved in the altercation, turning the supreme moment of crisis into a political food-fight.

Jesus clearly goes on to explain the parable in this sense of opposition-for-opposition's-sake: 'For John the Baptist came neither eating food nor drinking wine, and you said, 'He is possessed by a demon.' The Son of Man came eating and drinking and you said, 'Look, he is a glutton and a drunkard, a friend of tax collectors and sinners'' (7:33-34). But built in here also is the vast difference between John's practice and that of Jesus and this should not be lost sight of. Jesus in fact is stating it explicitly. Of course the difference provides successive sources for comment and scandal, for the *skandalon* is the only thing 'this generation' really wants, the power to overwhelm the other in violence. But beyond the way it is used the difference remains and that must be borne in mind in the final statement: 'Nevertheless, Wisdom is vindicated by all her children.' It could be that Luke has added 'all' here in order to include John, and so reduce the contrast. But that makes it even harder to deny that in the original Q material, and very likely Jesus' own language, this statement parallels and contrasts both with the children of the marketplace and those 'born of women' at 7:28 which includes John. The saying in its positive sense refers to all those invited into the kingdom, above all the sinners with whom Jesus is a friend, but in terms of the discourse on John it must exclude him.

This has to be the final sense of the chain of associations. It is highly implausible that Jesus would have ended the pronouncement with the exclusive company of himself and John as 'children of Wisdom,' as the saints of divine Wisdom; this is pure hagiography. Much more consistent is a sustained theme of difference from John who though 'more than a prophet' still lies outside the new generation of Wisdom. The difference between them would likely itself have been a talking point among the children of the marketplace, a source of pleasant contradiction-finding. But the fact that mimetic children use it this way does not lessen its own truth. Jesus was hugely different from John, to the degree that even though John was a prophet and more than a prophet he still risked being part of 'this generation' (those born of women). John is the tipping point between two profoundly different orders, but while dwelling in that painful undetermined space he really did provide the opportunity for something new to come forth. That is why he is the greatest of all the old order.

Wisdom the Core Sign

Meanwhile the decisive new element is Wisdom and with it we are, I think, in the true orbit of Jesus' self-differentiation. Here is the solar sign or meaning which lies at the heart of his astonishing preaching and praxis. As I pointed out in the fifth chapter Wisdom is a personalized figure in the Old Testament, one who speaks and acts in her own right in the book of Proverbs and the deuterocanonical book of Sirach. She delights in human company and invites all who are foolish or uneducated to share a meal (Proverbs 9:1-6). Jesus' eating and drinking with sinners fits fully with this persona of Wisdom. We also saw in Sirach that the author recommends his pupils to 'put your neck under her yoke' (51:26), and we read in the same author the personal address of Wisdom saying 'Come to me, you who desire me, and eat your fill of my fruits' (24:19). At the end of the extended Wisdom material that we noted in Matthew Jesus says: 'Come to me, all you that are weary…and I will give you rest. Take my yoke upon you, and learn from me; for I am gentle and humble in heart, and you will find rest for your souls…' (Matt. 11:28-9). The conjunction of this startling first-person identification with Wisdom and the fact that it played little to no part in mainline New Testament theology, makes these words very plausibly

Jesus' own. And, again, in general terms of the Hebrew bible what else but the personal figure of Wisdom and her hospitality to the foolish could warrant Jesus' down-and-dirty practice of mixing with the wicked? The only thing that Jesus adds to the language—and this also warrants seeing the statement as authentic—is an explicit note of nonviolence. When he says he is 'gentle' the word in Greek is *praus*, the same word used by Matthew describing Jesus' triumphal entry to Jerusalem. It is taken from the prophecy of Zechariah, 'Look, your king is coming to you, humble (*praus*), and mounted on a donkey' (Matt. 21:5, Zechariah 9:9). The Zechariah text goes on to say that 'He will cut off the chariot from Ephraim and the war-horse from Jerusalem; and the battle bow shall be cut off, and he shall command peace to the nations' (Zechariah 9:10). When Jesus speaks as Wisdom he speaks in language with key scriptural associations of an end to violence. The statement in today's language should therefore read: 'Take my yoke upon you, and learn from me; for I am nonviolent and humble in heart, and you will find rest for your souls.'

We have reached a central seam of meaning as regards Jesus. He identified with Wisdom as his first-person truth and he understood that in terms of nonviolence. Here is surely the sign from which all I have been talking about regarding the transformative meaning of Christ in the world derives. Because Jesus took on this identity in the depth of his soul and he understood it as direct person-to-person nonviolence the meaning of humanity was changed at root. Following the frame of chapter five it is not necessary that Jesus thought of this in metaphysical terms. It was enough that Wisdom provided the effective sign for his personal identity. His relationship with the Father flowed into that sign and the sign worked positively with generative power to confirm that relationship. Anything more and Jesus would have tied his brain in the knots that the fathers of Chalcedon tied theirs!

There was, however, a singular test to which this identity had to be submitted before its sign value could be truly infectious in the human system, before its transformation could take hold. First-person Wisdom welcoming sinners is very well and fine but what happens to the previously systemic values like law, nation, temple and empire? Are they just going to go away because Wisdom has a dinner party? Absolutely not. If Jesus was serious about his meaning as God's Wisdom present among humans then he had to follow the challenge to its last consequence, to its last terrifying implication before all the boundary-creating institutions. It implied confronting the will-to-kill that lurks at their root. And so there is the gospel passion story, following on from Jesus' ministry, and it has a consistency of almost unbelievable generosity and courage.

In preparation for this story we are used to Jesus' journey to Jerusalem during which he predicted a destiny of suffering and death. But is there anything more at the level of the self-differentiation we have been studying? Is there a further sign with a certain wisdom flavor that can bring us to the radical heart of Wisdom working from below? Asking this question allows us to leapfrog quite naturally from what I have called Jesus' manifesto to a passage that shows the literal depth to which he brought his Wisdom identity. It leads us to a sign which we might see as Wisdom's calling-card in a world of violence and it shows the way in which Jesus understood himself at this level before we ever get to any formal plan or destiny that he should die. As such it operates as the interpretive code by which Jesus read his own identity at its most critical point. It is a sign which can take hold of all the old God-directed legal formulae about the meaning of Christ's death and plunge them into the depths of human violence and its transformation.

The Universal Jonah
The standard foreshadowing of Jesus' coming ordeal in Jerusalem

is the prediction of the passion at Mark 8:31, 9:31 and 10:33-4, and parallels. Mark's triple and explicit prediction is a literary device enabling the reader to appropriate the shock of the passion in advance, giving it a kind of objectivity. A threefold structure is also standard bible-speak for something divinely willed and all the evangelists employ it in setting up the story of the passion. There is, however, a saying more characteristic of Jesus' story-telling and which conveys a less formal and more graphic sense of his existential decision and pathway. Tellingly the remarks are made yet again in response to 'this generation' and it is this note that first connects it as meaning to the figure of Wisdom.

> This generation is an evil generation; it asks for a sign but no sign will be given to it, except the sign of Jonah. (30) For just as Jonah became a sign to the people of Nineveh, so the Son of Man will be to this generation. (31) The queen of the south will rise at the judgment with the people of this generation and condemn them, because she came from the ends of the earth to listen to the wisdom of Solomon, and see, something greater than Solomon is here! (32) The people of Nineveh will rise up at the judgment with this generation and condemn it, because they repented at the proclamation of Jonah, and see, something greater than Jonah is here! (Luke 11:29-32, par. Matt. 12:38-42.)

This statement is perhaps composed of two separate sayings, one in answer to a request for a sign and the other on future judgment. They are brought together by the common motif of Jonah and linked by verse 30. Jonah is the primary theme in response to the question about a sign. In the saying in 31 and 32 he is secondary both to the queen of the south and the Ninevites who are the primary subjects in connection to future judgment.

The request for a sign is a standard reaction to Jesus in all the gospels. The Pharisees seek it at Mark 8:11, scribes and Pharisees at Matthew 12:38, Pharisees and Sadducees at Matthew 16:1, the crowd at John 6:30, and the people in the present context of Luke at 11:29a. In all examples from the synoptics Jesus replies condemning the 'generation' that seeks a sign. The key anthropology is a demand for a show of superior force, something like an Elijah-style fire from heaven. It also corresponds to the temptation of Jesus in the desert, third in Luke's account, second in Matthew's. In Luke's account we read the devil led Jesus to Jerusalem and 'made him stand on the parapet of the temple, and said to him, 'If you are the Son of God, throw yourself down from here''(4:9). The choice of location, the temple, and the circus-style plunge from the parapet speak to the possibility of overawing the crowd at the national-religious center of Judaism and immediately recruiting their national-religious devotion.

The somewhat absurd gesture also suggests the volatile mentality of the crowd at this time and it is this which Jesus is resisting. There was a longing for a figure with transcendent physical and religious power able to break the impasse of history into which Judaism had been brought. In his response to the request for a sign Jesus denounces the present generation as evil and we are reminded at once of his parable at Luke 7:31-35. There 'the people of this generation' are only interested in the drumbeat of rivalry and violence, in contrast to the children of Wisdom. Putting together this parable and his reaction to the request for a sign we get an understanding of Jesus' profound opposition to the anthropology of mimetic rivalry. But before we can fully appreciate his meaning we should look at one further occasion in the gospels in which the issue of 'this generation' arises. A moment is described where the disciples have been unable to cast out a demon and they seem to be included under the general judgment of Jesus' response: 'You faithless and perverse generation, how much longer must I be with you and bear with you?' (Luke 9:41) What he intends by this cannot then be simply a criticism of a particular sociological group (i.e. that particular generation of Judaism), because he had called his disciples out of contact with their peers in order to become something new. It must refer more to the generative principle at the heart of that society which his followers continued to imitate. It is because the disciples are themselves deeply identified in and with the culture of violence that they have been unable to deal with a child presented to them who is overwhelmed by it. A child has been placed before them suffering from 'a spirit' which seizes the child and then the boy 'suddenly screams and it convulses him until he foams at the mouth; it releases him only with difficulty, wearing him out' (9:37-41). It is of course possible to give a 'medical' explanation for this but we also well aware of the way in which trauma produces acting-out, dissociation and psychosis. In the contextual crisis of first century Judaism occupied by the violence of Rome, and for six hundred years before that living in the shadow of exile and empire, the people themselves saw the phenomenon strictly in terms of violence (it 'seizes', 'convulses', 'releases only with difficulty', 'wears out'). Jesus' multiple encounters with demons and his instant power over them have to be understood in this anthropological context, as an ability to offer from his own person an entirely different way of peace. In contrast the character of the generation surrounding him, this *genea*, can only be the crisis of violence which defines them and in which they are plunging ever deeper. If we now put this character together with their search for a validating sign we can see its meaning cannot be constituted by anything else but by violence. What they are requesting is a symbol of superior violent power.

Jesus consistently refused to give such a sign but instead provides a totally different semiotics. Culled from the Hebrew scriptures these follow an alternative generativity of Wisdom, one able to lead humanity out of its most fundamental problem. It is unthinkable that Jesus, a master of his tradition's language and range of allusions, would not have found an alternative figure to the semiotics of violence. And find it he did in the startling wisdom prophecy of the Book of Jonah. I say it is a 'wisdom prophecy' because unlike any other of the minor or major prophets this book contains none of the usual pronouncements of curse or blessing and, on reflection, is a piece of highly creative fiction. There is no corroborating evidence of a mass conversion of the Ninevites either in the bible or outside of it. Instead, read the prophet Nahum for a description of Nineveh, the 'city of bloodshed', and its terrifying final downfall! The writer of Jonah clearly enjoyed fictionalizing the conversion of the violent Ninevites in order to turn all standard expectations of the character of Israel's God on their head. The story is itself a *mashal*, a parable, close in sympathy to Jesus' type of story-telling. It represents a subversive wisdom, and the genius of those who formed the Hebrew canon of scriptures recognized the depth of that subversion as prophetic. It is totally credible for Jesus to choose this text as a sign of his own world-overturning wisdom. In fact, I believe, for Jesus the figure of Jonah is the chosen alternative to Elijah as the prophet-sign of God's imminent action in the world. He chose the castaway-from-God who found in the deeps God's endless gift of life, because this was to be his own final pathway. Let me now show how various gospel texts related to the figure of Jonah serve to flesh out and give meaning to this relationship of Jesus and the prophet of the deeps.

Jesus replies that 'no sign will be given … except the sign of Jonah.' In Matthew's version this is elaborated with the gloss, 'Just as Jonah was three days and three nights in the belly of the sea monster, so for three days and three nights the Son of Man will be in the heart of the earth' (12:40). This seems plainly editorial, spelling out a post-Easter explanation to the parable. Most commentators think that Luke's pithier version is the original, missing the belly of the fish, the three days and nights and the heart of the earth, and simply stating the sign. The shorter form is corroborated by a second Matthean example of the saying at 16:4, which has the statement of Luke 11:29b almost word for word: 'An evil and unfaithful generation seeks a sign, but no sign will be given it except the sign of Jonah.' This in turn is part of Matthew's version of the episode at Mark 8:11-13 which records the sign request but has no mention of Jonah at all. Instead we have: 'He sighed from the depth of his spirit and said, 'Why does this generation seek a sign? Amen, I say to you, no sign will be given to this generation.' Then he left them, got into the boat again, and went off to the other shore.'

Commentators believe that here Mark has truncated the saying because of his own tendency to keep the 'secret' of Jesus from those who are not disciples, but even here there is a hint of the abyssal content of Jesus' response. Jesus sighs from the depth of his spirit, a depth that in literary terms echoes Jonah's descent. We remember Jonah's heartfelt prayer: 'Out of my distress I called to the Lord … for you cast me into the deep, into the heart of the sea' (2:3a, 4a). There is also a further hint in Jesus' immediate embarking in the boat. Mark could easily be giving a coded reference to 'the sign of Jonah' present in the tradition. If this is true it illustrates how the sign of Jonah was by no means a mechanical figure of Jesus' period in the grave, but corresponded to the depths of anguish to which Jesus would sink in following his chosen road. However, we don't have to rely simply on literary guesswork to link Mark's gospel to the theme of Jonah. It is reinforced by verbal material elsewhere which shows a remarkable dependence on the Old Testament narrative.

At Mark 4:35-41 Jesus is crossing the lake asleep in the stern while a violent storm breaks upon the boat. The disciples are terrified and turn to Jesus with a reproach, 'Teacher, do you not care that we are perishing?' (v.38). The points of identity with the Jonah story are striking. The storm is introduced in similar terms: 'A mighty storm came upon the sea' (Jonah 1:4), 'A great windstorm arose' (Mk.4:37). Jonah is asleep in the hold of the ship (1:5), Jesus in the stern. The word that the disciples use of their imminent danger, 'perishing' (*apollumetha*) is the same as used by the sailors in Jonah's boat: 'Rise up, call upon your God. Perhaps God will be mindful of us so that we may not perish' (1:6 LXX *apolōmetha*). Calm returns to the waters at Jonah's being cast in by the sailors and the same in Mark, at Jesus' command. Finally in both accounts the other people in the boat, sailors and disciples, all fear with a great fear (Jonah 1:16 LXX *ephobēthēsan phobō megalō*, Mark 4:41 *ephobēthēsan phobon megan*). The difference is that fear is the fear of the Lord in the Jonah story, and in Mark it is a fear in reaction to Jesus' own power: 'Who then is this whom even wind and sea obey?' (v. 41b). These words have always been read as an implied suggestion of the divine nature of Jesus and this is indeed a possible inference. The Lord is the cause of the great storm and so presumably he brings it to an end, and Jesus does the same thing. But in the Book of Jonah there is a direct connection between the casting in of Jonah and the cessation of the storm. 'So they picked Jonah up and threw him into the sea; and the sea ceased from its raging' (1:15). It's more likely, therefore, given the other points of connection that Jesus is seen as the one who brings a cessation to the violent storms of this world because he is the one cast in the deep in the final trajectory of the gospel. From this perspective Mark is suggesting Jesus' return of peace to the seas is a profoundly 'human' gesture rather than simply a fiat of divine power. Jesus' power to bring peace in the violent tempest is an effect of his Jonah-like descent into the abyss.

Overall we have to ask ourselves why would the evangelist use elements of a story about such a disreputable figure as Jonah to frame the account of the calming of the waters if the connection were not already made in the tradition? For Mark himself to make the symbolic connection to the abyss of the world's violence would have taken great literary creativity allied to a baffling lack of commentary. I believe, therefore, the Jonah motif is only present because it was present in the tradition and at the most primitive level. Jesus so strongly identified with Jonah in the abyss that the two narratives were merged at a formative level of the tradition. Mark simply echoed what he had first heard.

Here then is a sign of enormous resonance, but it has been almost hidden from us by all the high metaphysics of Jesus as the Son of God. It is only today with the possibility of an anthropological reading that we are in a position to recover Jesus' profound intention and meaning. Here is the sign in Jesus' thought and teaching that carries us into the radical heart of his project. Jonah represents for Jesus the sojourn of Wisdom in the depths, the deepest darkest alienation of death, and death too at the hands of the community which is the action on which all boundary making is premised. It is the ultimate boundary and to cross over into that space willingly, in faith, forgiveness and love is to will the absolute liberation of a humanity based in the violence of exclusion.

Jonah Jesus and Roman Nineveh

This thought is made emphatic by the narrative that follows directly on the calming of the storm and we cannot finish with the figure of Jonah in the gospels without describing its structuring role here too. In all three synoptics the episode of the storm is followed by the healing of a possessed man, the famous 'Gerasene demoniac'. It cannot be by accident that this dramatic encounter takes place immediately consequent on the calming of the storm. The word characterizing Jesus' address to the tempest is 'rebuke' (*epitimaō*), the same word used when he silences and drives out demons. If we read the two accounts as linked narratives we can see both how the Jonah semiotics are reinforced and what the story of the demoniac therefore conveys.

As already suggested, a demon should be understood not as some independent spiritual entity strangely let loose on earth to bedevil humanity. The high incidence of demon possession in the gospels indicates an historical moment of incredible intensity and stress. At the time of Jesus the cumulative effect of violence must have been staggering, a product both of the brutal Roman occupation, the succession of empires before it, and a theological viewpoint that saw all this as under God's imminent judgment. The result was what can be described as mimetic crisis, the accumulation of violence within a human system with no place for it to go. To protect oneself from this imploding cosmos entailed for some a concentration of cultic observance and for others a deeply-nourished intent of rebellion. Other, vulnerable individuals, without resources or strength, and perhaps with personal histories as victims of violence, would have been overwhelmed, afflicted with a poisoned cocktail of shame and anger in constant flux. The crisis was concentrated with full force in them and the only human possibility was to transform themselves into the whole battleground, taking sides with the violence itself against themselves, and so gain a measure of control. In the presence of Jesus these persons were confronted with an existence free from the hostile interference that oppressed them, because it was plunged completely in a divine abyss of self-giving and trust. This abyss was already a new form of human historical existence in Jesus; to be touched by it was to know a power that could dispel all internalized violence, replacing it with complete peace.

Again there is a symmetry between the events of the Gerasene story and the Jonah story and it has to arise at some point—evangelist, oral tradition, Jesus himself—where the connection was understood and made. At the least it is Jesus' own linking of himself with the story of Jonah together with the key role of violence in that story that made the connection inevitable. I already said that the role of violence was implicit in Mark's Jonah-structured account of the storm. Let me show briefly how the *mashal* of Jonah is suffused with the theme of violence in order to support this first linking and then draw a vital parallel with the episode of the demoniac. It will serve to integrate the two gospel narratives—storm and demoniac—into a single re-reading of the Jonah prophecy / parable.

The text of the book of Jonah has an interplay of terms which place the theme of violence front and center. The Hebrew word *rā'āh* is used at multiple points, translated by 'calamity', as descriptor of the storm (1:7), and by 'evil' in reference to the doom the Lord had determined to bring on the Ninevites (3:10) and the practices from which the Ninevites turned away at the urging of their king (3:8, 10). When the king speaks to the citizens he parallels this word with violence. 'Man and beast shall be covered with sackcloth and call loudly to God; every man shall turn from his evil way and from the violence he has in hand' (3:8). In contrast, Jonah falls into an evil rage, and again the same word, *rā'āh*, is used (4:1). This word in turn is paralleled with another fierce word for anger (Hebrew root *hrh*, 4:1). It is this 'burning anger' from which God relents (3:9) while Jonah is on fire with it. All in all the text speaks four times of this murderous anger in Jonah (4:1, 4, 9 twice). This same term is used for Cain's anger just before murdering Abel (Genesis 4;5), and the Lord questions Cain about it just as he does Jonah here (4:4).[4] The interlaced language of anger, disaster and violence binds the story into a whole, and it is impossible for an alert reader, especially in Hebrew, to miss the themes that give it unity. The placing of the episode of the intensely violent Gerasene demoniac directly after the Jonah-structured story of the storm is itself an illustration of this understanding.

The possessed man meets Jesus directly he gets out of the boat. In a sense Jesus never gets out of the boat because the man is so powerfully a figure of chaos. He lives among tombs, among the dead, a condition that fits the diagnosis of 'with an unclean spirit' (*en pneumati akathartō*, Mark 5:2). In his case it clearly also means intense violence. '(H)e had frequently been bound with shackles and chains, but the chains had been pulled apart by him and the shackles smashed, and no one was strong enough to subdue him. Night and day among the tombs and on the hillsides he was always crying out and bruising himself with stones' (5:4-5). Here is chaotic violence beyond cultural control, invested in a single individual. The man runs up to Jesus and demands in the name of God that Jesus not torment him even as he also calls Jesus 'Son of the Most High God'. The emerging distinction between 'God' as the progenitor and protector of violence and 'God' in relation to Jesus is summarized in this brief gospel sentence, and it is underlined by the fact the man cannot remain indifferent. Jesus represents a mode of existence antithetical to the existence of the man. Jesus asks him his name and now the jig is up completely. A name asserts existence and so the man cannot but give it in defiance: 'Legion is my name. There are many of us' (9b). The gloss 'many of us' indicates an editor's hand: how likely is it that a mob of demons would provide a handy self-definition? Unless of course they're trying to throw the questioner off the track! In reality it is the military meaning that is confessed and it is probable the gospel tradition provided the gloss to avoid making the story an explicitly anti-imperial text.

The Roman legion was the sovereign instrument of violence from the Rhine to the Euphrates. Josephus always includes mention of the legions in describing the troops sent by Rome to subdue Jewish rebellion. His description of Roman militarism is famous and the legion was its standard instrument: 'Their exercises are unbloody battles, and their battles bloody exercises.' This Latin name in the Jewish context—and indeed anywhere at that time—would unmistakably have had this connotation. As it stands in Mark 'legion' refers immediately to Roman violence, and when the man confesses to this name we see Jesus confronted by a one-man condensation of the Roman hurricane in Palestine and throughout the whole western world of that day.

The military connotation is reinforced by the number of swine into which the legion enters; two thousand is an improbably large number for a herd of pigs; it would represent a major industrial business even in modern times. But in Hebrew history a 'thousand' is a technical term for a military unit (for example at Numbers 1:20-46). And Roman legions were always numbered in the thousands. The number should almost certainly be taken in this technical sense. The fate of the pigs has also always concerned readers but this is only because the scandal of the legion has been transferred to plurality away from military violence. If we think of the thousands upon thousands killed in military actions in that area alone and then, expanding from there throughout history, the pigs are simply an anthropological code for the immense violence of humanity that always seeks to displace itself in a surrogate.

The final vision of the story is the terrifying rush of the pigs over a precipice into the sea. In Luke the demons explicitly asked not to be sent 'to the abyss' (*eis tēn abusson*, 8:31) but in the event of entering the swine they go there anyway. The appalling human violence that had been constitutive of the man's personality heads straightway to the very place to which Jesus has just brought calm. There is now a symbolic identity going in a reverse direction, between the final abode of the demons of violence and the realm of the storm. We have returned to the chaos of the abyss and the complex of language and themes shared between the Jonah story and these two gospel episodes make the interpretive force of Jonah conclusive. Within this framework Jesus has been assigned his future in the place where the demons have just gone. The pigs have become monsters of the deep invested with displaced human violence, exactly as Jonah became. And Jesus would be no less dispatched as Jonah was; not however with the sacrificial swiftness of drowning but in full crucified display, a Roman theater of exponential cruelty. Thus the semiotics of Jonah—of storm and violence—can be seen to structure and give content to these episodes and consequently to Jesus' chosen sign.

Greater Than Solomon / Jonah

Following this chain of meaning has brought us to the seminal heart of Jesus' ministry and meaning. From his use of the 'sign of Jonah', through the calming of the storm, to the encounter with 'Legion', we have pursued what might be called a subterranean pathway in which to discover his aims and intentions. The 'sign of Jonah' should be considered a kind of minority report within the gospels, lying below the radar which gives us the much more familiar figures of 'Son of Man', 'Son of God', and 'Messiah'. Of course the Jonah pathway is not exclusive. The gospels use many registers to convey Jesus' meaning, and these other, better known titles carried much more of his public significance, whether used by himself or by others about him. But it should also be expected that he had more intimate or personal images to convey his self-identity. The Jonah figure is bound closely to his pattern of Wisdom identity and in this connection it speaks eloquently of the profound human transformation that he was bringing about. Its enigmatic and oblique character speaks also to the strangeness and challenge of what he was doing, something that could only be signaled in the biblically odd figure of Jonah. It has taken a long time to arrive at the anthropology which could make sense of that sign. It can now be understood as the core symbol of Jesus' encounter with the human condition of violence, a meaning that has been waiting for millennia to break to the surface.

In this light we now return a final time to the passage where we introduced the sign, Luke 11:29-32. We are in a position to appreciate a linking that underlines the whole argument. After the saying 'no sign will be given except the sign of Jonah' we pass to the second saying via the editorial verse at 11:30.

The second saying is an oracle of judgment which represents a separate tradition but its content both confirms and expands the resonance of the sign. 'The queen of the south will rise at the judgment with the people of this generation and condemn them, because she came from the ends of the earth to listen to the wisdom of Solomon, and see, there is something greater than Solomon here! The people of Nineveh will rise up at the judgment with this generation and condemn it, because they repented at the proclamation of Jonah, and see, there is something greater than Jonah here!' (31-2). There is a detailed parallelism contained in the two segments, consisting of a rising from the depths to a place of wisdom and judgment. Both the queen of the south and the people of Nineveh come 'from the ends of the earth', one geographically and the others in their relationship to violence. The element that brought them to this point is respectively the wisdom of Solomon and the proclamation of Jonah, the prophet who himself had risen from the depths. Finally all three figures, the queen of the south, the people of Nineveh and this generation, will all rise at a coming judgment to a final witness to the truth.

Solomon and Jonah are placed in parallelism as the keys of transformation, and in both cases they are followed by the ringing phrase 'And see, there is something greater...here!' They are somehow on a par and yet for both of them 'look, something greater is here!' Jesus is thus claiming that he both repeats and exceeds the composite figure of Solomon and Jonah. In the Hebrew tradition it is impossible to imagine a figure of wisdom greater than Solomon if is not Wisdom herself; Solomon is her classic lover and disciple, second only to her. But by placing the extraordinary claim of identity with Wisdom in connection to Jonah this becomes something other than a purely transcendent claim. Jonah in contrast to Solomon is a continual disgrace; his greatness is achieved only by his extraordinary descent to the depths and his liberation from them. By putting this complex of figures and themes—of height and depth—together Jesus is saying unmistakably that rising and judgment will center upon a

Wisdom that finds itself in the depths of human violence and yet overcomes it. The Wisdom he is presenting is in fact a hybrid of the figure evoked by Solomon and the abyss of violence transformed in the story of Jonah. To ignore this is indeed to invite judgment upon oneself, for what other way is there for humanity to escape our historic anger and murder?

This passage, therefore, represents probably the most densely packed set of signs presenting us Jesus' meaning of human transformation. With this weaving of signs and their meaning, fulfilled in the cross and resurrection, we can draw to a close both this New Testament excursus and the overall study. Jesus is Solomon and Jonah and something greater still. His aims and intentions are wrapped up in these figures and signs and their intrinsic ability to transform human meaning. They differentiate him absolutely from John the Baptist who, nevertheless, opened the doors of sign-making for this radically new condensation of meaning. Jesus' signs renounce the old order based in violence and they replace it with a Wisdom in the depths. They refer in fact to himself as the transfiguring of our human condition from within, and so also of all creation. They are able to bring creation to its intended goal of fullness of life, the New Jerusalem come down out of heaven into the depths dressed as a bride for her husband.

We have followed this amazing possibility from its anthropological bases, through the progressive traces it has left on actual human culture, the implications this has for the concept of church, and then finally in a great loop back to the gospel account of Jesus itself. The signs from the gospels I have presented fit with the reconstruction of human meaning that I have attempted to describe in the rest of the book. They fit as a consistent set of signs wresting human meaning from its violent foundations and reprogramming it as compassion, forgiveness, life and peace. To see and understand Jesus in this seminal way, either in his gospel story or in the multiple ways he has impacted subsequent history, is to begin to be changed as a human being and in a human manner. It is to become virtually Christian.

Notes

Chapter One: No Name for a Non-Violent God

1. Girard's thought will be described in detail in the next chapter. There are a number of books today tracing an endemic link between religion and violence, for example, Jack Nelson-Pallmeyer's, *Is Religion Killing Us? Violence in the Bible and the Quran* (London, New York: Continuum, 2005), and Christopher Hitchens' *God is Not Great: How Religion Poisons Everything* (New York: Twelve, Hachette Books, 2007).

2. Anthony W. Bartlett, *Cross Purposes: The Violent Grammar of Christian Atonement* (Harrisburg, PA: Trinity Press International, 2001).

3. For the essential nonviolence of Revelation see Steven J. Friesen *Imperial Cults and the Apocalypse of John, Reading Revelation in the Ruins* (Oxford: Oxford University Press, 2001), 176-7, 189-91. E. Schüssler Fiorenza describes Revelation's rhetorical character, its construction of a symbolic universe enabling continued commitment and hope. See *Revelation, Vision of a Just World*, Proclamation Commentaries (MN: Fortress Press, 1991), 119-30; and *The Book of Revelation, Justice and Judgment* (Philadelphia: Fortress Press, 1985), 198: 'In taking his audience on the dramatic-cathartic journey of Rev., John seeks to 'move' them to control their fear and to sustain their vision.'

4. Story from Andrew Chaikin, *A Man on the Moon* (New York: Penguin Group, 1998), 204-5.

Chapter Two: The Sign that Means the World

1. N.T Wright's *Surprised By Hope* (New York: HarperOne, 2008) describes and debunks this popular and quite vaguely conceived viewpoint.

2. For the curious the movie I'm referring to is *Jesus' Son* (1999) with Billy Crudup.

3. There is already a large number of books examining the relationship of Christianity to contemporary culture and media; representative are *Matrix of Meanings: Finding God in Pop Culture*, Craig Detweiler and Barry Taylor (Grand Rapids, MI: Baker Academic, 2003) and *The Hidden Power of Electronic Culture: How Media Shapes Faith, the Gospel, and Church*, Shane Hipps (Grand Rapids, MI: Zondervan, 2006). The present study shares their attention to the way in which the media are currently affecting the whole context of faith and church life, but continues the analysis to the generative roots of culture affected themselves by Christianity.

4. The following give probably the best overall account of Girard's thought: René Girard with Jean-Michel Ougghoulian and Guy Lefort, *Things Hidden since the Foundation of the World*, trans. Stephen Bann and Michael Metteer (Stanford, Calif.: Stanford University Press, 1987), and René Girard, *I See Satan Fall Like Lightning*, trans. and foreword James G. Williams (Maryknoll, New York: Orbis Books, 2001).

5. René Girard with Pierpaolo Antonello and João de Castro Rocha, *Evolution and Conversion, Dialogues on the Origin of Culture* (London & New York: Continuum, 2007), 237.

6. See Andreas Capellanus' classic twelfth-century treatise, *De Amore*: 'This is the kind [of love] that anyone who is intent upon love ought to embrace with all his might, for this love goes on increasing without end, and we know that no one ever regretted practicing it, and the more of it one has the more one wants. This love is distinguished by being of such virtue that from it arises all excellence of character, and no injury comes from it, and God sees very little offense in it. No maiden can ever be corrupted by such a love, nor can a widow or a wife receive any harm or suffer any injury to her

reputation. This is the love I cherish, this I follow and ever adore and never cease urgently to demand of you. But that is called mixed love which gets its effect from every delight of the flesh and culminates in the final act of Venus. What sort of love this is you may clearly see from what I have already said, for this kind quickly fails, and lasts but a short time, and one often regrets having practiced it; by it one's neighbor is injured, the Heavenly King is offended, and from it come very grave dangers'. (*The Art of Courtly Love,* trans. John Jay Parry [Reprinted: New York: Norton, 1969], Book 1, Dialogue 8, 122.) Note the comment: 'The concept of love as desire never to be fulfilled is at times implied by the [Arabic] poets, but never endowed with the weight of a doctrine.' (G.. E. Von Grunebaum, 'Avicenna's Risâla Fî 'l-'išq and Courtly Love,' *Journal of Near Eastern Studies* 11 (4), 1952: 233-8 [234].)

7.   The standard Christian reaction to courtly love has been hostile. C.S. Lewis regarded it as a formal rival to Christianity: '(T)his erotic religion arises as a rival or parody of the real religion and emphasizes the antagonism of the two ideals [courtly love and true religion]'. (*The Allegory of Love, A Study In Medieval Tradition*' [Oxford: Oxford University Press, paperback 1958], 18.) But where there is rivalry there are shared values, in this case attitudes of devotion, humility, surrender, non-possession. The point again is not that courtly love, like Caesar's wife, is beyond reproach, but that the structure of human desire learned a possibility of nonviolent relation to the object through the cultural impact of Christianity. It is the virtual object as non-possessive desire, otherwise called love. C.S. Lewis himself employed courtly-romantic motifs of chivalry in his *Narnia* series, as a vehicle for the Christian story as he understood it.

8.   Friedrich Heer, trans. Janet Sondheimer, *The Medieval World* (London: Weidenfeld and Nicolson, 1990), 125.

9.   Although Chrétien de Troyes' original tale about Perceval

and the Grail remains unfinished it is taken up in numerous adaptations. In Wolfram von Eschenbach's *Parzival*, from the beginning of the 13th century, the story reaches a peak moment of nonviolence. Toward the end of Eschenbach's account Parzival fights with a 'heathen' knight who is more skilled than he. Parzival's sword breaks, but the other knight refuses to slay him, seeing no honor in this. They subsequently learn that they share the same father. The foreign knight says to Parzival 'You have done combat here against yourself. I came riding into combat against myself'. (*Wolfram von Eschenbach, Parzival*, ed. & trans. André Lefevere, The German Library, Vol 2 [New York: Continuum, 1991], bk. 15, 203.)

10. R. W. Southern, *Saint Anselm, Portrait In A Landscape* (Cambridge: Cambridge University Press, 1990), 107.

11. Herr, *The Medieval* World, 15.

12. Caroline Walker Bynum, *Holy Feast and Holy Fast, The Religious Significance of Food to Medieval Women* (Berkeley & London: University of California Press, 1987), 50-53. Manifestations of popular devotion were going on for at least a hundred years before the Fourth Lateran Council (1215) defined the doctrine of transubstantiation. See also 54-5 for devotional practice.

13. *Anne Astell, Eating Beauty, The Eucharist and the Spiritual Arts of the Middle Ages* (Ithaca & London: Cornell University Press, 2006), 3. See p.14: 'Eating the Eucharist was thus simultaneously to 'see' Christ and to 'touch' this vision, to reach out for it...'

14. German knights and peasants even brought their horses to reverence Christ in the host, 'in a kind of equine communion' (*Holy Feast and Holy Fast*, 54).

Chapter Three: Motion Pictures

1. David McIntee, *Beautiful Monsters: The Unofficial and*

Unauthorized Gudie to the Alien and Predator Films (Surrey, England: Telos Publishing), 27.

2. The shooting of Ripley's death, 'ironically when one considers the religious imagery used, took place on Good Friday'. (*Beautiful Monsters*, 101.)

3. Mel Gibson and Ken Duncan, *The Passion: Photography from the Movie 'The Passion of the Christ'* (Tyndale House Publishers, 2004).

4. René Girard, trans. Patrick Gregory, *Violence and the Sacred* (Baltimore & London: The Johns Hopkins University Press, 1979), 39-41.

5. His first post-Christian album, *Infidels* (1983), strongly suggests a reaction like this. See in particular a song that was an outtake but eventually showed up in *The Bootleg Series* (Vols. 1-3, 1991), *Foot of Pride*.

Chapter Four: Alpha to Omega

1. Teilhard de Chardin, trans. Bernard Wall, *Phenomenon of Man* (originally published in English by Wm. Collins & Co. Ltd., London, and Harper & Row, New York; Harper Colophon edition 1975, reprinted in Perennial, 2002), 146.

2. Ibid. 294, italics mine.

3. Ibid. 182.

4. Marco Iacoboni, *Mirroring People: The New Science of How We Connect with Others* (New York: Farrar, Straus and Giroux, 2008), 10.

5. Scott Garrels, 'Imitation, Mirror Neurons, And Mimetic Desire. Convergence Between The Mimetic Theory Of René Girard And Empirical Research On Imitation' in *Contagion, Journal of Violence, Mimesis and Culture*, vol. 12-13 (Michigan State University Press, 2006), 56.

6. Barna Research Group, Ventura, California, October 2003, http://www.barna.org/barna-update/article/5-barna-update/128-americans-describe-their-views-about-life-after-

death

7. Jacques Derrida, *The Gift of Death*, trans. David Wills (Chicago & London: University of Chicago Press, 1995), 23. For forgiveness see Jacques Derrida, *On Cosmopolitanism and Forgiveness (Thinking in Action)* (New York: Routledge, 2001). Heidegger studied theology at the University of Freiburg for four semesters with the intention of becoming a Roman Catholic priest. See his statement in *Unterwegs zur Sprache* (Pfullingen: Neske, 1959; p. 96): *'Without this theological background I would never have got to the pathway of thought. But what came before remains always to come.'* Quoted in *Martin Heidegger and the Pre-Socratics* by George Joseph Seidel O.S.B (Lincoln: University of Nebraska Press, 1964, p. 7; my translation).

8. John D. Caputo, *Prayers and Tears of Jacques Derrida* (Bloomington & Indianapolis: Indiana University Press, 1997), 140. The Freiburg course was 1920-21, 'Einleitung in die Phänomenologie der Religion.'

9. John D. Caputo, *Demythologizing Heidegger* (Bloomington: Indiana University Press), 181.

10. Jacques Derrida, *Of Spirit, Heidegger And The Question*, trans. Geoffrey Bennington and Rachel Bowlby (Chicago and London: University of Chicago Press, 1989), 111.

11. Martin Heidegger, trans. Joan Stambaugh, *Being and Time* (Albany: State University of New York Press, 1996), 398, italics original.

Chapter Five: God Save Me from God!

1. *God Is Not Great: How Religion Poisons Everything*, 10. Richard Dawkins, *The God Delusion* (Boston, New York: A Mariner Book, Houghton Mifflin paperback, 2008), 51.

2. Ibid., 284-5.

3. Marcus Borg has most clearly described the clash between Jesus and the purity world of first century Judaism,

including an organic connection to the temple. See *Conflict, Holiness and Politics in the Teachings of Jesus* (New York & Toronto: The Edwin Mellen Press, 1984); *Jesus in Contemporary Scholarship* (Valley Forge, PA: Trinity Press Intnl, 1994). Dominic Crossan has argued strongly for Jesus' action in the temple as the proximate cause for his death. See *The Historical Jesus: The Life of a Mediterranean Jewish Peasant* (San Francisco: Harper Collins, 1991) & *Who Killed Jesus? Exposing the Roots of Anti-Semitism in the Gospel Story of the Death of Jesus* (San Francisco: HarperSanFrancisco, 1995). The basic analysis was already in E.P. Sanders *Jesus and Judaism* (Philadelphia: Fortress, 1985). N.T Wright has a more creative sense of Jesus' work, combining both challenge to the purity context and displacement of the temple in a concerted action to restructure the core symbols of Israel in and around his own self and meaning. See *Jesus and the Victory of God* (Minneapolis: Fortress Press, 1996).

4.   The text is common coin of Christian tradition, seen by its placement at the back of the Anglican Book of Common Prayer in the Historical Documents section, whence this translation. (*The Book of Common Prayer* [New York: The Church Hymnal Corporation and The Seabury Press, 1977], 864.)

5.   Ben Witherington III, *The Christology of Jesus* (Minneapolis: Augsburg Fortress, 1990); *Jesus the Sage: The Pilgrimage of Wisdom* (Minneapolis: Augsburg Fortress, 1994).

6.   *The God Delusion*, 287.

7.   Raymond E. Brown, Intro., Trans. & Notes, *The Anchor Bible, The Gospel According to John*, Vol. 29A (New York: Doubleday & Co., Inc., 1970), 1047.

8.   Giovanna Negrotto Cambiaso, *I sentieri inesplorati. Autobiografia di una pellegrina dietro l'invisibile*, 2nd. ed. (Padova: Edizioni Messaggero, 2009), 25, my translation.

9.   Gandhi frequently paired these two names, especially in the

years proximate to his death: cf. *The Collected Works of Mahatma Gandhi* (Publications Division New Delhi, 1982 & 1983), vol. 86, pp. 419, 433, vol. 87, pp. 237, 409.

10. Étienne Gilson, *God and Philosophy*, 2nd. ed. with foreword by Jaroslav Pelikan (New Haven & London: Yale Nota Bene, Yale University Press, 2002).

11. Ibid. quoted p. 36.

12. Ibid. quoted p. 42.

13. Ibid. 63.

14. Cornelius Plantinga Jr., *Engaging God's Word: A Christian Vision of Faith, Learning and Living* (Grand Rapids, MI: Eerdmans, 2002), 20-1, italics in original.

15. John D. Zizioulas, *Being as Communion: Studies in Personhood and the* Church, Contemporary Greek Theologians Series, No 4 (New York: St. Vladimirs Seminary Press, 1997), 40-1, italics in original.

Chapter Six: A Virtual Church

1. http://www.forbes.com/2009/06/26/americas-biggest-megachurches-business-megachurches.html

2. A monograph by Sean Freyne from the Center for the Study of James the Brother, Institute of Advanced Theology at Bard College, New York, entitled *Retrieving James / Yakov, The Brother of Jesus* (Bard College, 2008), provides a succinct review of the evidence on James. Freyne states that the circumstances that led to James' emergence as Jerusalem leader 'are hidden from view' but 'the idea of blood brothers sharing the leadership of Israel, following the pattern of Moses and Aaron, has considerable merit' (p. 33).

3. For a statement of Paul's continued theological relation to Israel see N.T. Wright, *What Saint Paul Really Said: Was Paul of Tarsus the Real Founder of Christianity?* (Grand Rapids, MI: W.B. Eerdmans, 1997).

4. See Raymond E. Brown, *The Community of the Beloved*

Disciple. The Live, Loves and Hates of an Individual Church in New Testament Times (New York: Paulist Press, 1979). Also his *Introduction to the New Testament* (New York: Doubleday, 1997).

5. Brian McLaren is one of the leading thinkers and writers in the field of emerging church. His many books focus on Jesus' intense human involvement, the kingdom of God as a this-world theme, the priority for Christians of peacemaking, justice, compassion and care for creation. See particularly *The Secret Message of Jesus: Uncovering the Truth that Could Change Everything* (Nashville: Thomas Nelson, 2007), and *Everything Must Change: Jesus, Global Crises, and a Revolution of Hope* (Nashville :Thomas Nelson, 2007).

6. *The Community of the Beloved Disciple*, 102.

7. http://www.theage.com.au/news/world/church-chief-blasts-megachurches/2006/02/22/1140563843279.html

8. http://www.marshill.org/

9. http://www.crcc.org/section.php?SectionID=164

10. See *Man On Wire* (Magnolia Home Entertainment, 2008), a movie dedicated to Petit's high-wire crossing of the Twin Towers on August 7th 1974.

11. There are a number of resources that can assist an anthropological bible study. James G. Williams' *The Bible, Violence And The Sacred* (New York: HarperCollins, 1991) is a classic treatment of both Old and New Testaments from the perspective of Girardian anthropology. Acquiring a good bible dictionary is an important first step in becoming historically literate about the bible. *HarperCollins Bible Dictionary*, ed. Paul J. Achtemeier, is a one volume work with concise informative articles. *The Anchor Bible Dictionary* (6 Volumes), ed. David Noel Freedman, is a heavyweight with extensive and wide-ranging topics. My own study of Isaiah 40-53 may be offered as detailed demonstration of the anthropological approach, found at http://www.preaching-

peace.org/biblestudies.htm. The website of Preaching Peace, http://www.preachingpeace.org/, also provides a lectionary commentary covering the readings of the church year, another effective path into reading the bible this way.

Chapter Seven: What Signs Did He Give?

1. Bultmann, Rudolf, *New Testament & Mythology And Other Basic Writings* (Philadelphia: Fortress Press, 1984), 23.
2. N.T. Wright, *Jesus and the Victory of God* (MN: Fortress Press, 1996), 84. This book is essential reading for its own critical historical argument from this perspective. See also Wright's *The Resurrection of the Son of God* (MN: Fortress Press, 2003).
3. For example, Robert L. Webb, *John the Baptizer and Prophet: A Socio-Historical Study*, JSNTSS vol. 62 (Sheffield: Sheffield Academic Press, 1991); John P. Meier, *A Marginal Jew: Rethinking the Historical Jesus. Vol. 2. Mentor, Message and Miracles* (New York; Doubleday, 1994); Walter Wink, *John the Baptist in the Gospel Tradition* (OR: Wipf & Stock Publishers, 2001).
4. Hebrew text from James Limburg, *Jonah, A Commentary*, (Louisville, Kentucky: Westminster / John Knox Press, 1993), 89.

Index

BOOKS

O is a symbol of the world, of oneness and unity. In different cultures it also means the "eye," symbolizing knowledge and insight. We aim to publish books that are accessible, constructive and that challenge accepted opinion, both that of academia and the "moral majority."

Our books are available in all good English language bookstores worldwide. If you don't see the book on the shelves ask the bookstore to order it for you, quoting the ISBN number and title. Alternatively you can order online (all major online retail sites carry our titles) or contact the distributor in the relevant country, listed on the copyright page.

See our website **www.o-books.net** for a full list of over 500 titles, growing by 100 a year.

And tune in to myspiritradio.com for our book review radio show, hosted by June-Elleni Laine, where you can listen to the authors discussing their books.

MySpiritRadio